THE CIVIL SERVICE
OF CANADA

OXFORD UNIVERSITY PRESS
AMEN HOUSE, E.C. 4
LONDON EDINBURGH GLASGOW
LEIPZIG NEW YORK TORONTO
MELBOURNE CAPETOWN BOMBAY
CALCUTTA MADRAS SHANGHAI
HUMPHREY MILFORD
PUBLISHER TO THE
UNIVERSITY

THE CIVIL SERVICE
OF CANADA

BY

ROBERT MacGREGOR DAWSON
M.A., D.Sc. (Econ.)

PROFESSOR OF POLITICAL SCIENCE, UNIVERSITY
OF SASKATCHEWAN

OXFORD UNIVERSITY PRESS
LONDON : HUMPHREY MILFORD
1929

Printed in Great Britain

TO
MY WIFE

PREFACE

I WISH to thank many friends who have assisted me in the production of this book. My greatest indebtedness is to Professor Graham Wallas who first aroused my interest in the subject and whose lectures, discussion, and criticism have been of incalculable benefit to me. I have received further help from numerous suggestions made by Professor A. Berriedale Keith, and from conversations which I have held with members of the Canadian Civil Service. I desire also to express my appreciation of the courteous assistance rendered by Mr. M. C. McCormac, Mr. F. A. Hardy, and other members of the staff of the Parliamentary Library, Ottawa.

The editors of the *Canadian Historical Review* have kindly given their permission to reprint large parts of Chapters I and II, and the editors of the *Dalhousie Review* have done the same in respect to parts of Chapter VII.

R. MacG. D.

UNIVERSITY OF SASKATCHEWAN,
January 1929.

CONTENTS

PART I. THE HISTORY OF THE CANADIAN CIVIL
SERVICE

   I. Canadian Civil Services before Confederation . 3

  II. The Spoils System and Proposals for Reform:
1867–80 19

 III. The First Gesture towards Reform: 1880–2 . 44

  IV. The Period of Stagnation: 1882–1908 . . 56

   V. The Reform of the Inside Service: 1908–17 . 78

  VI. The Flow and Ebb of Reform: 1917–28 . 90

PART II. PRINCIPLES OF CIVIL SERVICE
ORGANIZATION

 VII. The Place of the Civil Service in Government . 109

VIII. Selection 128

  IX. Gradation: Promotion: Salary . . 154

   X. Tenure: Removal: Retirement: Women . 179

  XI. The Civil Service Commission: Parliamentary
Responsibility 195

 XII. The Civil Service as a Large Scale Organization . 220

XIII. Conclusion 252

PART I
THE HISTORY OF THE CANADIAN CIVIL SERVICE

I. CANADIAN CIVIL SERVICES BEFORE CON-FEDERATION

'Ah, take one consideration with another,
A policeman's lot is not a happy one.'
The Pirates of Penzance.

THE Canadian civil service began with the Confederation; but its future was to a large degree determined by the influence of institutions existing at that time. Its external form was governed by the terms of the *British North America Act*, which incorporated and centralized the most important functions of the component colonial governments, and brought at the same time the majority of the civil servants under federal control. The living spirit of the service, however, did not come from the statute, but from earlier colonial experience. The old provincial services contributed in addition to their personnel certain traditions and customs which were passed on to their successor and which have influenced enormously subsequent Canadian history. Some of these traits were beneficial, some might have been called taints, but all can be traced back to some early provincial ancestor. The idea of office as a reward for political usefulness, the custom of interpreting civil service tenure as one 'during good behaviour' and not 'at pleasure', the understanding that political activity on the part of civil servants meant loss of office if the other party were returned—these were a part of the inheritance which the Dominion received from the colonial governments. It is, therefore, a matter of some interest to investigate the circumstances under which these customs arose and to discover how firmly they were established at the time of Confederation.

The formative period of the civil service was broadly coincident with the winning of responsible government: it was one phase of the confused struggle which culminated in colonial home rule. Any discussion of these conditions naturally stresses the lack of executive and legislative co-operation and omits or slurs over the equal confusion existing within the administration. Before responsible government any organized civil service, such as exists to-day, was unknown. In the first place, in accordance with the precedent set in the American colonies before the Revolution, part of the administration was controlled by the Governor and his supporters, part by the Assembly. The officers of the Crown were not given a representative character even in theory, and unpopularity was a real recommendation for appointment at the hands of the Governor.

'The principal officers of the local government', wrote Lord Glenelg in 1835, 'have frequently unpopular duties to perform; they are not seldom called to oppose the passions and emotions of the day; and, for the permanent well-being of society, to brave the displeasure of the popular leaders. . . . I will not allow myself to suppose that, on this subject (pensions) any difference of opinion can arise between the executive government and the representatives of the Canadian people.'[1]

Lord Durham was even more emphatic:

'The Assembly . . . could exercise no influence on the nomination of a single servant of the Crown. The Executive Council, the law officers, and whatever heads of departments are known to the administrative system of the Province, were placed in power, without any regard to the wishes of the people or their representatives; nor indeed are there wanting instances in which a mere hostility to the majority of the Assembly elevated the most incompetent persons to posts of honour and trust.'[2]

The administration appointed by the Assembly was of minor importance, but in expending the monies voted by the popular body it made no pretence at co-operation with the executive. Had the Crown not enjoyed an independent revenue, the Assembly's control would undoubtedly have extended over the entire field; but they were limited for the most part to expenditures on public works, and this gave them a patronage which they used without scruple. Eight

[1] Lord Glenelg to the Commissioners in Lower Canada, 17 July 1835, *Brit. H. of C. Papers* (113), xxxix, 1836, pp. 7–9.
[2] *Lord Durham's Report* (*Lucas*), ii, p. 77. Cf. Petition of House of Assembly (Lower Canada) to the House of Commons, December, 1834; *Brit. H. of C. Papers* (113), xxxix, 1836, p. 22.

hundred and fifty commissioners were appointed in Nova Scotia to pay out £10,000 on local improvements. In Lower Canada £25,000 a year was spent on education, and a large proportion of the teachers appointed could neither read nor write.[1]

Another cause of disorganization lay within the Council itself. No member of that body assumed political responsibility for the work of any department. The Council advised as a whole, and the civil service was not subject to the supervision of any special political officer.

'There is', said Lord Durham, ' no head of any of the most important departments of public business in the Colony. The limited powers of the local government in a Colony necessarily obviate the necessity of any provision for some of the most important departments which elsewhere require a superintending mind. But the mere ordinary administration of justice, police, education, public works and internal communications, of finance and of trade, would require the superintendence of persons competent to advise the Governor, on their own responsibility, as to the measures which should be adopted. . . . Yet, of no one of these departments is there any responsible head, by whose advice the Governor may safely be guided. There are some subordinate and very capable officers in each department, from whom he is, in fact, compelled to get information from time to time. But there is no one to whom he, or the public, can look for the correct management and sound decision on the policy of each of these important departments. . . . There is no division into departments in the Council, there is no individual responsibility, and no individual superintendence. Each member of the Council takes an equal part in all the business brought before it.'[2]

During the transition to responsible government the relations of Cabinet and civil service were even more confused. In Nova Scotia in 1847, for example, two heads of departments were in both the Executive Council and the legislature, others were not in either body, while the Council also contained some men who held no other office whatever.[3]

---

[1] *Lord Durham's Report (Lucas)*, ii, pp. 93–6.
[2] *Ibid.*, ii, pp. 108–10.
[3] Letter to Sir John Harvey from his Executive Council, 30 Jan. 1847, *Brit. H. of C. Papers* (621), xlii, 1847–8, p. 65.

The confusion in Canada was even more marked. In 1842, during the negotiations preceding the reconstruction of the Government, La Fontaine steadily refused to concede that any Cabinet officer who was compelled to retire had a right to a pension.[1] One of the ministers eventually forced out was C. R. Ogden, who had accepted the Attorney-Generalship of Lower Canada when the office was non-political.[2] At the same time the Commissioner of Crown Lands, John Davidson, was displaced by a new member of the Cabinet. This office had not been regarded as political and Davidson had not even a seat in Parliament, although Lord Sydenham had suggested in 1841 that he obtain one.[3] The career of Dominick Daly, 'the permanent secretary, the Vicar of Bray of Canadian politics', is most instructive: he combined a political office with a permanent tenure. He began as Provincial Secretary of Lower Canada in 1827, an office which he held until the Union. Lord Sydenham retained him as Provincial Secretary for Canada. He remained in that position under the first Baldwin-La Fontaine Government, and in the dispute between Sir Charles Metcalfe and the Cabinet he remained in office after nine ministers resigned. For sixteen days he was sole minister, and for nine months was one of three. Later, when a genuine Government was formed under Draper, he continued as Provincial Secretary. In 1847 the Draper Government attempted to strengthen itself by including several French Canadians, but they declined to come in unless Daly went out. He refused to leave; and the French Canadians remained outside the Cabinet. In the reorganization of May 1847, Daly still kept his post, and it was not until the formation of the second Baldwin-La Fontaine ministry that he finally resigned. The Imperial Government took pity on him and made him an Imperial civil servant as Commissioner of Tobago, and later Governor of Tobago, Prince Edward Island, and South Australia successively.

The struggle for responsible government found expression in the civil service over the right of patronage. All the

[1] Dent, J. C., *Canada since the Union of 1841*, pp. 239, 243.
[2] *Ibid.*, pp. 87–8, 244.   [3] *Ibid.*, pp. 235, 245.

highest positions were at the disposal of the Governor, who was generously assisted in his task by the Family Compact groups, consisting of the colonial bureaucracy, who naturally recommended those who were sympathetic towards the governing class. Lord Durham described the conditions of patronage existing in the two Canadas in 1838:

'For a long time this body of men (the Family Compact) receiving at times accessions to its numbers, possessed almost all the highest public offices, by means of which, and of its influence in the Executive Council, it wielded all the powers of government; it maintained influence in the legislature by means of its predominance in the Legislative Council; and it disposed of the large number of petty posts which are in the patronage of the Government all over the province. Successive Governors, as they came in their turn, are said to have either submitted quietly to its influence, or, after a short and unavailing struggle, to have yielded to this well-organised party the real conduct of affairs. The bench, the magistracy, the high offices of the Episcopal Church, and a great part of the legal profession, are filled by the adherents of this Party'.[1]

'His (the Governor's) position compelled him to seek the support of some party against the Assembly; and his feelings and his necessities thus combined to induce him to bestow his patronage and to shape his measures to promote the interests of the party on which he was obliged to lean.'[2]

It was this appointing power that was demanded by the Assembly as part of responsible government: if they were to govern, they must of necessity appoint. Although this was clearly seen by Lord Durham,[3] it was not at first admitted by the governors, the Colonial Office, or some of the Assemblies. The classic example was the dispute between Sir Charles Metcalfe and the Baldwin-LaFontaine administration, when responsible government and patronage were made one issue. La Fontaine and Baldwin demanded of the Governor that he should make no appointments without first consulting them,

[1] *Lord Durham's Report (Lucas)*, ii, p. 148.
[2] *Ibid.*, ii, p. 78. Cf. Christie, R., *History of Lower Canada*, i, pp. 349–50; *Brit. H. of C. Papers* (113), xxxix, 1836, pp. 22, 56; *Lower Can. Ass. Journals*, 27 Oct. 1835, pp. 8–9.
[3] *Lord Durham's Report (Lucas)*, ii, pp. 283–4.

and that such appointments should help their political influence in the colony.

'The Governor replied, that he would not make any such stipulation, and could not degrade the character of his office, nor violate his duty by such a surrender of the Prerogative of the Crown. He objected, as he had always done, to the exclusive distribution of Patronage with party views, and maintained the principle that Office ought, in every instance, to be given to the man best qualified to render efficient service to the State; and where there was no such pre-eminence, he asserted his right to exercise his discretion.'[1]

The ministry resigned; and their action was approved by the Assembly as being in accord with the principles of responsible government.[2] The Colonial Secretary, Lord Stanley, defended the position of the Governor in resisting the 'extravagant demands', and said that Metcalfe had 'the entire concurrence and approbation of Her Majesty's Government'.[3] What was more surprising was the vote of the Nova Scotia and New Brunswick Assemblies, both of which supported Metcalfe's interpretation of responsible government.[4] Christie, writing in 1848, voiced the Tory fear that was evidently behind this vote:

'While they (the Cabinet) can secure their dominion in the Assembly . . . and sway it at pleasure, they shall be the responsible ministers, with the Treasury at command, and its attendant influences, and theirs the spoils of office, as the reward of corruption, and the means of perpetuating it. A fair understanding, in fact, that corruption shall be legal, and the people pay, provided always the representatives have their share; and this is responsible government!'[5]

Over a year after the Metcalfe affair the Lieutenant-Governor of New Brunswick appointed his own son-in-law, Alfred Reade, a native of England and a stranger to New

---

[1] Metcalfe's statement to the Assembly, *Can. Ass. Journals*, 1 Dec. 1843, p. 182.　　　　　　　[2] *Ibid.*, 2 Dec. 1843, pp. 186–8.

[3] *Brit. H. of C. Debates*, 2 Feb. 1844, pp. 144–5. Cf. *Ibid.*, 30 May 1844, pp. 31–77.

[4] *N.S. Ass. Journals*, 5 Mar. 1844, pp. 66–71; *N.B. Ass. Journals*, 22 Feb. 1844, pp. 87–8. The Reform party was in a minority in both Assemblies.

[5] Christie, R., *History of Lower Canada*, ii, p. 351.

Brunswick, as Provincial Secretary. Four members of the
Executive Council resigned in protest. Their action was sustained by the House because the appointment was an injustice to members of the colony; but more radical motions as to
its violation of the principles of responsible government were
defeated.[1] When the matter was referred to England,[2] Lord
Stanley went against the Governor, as the appointment had
broken a rule laid down in earlier instructions that employment should be bestowed only on 'settled inhabitants' of the
colony.[3] 'I observe with satisfaction', he continued, 'that the
House of Assembly have not only abstained from complica-
ting the subject with any abstract question of government,
but have rejected every proposal for laying down formal principles upon such questions.'[4] It was not until 1846 when Earl
Grey became Colonial Secretary that patronage was definitely
acknowledged to be in the hands of the Governor's advisers.

The winning of responsible government and the transfer
of patronage from the Governor to his Cabinet did not bring
peace to the civil service. Two questions immediately pressed
for settlement: first, the need for a definite distinction between political and civil office by means of tenure; second,
the conditions which would justify removal from civil office.
The answers in both cases were given by colonial experience
and by English precedents enunciated in the dispatches of
the Colonial Office.

Before the coming of responsible government all offices
were held at the pleasure of the Crown, a concession to the
theory that the Governor was to be completely accountable
to England, but this tenure was interpreted in practice as
meaning during good behaviour.

'No public officer', wrote Lord Glenelg to Sir Francis Bond

[1] Hannay, James, *L. A. Wilmot*, pp. 76–80; *N.B. Ass. Journals*, 13 Feb.
1845, pp. 89–93.

[2] *Ibid.*, 22 Feb. 1845, p. 143.

[3] Lord Stanley to Sir W. Colebrooke, 31 Mar. 1845; *N.B. Ass. Journals*,
5 Feb. 1846, pp. 24–5. Cf. Lord Glenelg to Earl of Gosford, 17 July 1835,
Brit. H. of C. Papers (113), xxxix, 1836, pp. 47–8; Lord Glenelg to Sir F. B.
Head, 5 Dec. 1835, *Ibid.*, pp. 57–8; Lord Glenelg to Sir A. Campbell,
31 Aug. 1836, *N.B. Ass. Journals*, 23 Dec. 1836, p. 199.

[4] Lord Stanley to Sir W. Colebrooke, 31 Mar. 1845, *N.B. Ass. Journals*,
5 Feb. 1846, p. 25.

Head, 'is in danger of losing his employment, except for misconduct or incompetency: but there are many kinds of misconduct
and incompetency which could never be made the subject of
judicial investigation, but which yet would be destructive of the
usefulness of a public officer, and ought therefore to be followed by
a dismissal from the public service.'[1]

The general rule was that appointments lasted for life, as
removal appeared to reflect on the character and integrity of
the incumbent.[2] The office of Provincial Secretary in New
Brunswick—to give an extreme example—was filled for sixty
years (1784–1844) by the two Odells, father and son.

This rule had obviously to be changed if responsible
government were to become effective: political offices had to
be distinguished from civil not only by seats in the legislature
and council but also by tenure strictly at pleasure. The
heads of departments must be prepared to move out when
they lost the legislature's confidence. A dispatch of Lord
John Russell to the Governor-General in 1839 calls attention
to this very necessary alteration. Lord John thought it
unwise that all offices held at pleasure should in fact be held
during good behaviour, but that 'sufficient motives of public
policy' might cause the retirement of some. This was intended
to apply 'rather to the heads of departments than to persons
serving as clerks or in similar capacities under them', such as
the Treasurer, Surveyor-General, Secretary, Attorney- and
Solicitor-General, and members of the Executive Council.
Lord John Russell added that the rule should not be enforced
too stringently with existing officers, but that it was to apply
for all future appointments.[3] Similar dispatches were sent to
Nova Scotia and New Brunswick.[4] The reform was a nominal
one. Lord John Russell had accepted Durham's Report with

[1] Lord Glenelg to Sir F. B. Head, 5 Dec. 1835, *Brit. H. of C. Papers* (113),
xxxix, 1836, p. 57.
[2] *Lord Durham's Report* (*Lucas*), ii, p. 284. Cf. Lord J. Russell to C. P.
Thompson, 16 Oct. 1839, *Brit. H. of C. Papers* (211), xxxi, 1840, p. 15.
[3] Lord J. Russell to C. P. Thompson, 16 Oct. 1839, *Brit. H. of C. Papers*
(211), xxxi, 1840, pp. 15–16. Cf. also *Upper Can. Ass. Journals*, 13 Dec.
1839, pp. 40–1.
[4] *N.S. Ass. Journals*, 4 Jan. 1840, p. 649. Appendix, § 10, pp. 31–2;
N.B. Ass. Journals, 5 Feb. 1840, p. 42.

reservations, and he was using it only as a threat against the Family Compact interests: he was not prepared to advocate the complete adoption of the new system.

For the next eight years colonial administration was in the confusion of the transitionary period. A dispute in Nova Scotia finally brought a definite pronouncement from the Colonial Office in favour of responsible government and the new conditions of tenure. Sir John Harvey, Lieutenant Governor of Nova Scotia, attempted in 1846 to conduct a coalition Executive Council and distribute the offices of emolument between the parties. The claims of the reformers were met by the Council with an offer of the Solicitor-Generalship and four executive seats, with the understanding that all other positions were to be held for life. The Opposition declined the coalition, and objected to the Council's views on tenure, citing Lord John Russell's dispatch of 1839.[1] The Council thereupon wrote the Governor pointing out that the English system of government had not been adopted in Nova Scotia, that there was no administration by heads of departments, that many councillors held no other office, and that it would be most unfair to deprive men of their positions on account of party changes. They asked that their correspondence be forwarded to the Colonial Secretary and that he should declare how far 'the mode and principles of English administration, with their incidents as respects the tenure of offices as dependent on the changes of political parties, shall henceforth be held to be in practical operation in Nova Scotia'.[2] Earl Grey replied in a long dispatch, giving a warm adherence to the principle of parliamentary responsibility and advising a complete adoption in Nova Scotia of the English system and precedents.

'Though the legal tenure, "during good behaviour", is rare, tenure during good behaviour, in the popular sense of the term, may be said to be the general rule of our public service. The exception is in the case of those high public servants whom it is

---

[1] Letter of Howe, Doyle, M'Nab, and Young to Sir John Harvey, 17 Dec. 1846, *Brit. H. of C. Papers* (621), xlii, 1847–8, p. 14.

[2] Letters to Sir John Harvey from his Executive Council, 28 and 30 Jan. 1847, *Brit. H. of C. Papers* (621), xlii, 1847–8, pp. 65–8.

necessary to invest with such discretion as really to leave in their hands the whole direction of the policy of the empire in all its various departments. Such power must, with a representative government, be subject to constant control by Parliament.' [1]

'I regard this system as possessing upon the whole great advantages. We owe to it that the public servants of this country, as a body, are remarkable for their experience and knowledge of public affairs, and honourably distinguished by the zeal and integrity with which they discharge their duties, without reference to party feeling: we owe to it also, that as the transfer of power from one party in the State to another is followed by no change in the holders of any but a few of the highest offices, political animosities are not in general carried to the same height, and do not so deeply agitate the whole frame of society as in those countries in which a different practice prevails. The system with regard to the tenure of office which has been found to work so well here, seems well worthy of imitation in the British American colonies. . . . In order to keep the Executive Government in harmony with the Legislature, it is doubtless necessary that the direction of the internal policy of the colony should be entrusted to those who enjoy the confidence of the Provincial Parliament, but it is of great moment not to carry the practice of changing public officers further than is absolutely necessary for the attainment of that end, lest the administration of public affairs should be deranged by increasing the bitterness of party spirit, and subjecting the whole machinery of Government to perpetual change and uncertainty.' [2]

The dispatch further stated that the public offices which were to be regarded as political could be determined only by local conditions. 'The practical end of responsible government would be satisfied by the removability of a single public officer, provided that through him public opinion could influence the general administration of affairs.' Earl Grey, however, suggested that it would probably be necessary to change the Attorney-General, Solicitor-General, Provincial Secretary, and possibly a few others. The Executive Council, he added, should contain no officers who were not removable.[3]

'Those public servants, who hold their offices permanently, must upon that very ground be regarded as subordinate, and

---

[1] Earl Grey to Sir John Harvey, 31 Mar. 1847, *Ibid.*, p. 77.
[2] *Ibid.*, p. 78.   [3] *Ibid.*, p. 78.

ought not to be members of either house of the Legislature, by which they would necessarily be more or less mixed up in party struggles; and, on the other hand, those who are to have the general direction of affairs exercise that function by virtue of their responsibility to the Legislature, which implies their being removable from office, and also that they should be members either of the Assembly or of the Legislative Council.' [1]

Seldom has the theory of parliamentary government been so adequately expressed, or have the relations of the ministry and the civil service been so clearly defined. Nova Scotia was not slow to give a practical demonstration. On 28 January 1848 the Executive Council resigned; and the offices named by Earl Grey went to the incoming government, which expressed its willingness to leave others undisturbed until a general reorganization was effected.[2]

The second civil service problem presented by the growth of responsible government was the definition of the conditions justifying removal from civil office, a difficulty which found slight mention in the dispatch of Earl Grey. If the greater part of the administration were to be permanent, did this mean that civil servants were to be as politically active as they wished? The ideal attitude, Lord Glenelg had written in 1835,[3] was one of neutrality on party questions; and so long as the Governor both ruled and made appointments, official hostility to the government was easily prevented. But with a changing cabinet and a changing policy, it was not only possible but extremely likely that the civil service and the ministry would be politically opposed.

The period between the Governor's and the Cabinet's supremacy apparently allowed the civil servant great latitude in his party activity. In 1842 Robert Baldwin was admitted to the ministry as Attorney-General for Canada West and was compelled to seek re-election in Hastings. He was opposed, and defeated after a very violent election, by Edmund Murney, Clerk of the Peace in that district; but the latter was

[1] *Ibid.*, p. 79.
[2] Sir John Harvey to Earl Grey, 10 Feb. 1848, *Ibid.*, p. 87.
[3] Lord Glenelg to Sir F. B. Head, 5 Dec. 1835, *Brit. H. of C. Papers* (113), xxxix, 1836, p. 64.

not dismissed from office until after the contest. Sir Charles Bagot, in a letter to the Colonial Secretary, said that it seemed to him and his Council both inconsistent and highly injurious to the efficiency of government that such an office-holder should work against the ministry 'in the most obnoxious form by opposing the re-election of my principal law officer . . . proclaiming his intention of offering determined resistance to government policy'.[1] The Governor enclosed Murney's answer to his dismissal. In this letter Murney denied that the office of Clerk of the Peace came under Lord John Russell's dispatch of 1839, and stated that although he had resisted Lord Sydenham's scheme of union he had not been dismissed. He had opposed Baldwin in 1841, and would have succeeded but for the violence and intimidation used by Baldwin's friends, who threatened 'all who voted for Mr. Murney would be forthwith dismissed. Perhaps the wisdom of your Executive Council can draw the distinction between the intimidation of clubs and intimidation used by Executive threats.' He stated that he was also a major in the militia, and concluded: 'Believing that the one office as much comes within the meaning of the above dispatch as the other . . . I beg to tender the resignation of my commission.'[2]

As self-government gradually developed, the question of the political activity of civil servants became more and more serious. The Cabinet made all appointments to the service from its own political supporters, and as a result a new ministry was frequently confronted with hostile subordinates. These were protected to a great degree by the convention that their tenure was one during good behaviour; but this could be partially circumvented by increasing the number of avowedly political offices, and also by making political partisanship a kind of misbehaviour and a cause for removal. It was the latter policy that found most favour with the colonial governments, and their natural inclination was strengthened by the well-established American practice of dismissing all civil servants who were appointed by the opposite party.

Such action was at first strongly opposed by the Colonial

[1] Sir C. Bagot to Lord Stanley, 11 Nov. 1842, *Canadian Archives*, G. 457 (No. 235).   [2] *Ibid.*

Office, but a few years' experience compelled a modification of its views. In 1848, for example, the Reform government in Nova Scotia found that the civil service was hampering its work and opposing its candidates at elections. Inasmuch as Earl Grey's dispatch of 1847 had imposed restrictions on the power of removal,[1] the ministry wrote him for further advice. Earl Grey's reply showed how his earlier position had changed. He rebuked the civil servants for their conduct, intimated that a continuance would lead to a more strict application of the power of dismissal, and concluded with a suggestion that disfranchisement might prove the only possible solution.[2]

'I am aware of no remedy against what is termed "the concealed hostility" of persons holding permanent offices to an administration opposed to that to which they may have been indebted for their appointments. It is impossible but that such persons should, like all others, have their personal political feelings, and it is not unnatural that they should desire the advancement of the party to power to whom they are thus indebted, but these persons must be aware that the condition upon which they will be suffered to enjoy exemption from dismissal for any other cause but that of positive misconduct, will be that they should abstain from taking any active part in political contests. Such indeed is the well understood rule which prevails in this country, and I am of opinion that a similar rule should be enforced in Nova Scotia. In the smaller society of a Colony, it is not unreasonable to expect that party disputes should run higher than in the larger and more settled society of this Country ; and it becomes the more necessary, therefore, that in the Colonies neutrality in party contests should be observed on the part of holders of office not regarded as political. I should think it by no means unreasonable to make it known to such persons, that they would be expected to abstain from the exercise of their right of voting at Elections against any Member of the existing Administration for the time being, inasmuch as they could not give such votes without forfeiting that neutral position in politics which is the condition of their permanent tenure of their respective offices.'[3]

---

[1] Cf. *supra*, p. 12.
[2] Earl Grey to Sir John Harvey, 15 Nov. 1848, *N.S. Legis. Coun. Journals*, 1849, Appendix, § 11, pp. 123–5.
[3] *Ibid.*, pp. 124–5.

By 1860 colonial precedent and Colonial Office approval had established the custom that active political partisanship by a civil servant constituted valid grounds for dismissal. Nova Scotia again furnished the opportunity for the official pronouncement on the subject. The Conservative Government in 1859 appointed Peter Hamilton, a violent partisan,[1] Registrar of Deeds for Halifax. The following year, the Conservatives having been defeated, he was removed by the Liberals. Lord Mulgrave, the Lieutenant Governor, in reporting the incident to the Colonial Secretary, said that the removal was quite justifiable and in accord with Earl Grey's dispatch of 15 November 1848. He continued:

'No one can be more opposed than I am to the system of depriving persons of subordinate offices simply on account of their political feelings, but at the same time I feel that it would be impossible for Responsible Government to exist if persons holding these offices are permitted to become open and violent partisans and still to retain their offices in opposition to the party in power.'[2]

The Duke of Newcastle replied that 'the act was no more than consonant with generally received principles of administration. It would be manifestly unreasonable that any one should expect to be in active opposition to the Government and at the same time to remain a public servant. . . . It is competent to any man to choose between political life and official life, but not to attempt to combine in himself two incompatible conditions.'[3] A minute of the Nova Scotia Executive Council indicates that its view of the case was identical with that of the Governor and the Colonial Secretary.[4]

Two years later the removal of the Honourable E. B. Chandler from office in New Brunswick led to a further correspondence between the Lieutenant Governor and the ministry and the Lieutenant Governor and Colonial Office.[5]

---

[1] Lord Mulgrave considered him so extreme a politician that he told the Conservative Government in 1859 that he thought the appointment 'an injudicious one'.

[2] Lord Mulgrave to the Duke of Newcastle, 26 May 1860, *Toronto Globe*, 22 Sept. 1860.

[3] Duke of Newcastle to Lord Mulgrave, 5 July 1860; *Ibid.*

[4] *Ibid.*   [5] *N.B. Ass. Journals*, 1862, pp. 192–5.

Substantially the same principles were enunciated as in the earlier Nova Scotian case, though the Duke of Newcastle was somewhat more explicit in his warning for moderation.

'I cannot, however, but express my cordial concurrence in the principle you have laid down in your Minute, that in the case of offices not of a political nature, it is highly inexpedient and improper to remove their holders except for incompetency or misconduct. Should removals from such offices be made from political motives, the obvious consequence would be that opposite political parties, on succeeding to power, would retaliate, so as to produce a repetition of vindictive and extensive changes amongst the holders of government offices, and thus to prevent the growth of experience and destroy the efficiency of public administration. This is an evil which is so notorious in a neighbouring country that it may serve as a warning to the public men of the British Provinces of North America, where happily greater moderation has prevailed in political affairs, and a greater stability in the machinery of Government.'[1]

The Canadian civil service, therefore, owes much to the period before Confederation. It not only began at that time, it also took on some of its most important characteristics, the influence of which is still felt. In the early days before responsible government the civil service presented few problems: its administrative duties were slight, its personnel was the Governor and his adherents. The Crown Colony had to be ruled, and the Governor and Family Compact did it. Then appeared troublesome ideas about self-government, and the Governor's lot 'was not a happy one.' Patronage, instead of being a useful means of maintaining peace, became a storm centre around which the Crown and the Assembly fought for power. Responsible government was finally obtained, but it only accentuated the uncertainty in the civil service. Political and civil offices had to be clearly defined, and separated by tenure as well as by position in the Council, the patronage being given to the majority in the Assembly, who used it as selfishly as their predecessors. This in turn led to the further problem of the right of a civil servant to take part in politics. It was decided that as the civil servant should not actively

[1] *Ibid.*, pp. 193–4.

support any party, political partisanship would constitute valid grounds for removal. Lastly, throughout this period as in later years, the trend of events in the civil service was guided, not only by local conditions, but by the examples and precedents in Great Britain and the United States.

II. THE SPOILS SYSTEM AND PROPOSALS FOR REFORM

1867–80

'He's got 'em on the list—he's got 'em on the list;
And they'll none of 'em be missed—they'll none of 'em be missed!'
The Mikado.

THE opening period of Canadian civil service history naturally began by consolidating and fitting together the segments from the provincial services. An enabling Act had to be passed, new rules and a new organization had to be drawn up, and it was necessary to appoint a body which should report on the adequacy of the statute and suggest possible changes in the regulations. The same years saw also the appearance of the Canadian version of the spoils system, and, in reply to it, the beginning of the reform movement, which led in turn to the culminating act of the period, the appointment of an investigating Commission in 1880.

The *British North America Act, 1867*, provided that all colonial civil servants discharging duties which did not come under those assigned to the provinces should become Dominion officials until the Canadian Parliament provided otherwise.[1] In 1868 the *Canada Civil Service Act*[2] was passed, modelled to a great extent on the statute which had been in force in the colony of Canada before the Union.[3] Its purpose was 'to limit the age and ensure the proper qualification of candidates for positions in the public departments, to establish a regular classification, to provide for judicious promotion, to check the unnecessary employment of extra clerks, and guard against an undue expansion for civil government.'[4]

The Act divided the public officials into two classes, the Departmental Staff and the Outside Service.[5] The regulation of the latter was left to the Governor in Council,[6] and except

---

[1] Section 130.   [2] *Can. Stat.*, 31 Vic. c. 34.   [3] *Ibid.*, 20 Vic. c. 24.
[4] Royal Commission on the Civil Service, *Can. Sess. Pap.*, 1892, § 16c,
p. xvii.   [5] Sections 1, 2.   [6] Section 15.

for three minor exceptions[1] was not again mentioned in the
Act. The Departmental Staff consisted of Deputy Heads of
Departments, Chief Clerks, First, Second (Senior and Junior)
and Third Class Clerks, and Probationary Clerks.[2] The latter
were to enter at a fixed salary with a view to becoming Third
Class Clerks at the expiration of a year: failing to do this at
the end of two years, they would be compelled to leave.[3]
Promotion was to take place from the Third Class through
the various grades, presumably to the First Class.[4] The Act
did not state whether Chief Clerks were to be promoted from
the First Class or whether they were to be brought in from
outside.[5] The Deputy Heads were to be appointed under the
Great Seal and receive such salary as the Governor in
Council might assign them.[6] All offices were stated to be
held at pleasure.[7]

Every candidate for a position was required to produce
evidence of his age, health, and moral character. He next
secured the nomination of a Cabinet Minister, and came
before the Civil Service Board for examination. If successful,
he was admitted.[8] The examining Board was composed of all
the deputy heads of departments, five making a quorum. It
was to frame regulations for the service and for the examinations (which might differ for each department), though these
regulations had to be first approved by the Governor in
Council. The Board was also to examine candidates, keep
records of such candidates and examinations, grant certificates to the successful, and report on the length of service of
those eligible for promotion.[9] Appointments were to be made
of persons between the ages of eighteen and twenty-five, but
the Governor in Council might appoint any one over twenty-
five upon the application of a Minister specifying reasons
therefor. If such appointment was recommended on the
ground of special qualifications the candidate might be asked
to undergo a special examination. If he should be over forty
years of age, the reasons for his appointment were to be submitted to Parliament.[10] Private secretaries of Cabinet Minis-

---

[1] Sections 6, 16, 23.   [2] Sections, 1, 7–14, 19.   [3] Section 7.
[4] Sections 8–11.   [5] Section 11.   [6] Section 14.
[7] Section 5.   [8] Section 6.   [9] Section 25.   [10] Section 3.

ters were not limited as to age, but they retired with their principals.[1]

The Government, having passed the Act, was immediately confronted with the difficult task of making the old colonial civil servants fit into the new scheme of things. A Royal Commission was therefore appointed on 9 June 1868, 'to enquire into the present state and the probable requirements of the civil service', and was directed to report on the re-organization, classification, and adaptation of the old services in relation to the new wants and problems.[2] The Commission was composed of five deputy heads of departments and two members from outside the service—a personnel which represented so strongly the civil servant element that really valuable proposals could scarcely be expected. A knowledge of actual conditions was, however, very important, and what the Commission lost in originality and initiative was partially made up by a mastery of the subject under investigation.

The first report of the Commission was devoted to the Departmental Staff. It found a general lack of proportion between the salaries and the offices: the remuneration being too high for lower positions and too low for higher ones. Indiscriminate promotions had caused the distinction between important and minor offices to be even less significant. The natural result had followed. The service had attracted second-rate men who could not hope to do so well elsewhere, while the lack of any great future had discouraged really good men from entering. The new *Civil Service Act* had endeavoured to remedy these defects, but inasmuch as the Government had been forced to consider existing office-holders and had been unable by the terms of the Act to lower their salaries, little immediate improvement could be made.[3] The Commission also made the complaint, which in later years was to be many times repeated, that similar positions requiring the same qualifications drew different rates of pay.[4] Furthermore, owing to the wholesale method by which some services had been taken over at the time of Confederation,

[1] *Ibid.*   [2] *Can. Sess. Pap.*, 1869, § 19, p. 4.
[3] *Ibid.*, p. 5.   [4] *Ibid.*, p. 9.

certain departments were found to be overloaded with officials while at the same time other branches were under-manned.[1]

The Commission proposed as a solution a theoretical staff for each department, classifying each rank 'according to the importance and responsibility of the duties which would be assigned to them', and suggested the way in which these might be filled by the existing office-holders.[2] Three con-siderations were laid down as determining the position of each official, 'the nature of his duties, the length of his service, and the salary to which he has attained'.[3]

Another fault found by the Commission was the large number of so-called 'temporary clerks', who were kept on from year to year at a *per diem* salary and received, in some instances, almost double the emolument of a permanent official doing the same work. The report expressed the mild hope that the greater severity of the new Act would prevent this reoccurring.[4] The service was also hampered by the pre-sence of a large number of men who had become so old as to be of little use. This was mentioned by the Commission, but no remedy was suggested.[5]

In the second and third reports [6] the Commissioners dis-cussed the reorganization of the Outside Service. Their chief recommendation was that all employees here, as in the Departmental Staff, should be made to pass an entrance examination.[7] They were particularly insistent on the neces-sity for such tests in the Excise Department.

'In the Outside Branches of this Department, we find the formularies for the examination of candidates are very complete, and where the examination is rigidly carried out, no incompetent man can pass. We cannot too strongly urge the necessity for a strict adherence to the requirements called for by these examina-tions. The revenue must inevitably suffer where any relaxation of the rules is permitted, and the worst consequences must follow where men are appointed or allowed to remain in the Department without examination. Unfortunately, up to the present time the

[1] *Can. Sess. Pap.*, 1869, § 19, p. 6.   [2] *Ibid.*, pp. 6, 12–38, 44–59.
[3] *Ibid.*, p. 7.   [4] *Ibid.*, p. 8.
[5] *Ibid.*, pp. 6, 58–9.   [6] *Can. Sess. Pap.*, 1869, § 19. *Ibid.*, 1870, § 64.
[7] *Ibid.*, 1869, § 19, p. 4. *Ibid.*, 1870, § 64, p. 3.

rules have not been strictly adhered to, and in all the points which we have visited we have found many men in the service who have undergone no examination; but an improvement is gradually taking place in this respect.' [1]

Criticism of the Commission's reports must lie not against what they said, but what they left unsaid. Only one paragraph in all the findings dealt directly with the evil of patronage:

'It is not sufficient, however, to lay down a rule—it should be carried out. But it is to be regretted that in this country, as appears to have been the case, until comparatively late years, in the mother country, the rule has been overridden by parliamentary influence, and both appointments and promotions have been made in direct contravention of the salutary rule laid down for the advantage of the Customs Service.' [2]

The patronage evil had descended on the new Dominion from the old colonies; and a few months before the Commission's report was written, the statement had been made in the House of Commons that 'upon every change of ministry the incomers found that they had friends, and he was sorry to say relatives, whom it was necessary to provide for, and the number of offices was being continually augmented upon these considerations, it being the practice of the country to consider each public appointment as having been made for life, and no old ones therefore being cancelled to make room for the new.' [3] Such a state of affairs must have been known to the Commissioners, especially to those five who were deputy heads of departments, and they could scarcely have deceived themselves by prospects of improvement so long as the Act remained a virtual copy of the older one of the colony of Canada. It is probable that the Commission either took the patronage system for granted and thought it an indispensable concomitant of government, or considered the prospects of reform so remote as to be almost Utopian.

The report, it is true, approved of the examination system, but the idea of using it to curb patronage was never men-

[1] *Ibid.*, 1870, § 64, p. 9.   [2] *Ibid.*, 1869, § 19, p. 32.
[3] *Ottawa Times*, 19 Mar. 1868.

tioned. The Commissioners recommended pass examinations as a means of procuring more efficient officers, but they did not appear to realize that a competitive test would discover much better men than one where only a passing grade was required. It was also assumed as a matter of course that candidates should obtain a recommendation from a Cabinet Minister before either examination or appointment. In England the Northcote-Trevelyan Report was presented in 1853, and the Order in Council establishing the Civil Service Commission was passed in 1855. In the United States, in 1868, a committee of Congress had made an exhaustive report on civil services throughout the world. The Canadian Commissioners, if one may judge from their report, had never heard of any of them. The suggestions which they made for the classification and organization of the departments were valuable, but they failed to touch the fundamental needs of the service. The only reasonable explanation for such important omissions is that they deliberately confined their inquiry to the adjustment of the old officials to the new Act, although they had been distinctly empowered to go much farther and to investigate the general state of the service. Their report had one tangible result: the majority of the recommendations were accepted by the Government and a classification drawn up on that basis.[1]

The first part of Canadian civil service history extends from the *British North America Act* and the Act of 1868 to the Royal Commission of 1880, which preceded the second *Civil Service Act*. It was an inglorious period. The original difficulty was the Act of 1868, which was extremely unsatisfactory. It made no innovations and embodied no new principles: it was a stop-gap measure put through in a hurry to straighten out the confusion resulting from the Confederation. There was, therefore, no attempt to make any real improvements; and although the Act was passed as a temporary expedient, it became permanently established on the statute book. Its chief virtue was that it created a classification and provided a rough machine by means of which the business of government could be carried on.

[1] *Can. Sess. Pap.*, 1870, § 64, pp. 1–22.

If the provisions of the Act were unsatisfactory, its administration was even more so. It was observed by the party in power when convenient, and ignored when an opportunity arose for the party to consolidate its position in the constituencies. Political influence and party service became almost the sole tests for obtaining appointments to the service or making removals from it. The early British tradition of placing friends in office, which was introduced by the colonial governors, was loyally carried out, and it was even improved upon by adding to it the contemporary American idea that 'to the victor belong the spoils of the enemy'. The influence of the latter theory upon the Canadian service has been so strong and persistent that a few of its essential features must be described. It was first introduced into American federal politics in 1829 by Andrew Jackson, though it had previously been freely used in state and local government. It has had many adherents, a number of attempted justifications, and a long practical demonstration in the United States which has not entirely ceased to-day.

'The essential features of the system are, that a place in the public service is held at the absolute pleasure of the appointing authority; that it is invariably bestowed from party motives on a party man, as a reward for party services (whether of the appointee or of some one who pushes him); that no man expects to hold it any longer than his party holds power; and that this gives him the strongest personal reasons for fighting in the party ranks.'[1]

The adoption of the spoils in the United States was made easier by the prevalence of the so-called democratic idea of rotation in office, and it was perpetuated because the party found it both convenient and necessary. Rotation in office, although 'a great American principle',[2] was a far call from the political beliefs of 1789. The Federalists considered that public office carried with it a vested right to hold that position during good behaviour, and the Republicans, although they did not stress this aspect, saw nothing undemocratic in a long and stable tenure. But the conception of any property in an office was completely repudiated by the Jacksonians,

[1] Bryce, James, *The American Commonwealth* (1911 ed.), ii, p. 138.
[2] Senator Allen, *Congressional Globe*, xv, p. 819.

who even went so far as to insist that a long tenure was detrimental to good public service.[1] Rotation was therefore first used only as a protection against abuse of power in elective offices, though it later grew in popular favour as applying to Government positions of all kinds.[2] The theory made two assumptions: first, that as an office in the civil service demanded no special ability, any one was competent to occupy it; and second, that no person had a greater right to an office than any one else. Government did not exist primarily to get things done well, but to provide jobs for the democracy; the public owned the Government, and it therefore had a right to pass the offices around. Efficiency might necessitate permanence, but equality could not tolerate it, and no one must be allowed to forget that all men were created equal. Jackson outlined the essential features of rotation in his first annual message to Congress:

'The duties of all public offices are, or at least admit of being made, so plain and simple that men of intelligence may readily qualify themselves for their performance; and I cannot but believe that more is lost by the long continuance of men in office than is generally to be gained by their experience. . . . In a country where offices are created solely for the benefit of the people no one man has any more intrinsic right to official station than another. Offices were not established to give support to particular men at the public expense. No individual wrong is, therefore, done by removal, since neither appointment to nor continuance in office is matter of right. . . . He who is removed has the same means of obtaining a living that are enjoyed by the millions who never held office.'[3]

This rotation, it was urged, held many advantages for a democratic people. It educated them in the operation of government. Every one was given an equal chance for office and political power. It prevented the growth of a stiff-necked official class and 'checked the overbearing insolence of office'. Finally, and perhaps most important of the alleged virtues, it was a constant reminder to the official that he was the ser-

[1] Merriam, C. E., *American Political Theories*, pp. 184–7.
[2] Fish, C. R., *The Civil Service and the Patronage*, pp. 80–5.
[3] Richardson, J. D., *Messages and Papers of the Presidents*, ii, p. 449.

vant of the people, and hence it was supposed in some
esoteric manner to prevent corruption.[1]

The second idea behind the spoils system was its cohesive
force in party management. It furnished a reward for deserving retainers, and the possibility of removal urged those
in office to exert themselves to the utmost for party success.
To such extremes was the principle carried that after 1857 a
change of President meant a change of offices, even though
the old and new administrations belonged to the same party.
Senator Marcy, who had christened the spoils system, rue-
fully observed that he had 'never recommended the policy
of pillaging his own camp'.[2]

'The true cause for the introduction of the spoils system was the
triumph of democracy. If the people as a whole are to exert any
tangible influence on the conduct of government, they must be
organized. . . . There must be drilling and training, hard work with
the awkward squad, and occasional dress parade. This work requires the labor of many men: there must be captains of hundreds
and the captains of tens, district chiefs and ward heelers. Now,
some men labor for love and some for glory; but glory comes only
to the leaders of ten thousands, to the very few—it cannot serve
as a general inducement, and even those who love must live. . . . If,
then, they are to devote their time to politics, politics must be
made to pay. It is here that the function of the spoils system
becomes evident; the civil service becomes the pay-roll of the
party leader; offices are apportioned according to the rank and
merits of his subordinates, and, if duties are too heavy or new
positions are needed, new offices may be created.'[3]

The sole requirement for a position, therefore, became
party service. 'Signatures' on a petition for an office became
exceedingly important, for the candidate who was able to
obtain the most names was likely to be successful.[4] Places
were promised by the bosses before the battle, so as to enlist
the greatest possible effort, and the whole party web of
primaries, conventions, and committees, whether of ward,

[1] *Ibid.*, ii, pp. 448–9.
[2] Ostrogorski, M., *Democracy and the Organization of Political Parties*, ii,
p. 83.
[3] Fish, C. R., *The Civil Service and the Patronage*, pp. 156–7.
[4] *Ibid.*, p. 113.

city, district, state, or nation, was bound together by patronage. Political activity did not cease with the acquisition of office: the fortunate one was expected to show his appreciation by even more strenuous efforts,[1] and his activity was watched and checked by other government agents.[2] Assessments to swell the party funds were levied on officials in proportion to the salary they received.[3]

The extent of the spoils system was limited only by the capacity of the service. All federal officers, from ambassadors to door-keepers, charwomen, and rural postmasters, might expect to be changed every four years. Frequently, of course, good appointments were made, either because the party happened to contain some talent or because it was not wise to outrage the moral element too greatly. The latter policy was known as 'sprinkling political perfumery'. It is scarcely necessary to mention the evil effect of the spoils on the public service. The party was better organized and better managed than the Government, for every office-holder was more attentive to his political success than to his administrative efficiency. The first affected his office and his pocket, the second merely his conscience—and he had not been chosen for his conscientiousness. The chief concern was not public duty but party loyalty: the great object sought was not the elevation of the office, but its retention.

Such was the spoils system at its worst, and it suffered no serious check in the United States until 1883. A thorough application of the idea, as stated above by Lord Bryce,[4] involved four things: appointments were given primarily for party service; officials were to work for the appointing party; tenure of office was strictly at pleasure; and wholesale dismissals followed each change of Government. To what extent did the Canadian service reproduce these characteristic features?

The attitude of the Canadian Government towards appointments was revealed in the building of the Intercolonial Railway, although it did not come under the provisions of the *Civil Service Act*. In 1874 an investigation was made into the

[1] Fish, C. R., *The Civil Service and the Patronage*, pp. 123–4.
[2] *Ibid.*, pp. 136–7.   [3] *Ibid.*, p. 180.   [4] Cf. *supra*, p. 25.

construction of the road, and the report discussed with un-
common frankness the patronage question. Political influence
was the cause of a 'very great redundancy of staff and the
employment of many incompetent men'. Employees were
frequently insubordinate because they knew their members
of Parliament would keep them in their positions. Inefficient
men were foisted on the engineers with no other qualification
save their political services, and they expected and demanded
promotion on the same grounds.[1]

Appointments in the civil service proper were made for the
same party reasons and rarely for any other. The independent *Canadian Monthly* gave a bitter account of the chief
qualities necessary to secure a position:

'Appointments to the civil service are theoretically supposed to
be based on individual competency; they are, in fact, the rewards
of political subserviency. Industry and intelligence ought to
ensure promotion in a steady and unbroken order as occasion
occurs; in practice, however, there exists a system of purchase
less defensible than that which Lord Cardwell abolished in the
army. The price of a commission in the government service is the
free exercise of a glib tongue, deftness in canvassing, unscrupulous-
ness in everything. Serve the party day and night, secure us an
electoral triumph by fair means or foul, and you shall be quar-
tered for life on the public treasury, is the bribe held out to those
who would live at ease. . . . The crowd of nondescript, and scarcely
reputable, politicians who hover about at pic-nics and declaim at
drill-shed "demonstrations" are the stuff of which, under the party
system, public servants are made. To the well-informed, trained,
and experienced member of the service there is little chance of
advancement when one of these gentry stands in his way. The
latter has paid his price for the office, the former has not; this one
has 'faithfully served his party', and should be recompensed, the
other has merely deserved well of his country, which has no means
left of rewarding him.'[2]

No one has ever accused Sir John A. Macdonald of an
excess of political morality or of expecting too much of his
associates, and this culpable tolerance may partially explain

[1] *Canadian Monthly*, Nov. 1874, p. 455.
[2] *Canadian Monthly*, Nov. 1876, p. 443; cf. *ibid.*, May 1875, p. 448.

the complacency with which he regarded the operation of the
Act of 1868. But even he was compelled to admit some
difficulties:

'It was quite true that the civil service was not worked with
that completeness here that it was in England, but there was a
very close and satisfactory approximation to it. . . . His experience
had been that the government had less trouble in carrying on the
whole administration of the affairs of the Dominion than they
had in arranging the contested claims of public servants. . . . When
the first Bill was introduced a great many persons said that it
could not be worked at all from the pressure that would be brought
on the government of the day by their political supporters and
others who had been accustomed to the old system. But by
degrees it was approaching perfection. . . . It was true the rules
were not carried out literally. Sometimes the pressure was so
great that the government might commit a breach of the provisions, but they were exceptional cases. He could say positively
that since the present Act had been in operation a very great
improvement had taken place in the civil service. The strictness
of its provisions assisted members of parliament in resisting undue
pressure from their supporters. When persons who from age or
incapacity of any kind had no right to expect an appointment
applied to them, they could point to the Act and say that they
would help them if they could, but that the law prevented it. In
time he thought the Act would be carried out as fully and faithfully as it now is in England.'[1]

It can be seen that Sir John's ideas as to what constituted
a good civil service were modest and easily satisfied. The
Act was useful as an aid in dodging those who were tactless
enough to remember election promises. He considered that
party support was the indispensable condition to appointment, and had little sympathy with idealistic attempts to
alter it. 'Every government', he said in 1878, 'selected for
the civil service their own friends and no one could object to
it.'[2] There is little wonder that Goldwin Smith wrote a few
years later: 'Sir John is disappointing. . . . He cannot resist
the solicitations of partisans, except perhaps in the case of

[1] *Can. H. of C. Debates*, 26 Apr. 1872, pp. 180–1. For a criticism of the
Act cf. *ibid.*, pp. 179–87.
[2] *Ibid.*, 27 Apr. 1878, p. 2229.

judicial appointments, in regard to which his best sentiment is peculiarly romantic.' [1]

The second characteristic of the spoils was also found in Canada. Each political party when in power expected the civil servants all over the country to support it and work against the Opposition. Each party accused the other of having dictated to the office-holders the way they should cast their votes.[2] Telegrams from Cabinet Ministers were cited in Parliament, which stated that the public servants should not work against the Government and implied that they were expected to support it.[3] Lucius Huntington, a prominent member of the Mackenzie Administration, said that no objection could be raised to Government officials interfering in provincial politics, so long as the service did not suffer.[4] Nine years later Sir Charles Tupper propounded the rather startling view that although no public officer should be allowed to oppose the Government of the day, he had 'a perfect right to take an active and open part' in supporting it.[5] This was equivalent to saying that the civil servants might be partisans provided they supported the Government and not the Opposition—a return to the idea held before responsible government. One conclusion seems to be unescapable: both parties were culpable, and each expected its appointees to use all the influence they could command to help win the election.

Inevitably dismissals from the service for party reasons became more and more common. The period from Confederation to 1880 saw two changes of Government: Macdonald resigned in 1873, and the Liberals were defeated in 1878. On each occasion changes in the personnel of the civil service followed closely the new party's accession to power.[6] The custom of pre-Confederation days, that political partisan-

---

[1] Smith, Goldwin, *Correspondence*, p. 128; cf. Pope, J., *Sir John Macdonald*, ii, pp. 73–5.

[2] *Can. H. of C. Debates*, 26 Apr. 1878, pp. 2215–19; *ibid.*, 27 Apr. 1878, pp. 2227–47.

[3] *Ibid.*, pp. 2238–40.   [4] *Ibid.*, pp. 2231–2.

[5] *Ibid.*, 31 May 1887, p. 661.

[6] *Toronto Mail*, 16 Apr., 8, 14, 19 May 1874; *Can. Sess. Pap.*, 1873, § 29, 1878, § 76; *Can. H. of C. Debates*, 16 Feb. 1877, pp. 88–93; *ibid.*, 22 Feb. 1877, pp. 204–47; *ibid.*, 19, 20 Mar. 1879, pp. 550–610.

ship would justify removal, was carried out with efficient thoroughness. And it was easy to excuse such dismissals. The original appointment had been poor, the office-holder had loyally worked for his benefactor, and there was an applicant clamouring for the position. Alexander Mackenzie stated in Parliament that 'the government had been obliged to exercise a great deal of forbearance when officials had been appointed for purely political reasons without any regard to their fitness for office'.[1] A couple of years later he said: 'I have known, under the old government, a public officer occupying a high position taking the course on a public platform of advocating the cause of the government of which he was a servant.'[2] These cases gave the opposing party no alternative but removal; the trouble was that the subsequent appointment was apt to be no better than the earlier one.

It was evident that Canada was only a step removed from the spoils system in the American sense. The idea of appointing for party service had been accepted unreservedly; and both parties also expected the civil servants to use their offices to promote the party cause. The legal tenure of all offices had always been at pleasure, but custom before Confederation had interpreted this to mean during good behaviour, provided the officials did not take an active part in politics. But as partisan appointments became more flagrant, and as the Governments exerted more pressure on their employees for open support, it became increasingly difficult for the civil servant to abstain from party contests. The result was that his tenure during good behaviour was frequently forfeited. This in turn led to the fourth characteristic of the spoils system, dismissal on a change of Government. If the Opposition were successful, it naturally removed all those who could be convicted of open hostility or gross inefficiency.

In spite of all this, it would be wrong to assume that Canada had a spoils system within the Jacksonian meaning of the word, though the application of the dictum of Sandfield Macdonald that 'we must support our supporters' was

---

[1] Can. H. of C. Debates, 23 Feb. 1875, p. 294.
[2] Ibid., 16 Feb. 1877, p. 91.

fast leading in that direction. The customary tenure during good behaviour was still recognized as a barrier, even if it were beginning to crumble under attack. Although the Government could and did fill offices with its supporters, vacancies were not created with the sweeping thoroughness that characterized the Jacksonian democracy and its successors. 'Rotation in office' was adopted in the United States as a principle and a right, but it never attained such a dignity in Canada. Rotation never became an end in itself or a political virtue about which to boast. When removals from the Canadian service occurred, they were made somewhat furtively, and the onus of proof always rested on the Government to justify its action. Alexander Mackenzie, when Prime Minister, went so far as to say that the Government 'endeavoured to act upon the principle that no person should be dismissed for political reasons, unless he was charged with something else that would afford a proper reason rather than an excuse for his dismissal'.[1] It is scarcely necessary to add that his opponents did not credit him with such forbearance, but his actions and his attitude were far removed from those of an American spoilsman.

There were, however, some members of Parliament who became so intoxicated with the election of 1878 that they declared themselves unequivocally in favour of a purely partisan service. It was stated in the House that 'the whole election was run on the question that "to the victors belong the spoils"'.[2] Another member frankly expressed his preference for Jacksonian methods in these words:

'The hon. member for Sheffield had charged the government with endeavouring to introduce the American system that "to the victors belong the spoils"; he wished that the charge so far as it would affect the province that he represented was true. All that he could say was, that he had been endeavouring to have certain political opponents dismissed from office, but had not as yet succeeded.'[3]

The growth in popular favour of the idea of wholesale removals was commented on a few weeks later in the House:

[1] *Ibid.*   [2] *Ibid.*, 19 Mar. 1879, p. 554.   [3] *Ibid.*, p. 553.

F

'If the present government had not distinctly initiated the American system of dismissing their political opponents, they had at least dismissed a great many—an unusually large proportion of them. . . . But even more significant than the mere number was the fact that members of this House had been found, for the first time, prepared to stand up here and demand the introduction of the American system—demand the dismissal of all those who were opposed to them at the late elections, and the substitution of their political friends.' [1]

Inefficiency in the service increased with each change of Government, and the cause was a political patronage that had lost its sense of proportion. The 'good behaviour' tradition and the moderation of the party leaders were both beginning to show signs of wear. But if the sinister example of the United States appealed to some, it also alarmed and repelled others. The better element in the Dominion saw in the spoils a grave warning against the whole idea of patronage, and the civil service of Great Britain furnished an incentive for reform. Inasmuch as the latter was to be during the next forty years the most important single influence in the reorganization and improvement of the Canadian service, a further digression will be made in order to sketch the chief lines of its development.

The civil servants in England were originally members of the king's household, and were as a consequence completely under his authority. They were largely composed of the king's followers and their retainers, who had been given office as a reward for services rendered. But as Parliament developed and assumed increasingly greater powers, the king was compelled to use the offices at his disposal for a more profitable purpose, either to influence elections, or to bribe the members who came from constituencies whose elections he could not control. Both devices were used extensively by the Tudors and Stuarts, and were common under the early Hanoverians. Corruption became the chief method of securing an acquiescent House of Commons. In the first Parliament of George I, for example, there were 271 members of the Commons holding offices, pensions, and sinecures under the

[1] *Can. H. of C. Debates*, 16 Apr. 1879, pp. 1269–70.

Government; in the first Parliament of George II, 257; and even as late as 1833 the number was 60.[1] This accentuated the difficulty (caused by the emergence of a Cabinet system) of distinguishing the civil servants from the political members; the inferior officials were on an equal parliamentary footing with the superior, and the permanent officials, who should have been kept out of the Legislature, were mixed up with the changing Cabinet officials, who should have been compelled to find seats there. It was the same embarrassing problem which was to cause confusion in Canada many years later, and it was solved in Britain in characteristic fashion. No sweeping changes were made, no revolutionary Act passed; but little by little the number of civil officers in Parliament was reduced by making the acceptance of certain positions inconsistent with the retention of a seat in the Legislature—a restriction which is still in force to-day. This policy led in time to a definite separation of civil and political offices along modern lines, and abolished one form of governmental bribery.

The Ministry, however, could still use public offices to buy support directly in the constituency by giving the office to the voter instead of to the member of Parliament. One remedy for this, which was tried as early as 1782,[2] was to disfranchise certain large groups of office-holders; but as the Ministry then gave the positions to the relatives of voters in place of the voters themselves, laws of this kind did little good. In the middle of the last century, for example, there were in Great Britain approximately 16,000 public offices filled by the relatives of voters, in order that indirectly they might bring support to the Government.[3] It must be remembered that the increase in the power of the Cabinet at the expense of the sovereign made no change in the manner in which public offices were used. The Ministry took over this function of kingship with the rest, and bought votes for its members in the constituencies with the moral recklessness of

---

[1] May, T. Erskine, *The Constitutional History of England* (1912), i, p. 251.

[2] This Act disfranchised revenue officers, who composed 11,500 out of 160,000 voters. The results of seventy seats depended on the votes of the former; *ibid*, i, p. 234.

[3] Muir, R., *Peers and Bureaucrats*, p. 41.

a Stuart. No general attempt was made, however, to dismiss the appointees of one party if the other happened to win the election; but when vacancies arose, they invariably were filled by those who had given the greatest help to the Government party.

Reform of the patronage evil came slowly. A start was made in 1834 and the following years when a few departments began to use pass examinations to weed out the utterly incompetent candidates. But the momentous year was 1853, which saw both the adoption of open competitive examinations for entrance to certain offices of the East India Company, and the report of Sir Stafford Northcote and Sir Charles Trevelyan, who had been appointed a Select Committee to investigate the organization of the English governmental service. The East India Company positions furnished a practical example of reform; the Northcote-Trevelyan Report[1] applied the same principles to England and provided a theoretical justification.

The Report emphasized the growing importance of public administration at that time, and indicated the necessity for a body of efficient permanent officers, subordinate to the Ministers, and yet with sufficient ability to advise the latter in an expert capacity. Such a body of men, the Report stated, was not found in the service at that time, due in part to the practice of recruiting at an early age, when ability could not be accurately tested, in part to the power of patronage carelessly exercised, in part to the feeling of security in the service and its resulting indolence, in part to the failure to promote men except to minor posts, while staff positions were filled by the appointment of strangers.

Two chief solutions were proposed: examinations for entrance, and a two-fold division of the service according to the nature of the work performed; the one aimed at securing the best material in the country, the other provided a way to use this material effectively after it had entered the service. The entrance examinations were to be open and competitive, and were to be administered by an independent board. They were to be on academic subjects, and those used to fill

[1] Reprinted in *Can. Sess. Pap.*, 1880–1, § 113, pp. 393–404.

administrative positions were to equal in difficulty the best educational standards of the universities, the object being to attract the brightest students and to eliminate the unfit. Technical positions were to be filled by tests on special subjects, inferior clerical positions by simple tests on academic subjects.

The second remedy proposed was a change in the organization of the service. Clerks were to be divided into those doing staff and those doing routine and inferior work, the former class being recruited by the severe examination, the latter by the easier one. The purpose of making the division was to enable the officer class to use their faculties to the best advantage and prevent the deadening of their minds by years of routine work. Promotion was to be strictly by merit within each class.[1]

The Report was not received with any great demonstration of enthusiasm, in fact, it was bitterly opposed in many quarters; but its recommendations were slowly adopted. A Civil Service Commission was appointed in 1855, which gave pass examinations to politically nominated candidates whenever a department signified its desire to try the scheme. Gradually the idea of examination increased in general favour until in 1870 open competition was definitely endorsed by Order of Council, and accepted by a number of departments. At the same time the other suggestion of the Report was also carried out, by dividing the service into two general classes according to the nature of the work and the difficulty of the entrance examinations. This Order in Council remains, in its essentials, in force to-day; indeed, the history of the British service since that time has been largely concerned with developing and applying the fundamental ideas contained in the Report and carried into effect by the Order.[2] As a result the entire organization has been built up anew, patronage has been almost completely eliminated, talent and ability have been so effectively attracted and utilized by the new plan that the British service has become second to none in the world.

Civil Service reform in Canada found for its spokesman

[1] A fuller exposition and development of the ideas of the Northcote-Trevelyan Report is given in Chapters VIII and IX.
[2] Moses, R., *The Civil Service of Great Britain*, pp. 106–29.

George Elliot Casey, a youth returned to Parliament in 1872 at the early age of twenty-two. In 1875 he began an intelligent and persistent agitation to improve the service along the lines adopted in Great Britain. In that year he introduced a motion for a Committee of the Whole House to consider the Act of 1868 and the advisibility of substituting a system of open competitive examinations. The motion was withdrawn on the suggestion of the Prime Minister that it was premature to ask for a Committee when the question had never been discussed before.[1] Two years later Mr. Casey resumed the attack, and succeeded in obtaining a Select Committee, with himself as chairman, to investigate the subject and make recommendations for improvement.[2]

Mr. Casey's opinions on reform are given in his speeches noted above, but a more complete and systematic exposition is found in an article which he wrote for the *Canadian Monthly* of January 1877.[3] Briefly, he advised the adoption of the British system with minor variations to suit Canadian conditions. Two qualities, according to the article, were needed in a civil servant: he must be efficient, and he must be patriotic and quite impartial, owing allegiance to no party or person but only to the state. Neither of these requirements was obtained under patronage. The idea that ministers and members of Parliament were politically responsible for dispensing public positions, Mr. Casey dismissed as 'a mere phantom of responsibility': they could not possibly be cognizant of the personal qualifications of all those whom they nominated for office, nor could they be trusted to recommend persons except for party and other irrelevant reasons. Not only appointments, but promotions, dismissals, and pensions were affected by the patronage evil to the detriment of others in the service who were more deserving. He cited the disastrous results of the spoils in the United States, pointed to the improvement which had accompanied reform in Britain, and urged that Canada should follow the latter.

'The service should be looked upon, not as a means of re-

---

[1] *Can. H. of C. Debates*, 15 Mar. 1875, pp. 708–15.
[2] *Ibid.*, 14 Mar. 1877, pp. 696–8 ; *ibid.*, 21 Mar. 1877, pp. 893–901.
[3] 'Civil Service Reform,' pp. 83–91.

warding friends, but simply as an organization for the transaction of public business, and as such should be conducted on "business principles ". The field of selection for its ranks should be made as wide as possible. Every consideration except character and ability should be disregarded, both in first appointments and subsequent promotions. In short, the service should be made a profession, offering as great attractions in pay and consideration combined as any other. . . . This ideal may not be at once attainable, but it should be the object of every change in the organization of the service.' [1]

This quotation indicates how thoroughly Mr. Casey had accepted the Northcote-Trevelyan Report. A more detailed study of his recommendations confirms this. He advised that the service be recruited by competitive examinations, preceded by qualifying examinations, which were to be open and competitive, and the object of which was to reduce the number eligible for the more difficult test. The service was to be divided into a Higher and a Lower Division, the latter holding office at pleasure and drawn from those who had passed the easier examination, the former being permanent and taken from the most successful candidates writing the difficult one. All appointments were to be provisional for one year. The duties of the service were to be divided so that mechanical work would be separated from that requiring special ability or skill, and this was to correspond (apparently) with the two-fold division of clerks noted above. Examination and appointments were to be supervised by Civil Service Commissioners, consisting of 'heads of departments' (presumably deputy heads) and others specially appointed.

The report of the Select Committee of 1877[2] was a rude shock to those who had been so unsophisticated as to believe with Sir John A. Macdonald that the service 'was approaching perfection'. The Committee found that patronage was the guiding principle of the whole organization, particularly in the making of appointments and promotions. In the Department of Marine (Outside Service), for example, on

[1] *Ibid.*, p. 87.
[2] *Can. H. of C. Journals*, 1877, Appendix, § 7.

31 December 1876, out of a total of 1596 employees at least 1350 were appointed on political nomination.[1]

'In the Outside Service with the exception of the Inland Revenue Department and the engineering branches the exercise of political patronage seems to be almost unchecked. . . . Employees remain as a rule in the positions to which they are first nominated, vacancies being filled by new appointments from outside the service, made, as usual, by political influence. . . . In the Customs and Post Office Departments . . . all the prizes go to outsiders, and those who enter in the lower grades have no prospect of promotion as a reward for their ability or zeal. . . . In the Inside Service a system of promotion is practised on the basis laid down in the Act, but with frequent suspensions and violations arising from political causes.'[2]

It may be wondered why this flow of patronage had not been stemmed by the Civil Service Board applying the examination provisions of the Act of 1868.[3] The evidence taken before the Committee was quite explicit on this point. The chairman of the Board said that candidates were not examined as a rule until after the appointment had actually been made ; in most cases there was no examination at all, and if a candidate happened to fail he was given a second chance. The Board examined all who presented themselves, but in 1875 none appeared, and in 1876 only one.

'The majority of nominees do not come before us. Only 72 have been examined by us since (the) Act of 1868. Those rejected do not bear a large proportion to those who pass. Two or three were rejected and tried over again, and only one was finally rejected. . . . The examination is only useful in excluding those who are utterly ignorant and entirely unfit for the service. . . . Any boy of 13 should be able to pass it. It is not nearly as severe as the entrance examinations of High Schools. We do not necessarily receive notice of any appointment. Any number of appointments might be made without our knowledge. We have no power to compel nominees to be examined. We have often represented to the government that the law has not been complied with in regard to examinations. Appointment before examination is a violation of the Act. The Act applies in terms to both Inside and Outside

---

[1] *Can. H. of C. Journals*, 1877, Appendix, § 7, pp. 53–4.
[2] *Ibid.*, pp. 3–4; cf. Evidence, p. 15.   [3] Cf. *supra*, p. 20.

Service, but the organization for the examination of the Outside Service as provided by Section 2 of this Act, has never been carried out.'[1]

The subjects of examination were penmanship, spelling, writing from dictation, and arithmetic, as far as vulgar fractions. Any or all of seven optional subjects might be taken if the candidate desired.[2] In making appointments no attention was paid to the standing obtained at the examination, and 'any person scraping through at all is in as good a position as any other, no matter how good'.[3] The Board was very rarely asked to determine special qualifications of men appointed to higher positions.[4] All these open breaches of the Act and the half-hearted application of some of its provisions made a mockery of the examinations, or, as a member of Parliament put it, 'the examination did not trouble, to any great extent, the slumbers of any candidate for office'.[5]

The Select Committee also reported that promotions, when not dictated by political considerations, were made slowly and by seniority, with the natural result that any stimulus to work was removed.[6] Inefficient and even insubordinate employees were kept on the staff because they had influence with their party.[7] The Committee concluded from all the evidence 'that the condition of the civil service has not been, and is not, satisfactory; that many of the most important provisions of the law in respect thereof have been systematically violated; and that that law is, in many particulars, insufficient to secure the highest efficiency of the service'.[8]

The recommendations of the report went immediately to the source of the trouble by advising a strict open examination, administered by a Commission composed of men outside the service, supplemented by a term of probation. Final appointment was to be made by another more severe and competitive examination or by personal selection by the

[1] *Can. H. of C. Journals*, 1877, Appendix, § 7, p. 18.
[2] *Ibid.*, p. 23.   [3] *Ibid.*, p. 19.
[4] *Ibid.*, p. 21; cf. *supra*, p. 20.
[5] *Can. H. of C. Debates*, 21 Mar. 1877, p. 895.
[6] *Can. H. of C. Journals*, 1877, Appendix, § 7, pp. 4–5; cf. Evidence, p. 26.
[7] *Ibid.*, p. 4.   [8] *Ibid.*, p. 5.

G

Commission.[1] The other suggestions as to a two-fold division of the service and staff followed the same lines outlined previously by Mr. Casey.[2] Parliament, however, took no legislative action on the proposals, and the general election was held the following year.

The return of the Macdonald Administration in 1878 led to so many dismissals from the service that the situation was felt to be intolerable. Lord Dufferin, shortly before relinquishing the Governor-Generalship, sounded a warning against the growing abuses.

'It is necessary that the civil servants should be given a status regulated by their requirements, their personal qualifications, their capacity for rendering the country efficient service, and that neither their original appointment nor their subsequent advancement should in any way have to depend upon their political connexions or opinions. The independence thus conceded to the members of the civil service imposes upon them a special obligation, namely, that they should serve their successive chiefs—no matter to which side they may belong—with a scrupulously impartial zeal and loyalty.'[3]

The caution was well timed, for it was during the next few years that the extremists began clamouring for a genuine spoils system. An anonymous cynic of the period defined appointments as 'political stock in trade, of which the supply is never equal to the demand. Political promissory notes with a large circulation, supposed to be payable on demand, but in point of fact irredeemable.'[4] Some change in the service was imperative if for no other reason than that given by another contemporary that 'the permanent conviction had forced itself upon the party members that there was not room for the entire male population of the country in the civil service', and the embarrassment caused to the member of Parliament 'who has only one vacancy and eleven hundred applicants'.[5]

The arguments of the indefatigable Mr. Casey fell therefore upon willing as well as deaf ears. He introduced a 'Public

[1] *Can. H. of C. Journals*, 1877, Appendix, § 7, p. 5.   [2] *Ibid.*, pp. 6–7.
[3] Stewart, G., *Canada under the Administration of the Earl of Dufferin*, pp. 658–9.
[4] *Manual for Public Men*, 1881.
[5] Collins, J. E., *Canada under the Administration of Lord Lorne*, p. 211.

Service Reform Bill' in 1878, 1879, and 1880, though with no greater success than a second reading. He had the satisfaction, however, of having a Civil Service Bill mentioned in the Speech from the Throne in 1880 ; [1] and later in the year the Prime Minister announced that although it had been drafted by the Government, pressure of business had caused its postponement.[2] On 16 June 1880 a Royal Commission was appointed to consider the condition and needs of the civil service.

[1] *Can. H. of C. Debates*, 12 Feb. 1880, p. 3.
[2] *Ibid.*, 28 Apr. 1880, p. 1830.

III. THE FIRST GESTURE TOWARDS REFORM

1880–2

'Her case may any day
Be yours, my dear, or mine;
Let her make her hay
While the sun doth shine.
Let us compromise
(Our hearts are not of leather):
Let us shut our eyes
And talk about the weather.'

The Pirates of Penzance.

THE Royal Commission of 1880 was expected to make a 'full, intelligent and painstaking inquiry' into the condition of the service, and to suggest suitable remedies.[1] The members travelled over the Dominion, heard a host of witnesses, asked them more than three thousand questions, received delegations from the lower ranks of employees, investigated the British and American civil services, and made a comprehensive study of superannuation. Two majority reports were submitted; and two members drew up a third, which disagreed with certain important findings of the others.[2]

The evidence taken in the inquiry showed that an investigation was badly needed. The Civil Service Board had not given any examinations or performed any duties since 1876, although the chairman continued to receive $400 a year.[3] The service was often 'a refuge for people, who by reason of their indolence or lack of intelligence, could not succeed in other employment'.[4] In the Postal Department thirty-five had been totally unfit for duty and were removed in the last few years; nine were drunkards, thirteen were guilty of robbery or dishonesty, and thirteen others were utterly incompetent, one being afflicted with epilepsy, and another, a letter carrier, did not know the letters of the alphabet.[5] Many inefficient clerks got in as temporary employees and were kept on

---

[1] *Can. Sess. Pap.*, 1880–1, § 113, p. 10.
[2] *Ibid.*, 1880–1, § 113; *ibid.*, 1882, § 32; *ibid.*, 1882, § 32a.
[3] *Ibid.*, 1880–1, § 113, pp. 12, 58, 71–2.
[4] *Ibid.*, p. 65.   [5] *Ibid.*, pp. 134–5.

through political influence.[1] The Department of Public Works had a number of men who had served as 'temporary' officers from five to twenty-one years, and were paid from the appropriations for the buildings which they were constructing.[2] Another abuse had arisen from the Act of 1868, which had forbidden a clerk to receive additional pay for extra work done in his own department. This had resulted in an interchange of clerks between departments when extra work had to be done, so that each could draw additional remuneration yet keep within the letter of the Act.[3]

The evidence of almost every witness disclosed the fact that political patronage was the cause of the major faults of the service;[4] and the Commission was not backward in repeating it:

'To this baneful influence, we believe, may be traced nearly all that demands change. It is responsible for admission to the Service of those who are too old to be efficient; of those whose impaired health and enfeebled constitutions forbid the hope that they can ever become useful public servants; of those whose personal habits are an equally fatal objection; of those whose lack of education should disqualify them; and of those whose mental qualities are of an order that has made it impossible for them to succeed in private business. It is responsible too for the appointment of those who desire to lead an easy and, what they deem, a genteel life.'

'To the same influence may be ascribed most of the appointments of men taken from beyond the Service to the best places over the heads of tried and efficient servants: and it may fairly be charged with all the discontent and demoralization arising out of the feeling, justified by bitter experience, that a faithful and zealous performance of duty establishes no sure claim to the prizes of the Service, which, as is abundantly shown by the evidence, are too often carried off by persons whose claim to office is mainly founded on the political service they have rendered to their party. . . . To this class of appointments and the consequent removal of the chief incentive to zeal may perhaps be attributed, more than to any other single cause, the languid interest which many of the public servants feel in the performance

---

[1] *Ibid.*, p. 187.   [2] *Ibid.*, pp. 228, 233.
[3] *Ibid.*, pp. 383–4.
[4] *Ibid.*, pp. 95, 125, 131, 142, 165, 187, 188, 199, &c.

of their duties. . . . Many unnecessary civil offices have been
retained, and . . . new places have been created, for no better purpose than to provide for the followers of influential politicians.'[1]

'Much that has been said with reference to first admission to the
Service applies with equal force to promotion therein. . . . Promotions in the Inside, and still more largely in the Outside Service,
have been made with but little regard to system. Sometimes
promotions have been made by seniority, regardless of merit. . . .
In other cases they have been made regardless of either merit or
seniority. . . . Any reform in the administration of the Public
Service must begin with an improvement in the mode of nominations, appointments and promotions.'[2]

The reports of the Commission contained general recom-
mendations for improvement[3] and a theoretical organization
for each department.[4] They suggested that the remedy lay in
open competitive examinations and promotion by merit.[5]
The new system was to be administered by a non-political
Board of Civil Service Commissioners, holding office on judicial tenure, and independent of party influence.[6] The Inside
Service was to be divided into four grades below the Deputy
Heads, viz. Chief Clerks, First, Second, and Third Class
Clerks, and the routine work was to be done by the latter.[7]
The Outside Service was to be classified differently in each
department according to duties performed.[8] The Commission
recommended open preliminary examinations followed by
more difficult competitive examinations, which were to determine first appointments to Third Class Clerkships in the
Inside and minor posts in the Outside Service.[9] Appointments were to be followed by six months' probation.[10] Promotions were to be made after special competitive tests open
to all those in the grade below the vacant office, but the
Civil Service Commission could choose from the first five
names on the list.[11] The report praised the Department of
Inland Revenue, Outside Service, for having consistently used

---

[1] *Can. Sess. Pap.*, 1880–1, § 113, pp. 16–17.   [2] *Ibid.*, p. 17.
[3] *Ibid.*, pp. 11–57.   [4] *Ibid.*, 1882, § 32, pp. 1–16.
[5] *Ibid.*, 1880–1, § 113, p. 20. This, as well as the Civil Service Commission,
was endorsed by the witnesses at the inquiry, e.g.; *ibid.*, pp. 91, 129, 135,
166, 188, 217, 269, &c.
[6] *Ibid.*, p. 21.   [7] *Ibid.*, pp. 27–8.   [8] *Ibid.*, pp. 34–45.
[9] *Ibid.*, pp. 22–3.   [10] *Ibid.*, p. 24.   [11] *Ibid.*, p. 24.

examinations both for entrance and promotion, and indicated the salutary effect they had had on producing efficiency.[1] The superannuation system[2] was approved, and a pension scheme proposed for the families of deceased officials.[3]

It will be seen that these proposals aimed at introducing several new elements into the Canadian civil service, some of which were directly copied from Great Britain while others were quite different. The idea of an independent Board of Commissioners to supervise entrances and promotions was inspired by the British example, and was worked out more courageously than by Mr. Casey or by the Select Committee of 1877. It had as its necessary corollary the abandonment of ministerial responsibility in making appointments to the service. On this point the Minority Report of the two Commissioners joined issue with a quixotic conscientiousness and valour.

'We feel it incumbent upon us, as Members of the Commission, to dissent from the recommendations, which have in view the establishing of an irresponsible body in a paid Board of Examiners, to supersede the action of the Executive as well as the legitimate exercise of influence on the part of the people's representatives. . . . In the spirit and practice of the English Constitution, the Crown is the fountain of all appointments, and among the duties and responsibilities of its advisers stand the proper and responsible selection of the servants of the State. If it be, at times, expedient for Constitutional Governments to institute Commissions to investigate, it is repugnant to them to devolve on such bodies, the duty of governing and administering, of which appointments and promotions form an essential part.'[4]

The phrase 'the spirit and practice of the English Constitution' is rather difficult to accept in the sense in which it was meant. It could not very well mean 'the Constitution as practised in England', for a similar body to that proposed had existed in England for years, and other bodies, analogous in this respect, such as the judiciary, had been recognized as integral parts of the Constitution for centuries. In fact, the

---

[1] *Ibid.*, p. 40; cf. pp. 133, 205, 215, 365.
[2] Established by *Can. Stat.*, 33 Vic. c. 4.
[3] *Can. Sess. Pap.*, 1882, § 32, pp. 13–16.   [4] *Ibid.*, 1882, § 32a, p. 87.

change proposed was not nearly so startling as it appeared. The responsibility of ministers and members in the matter of appointments had, in Mr. Casey's phrase, become 'a mere phantom'. Very few recommendations for positions were made with any exact knowledge as to qualifications or requirements, and any real responsibility for such acts had ceased to exist. Any great discernment, however, could scarcely be expected from the minority members of the Commission, who had gone so far as 'to stoutly affirm that this service as a whole is efficient'.[1] They evidently shared the same determined optimism and trust displayed by one of the witnesses: 'I do not think, from my long intercourse with men in Parliament, that they are frequently swayed in the use of their votes by such paltry considerations as the creation of patronage.'[2]

One other point in this connexion deserves mention. It was fully recognized by the Majority Report that the new proposals would place the civil servant himself in a far better position than formerly.

'The Civil Servants would be saved from the imputation of partisanship which is periodically brought against them in times of political excitement. Men who had obtained their places by merit alone, and as the result of impartial examination, could not possibly be open to any imputation of political partisanship in office; nor would they be in any degree influenced in the discharge of their duties by political considerations. . . . The Service would win the respect of the public and of the Government; and . . . it would obtain and preserve a dignity in the eyes of the whole country, which it does not now possess.'[3]

In other words, the civil servant would be divorced from politics so far as it was possible to do so. He would no longer owe his position to a party because of his political past, but to himself because of his own ability in fields other than those political. Allegiance would be owed and given to either or both parties instead of to one, and the service would command more respect from both the Ministry and the country.

The Commissioners departed from the British precedent in

---

[1] *Can. Sess. Pap.*, 1882, § 32 a, p. 89.
[2] *Ibid.*, 1880–1, § 113, p. 266.   [3] *Ibid.*, pp. 20–1.

some of their proposals because of alleged differences in the conditions of the two countries, but they failed to go into any greater detail in explaining the reason for the alterations. They stated that the two characteristic features of the British Service were open competitive examination and promotion by merit, yet they failed to apply either principle in its entirety. It will be remembered that the Northcote-Trevelyan Report had advised a twofold division of the service with separate sets of examinations to determine the entrance to each division. The intention had been to recruit an officer class by the severe examination and a class for routine work by the easy one. The Canadian Commission approved this distinction between intellectual and routine work, and advised that the former should be done by the Chief, First and Second Class Clerks, and the latter by those of the Third Class. The value of this differentiation, however, was largely destroyed by the excessive number of officers, the lack of gradation in the lower kind of work, and the admission of all candidates of whatever excellence to the Third Class Clerkships only—the work of which was avowedly mechanical. Any exceptionally clever young man would therefore have to spend a number of years in this class, filing letters, checking accounts, and copying documents, before he could get his promotion. There was also the further disadvantage that as all the clerks would come into the service by the same door, the test had to be a comparatively easy one. It would have been, therefore, much more difficult to ascertain what men really were of unusual ability, and this would have been all the more impracticable because the examinations proposed could not be called academic. The Commissioners may have thought that they had adopted the principle of the British Service, but they had so altered it as to rob it of a great part of its usefulness.

The danger of a clever Third Class Clerk remaining at routine work might have been obviated to some extent by a system of promotion examinations, but those advocated by the Commission would have had the opposite effect. Whatever be the evils of promotion examinations, and they are many, it is generally true that they must be set on the duties

H

of office and similar subjects. The Commission in this instance recommended that the subjects should be determined by the Board of Commissioners after consultation with the chief officers in each department, which clearly meant papers on official duties. For this reason it is extremely doubtful if the proposed scheme would have accelerated the promotion of any clever young clerk; on the contrary, it would probably have retarded it. He would have found himself at a hopeless disadvantage with a comparatively dull man who had laboured years at the routine of office. If the proposed examination for promotion had been an academic one, then the new clerk might quickly have won his advancement, but the time which he had already spent would have been to a large degree lost, and he might have entered directly to the Second Class at a greater profit.

Briefly, the proposals of the Commission, though excellent in some respects, were weak in many essentials. The abolition of the patronage system, the use of the competitive examination, the creation of an independent non-political board of supervision, were reforms sorely needed. But these could not be used with the greatest profit unless they were linked with other changes as well. The Commission's grasp of the British system appears to have been superficial: they had seized on the obvious points, but had missed those which lay below the surface. One thing can be said in their defence: they may have thought that the changes recommended were all that were feasible at that time, and the 'Canadian conditions', for which they professed to have made allowance, may have had reference to the difficulty of getting a Bill through Parliament. But this is perhaps a little too charitable. Everything points to the conclusion that they were so absorbed with the problem of shaking off patronage that they did not inquire very closely into other possible improvements: examination was the holy word which would exorcise the devil, and as soon as that was done the salvation of the service was assured.

The report of the Commissioners of 1880 ushered in a new era in the civil service, though it was not the era which they had tried to introduce. In 1882 a new *Civil Service Act* was passed,[1] and received various amendments during the next two years,[2] which were finally consolidated by the Act of 1885.[3]

The most important change was the creation of a Board of Examiners of three members, who received a salary and travelling expenses, and supervised all examinations. They held office at pleasure, and were appointed by the Governor in Council.[4] Two examinations were to be held, a preliminary to enter minor positions, and a qualifying for admittance to Third Class Clerkships in the Inside Service and certain offices in the Outside Service. The head of the department (i.e. the Minister) was to choose one from the successful candidates, who, subject to a probationary period, was then to be appointed.[5] Certain offices which were enumerated and others described as professional or technical were exempted from the examination.[6] Notices of all examinations for admission were to be advertised a month in advance in both the English and French languages, and were to state where and in what subjects such examinations would be held.[7] All promotions (with a few stated exceptions) were to be made only after special tests open to all holding positions below the vacancy. The subjects for such examinations were to be determined by the Governor in Council, and such additional ones might be required as agreed upon by the deputy head and the head of the department.[8] The Minister was to select for the promotion any one of the successful candidates, paying due attention to any special duties attached to the office, to any qualifications shown by the candidate in the examination, and to his past record.[9] Transfers from one division to the other or from one department to another, or an exchange of officers in such divisions or departments, might be authorized by the Governor in Council to be made without examination.[10] The deputy heads were to hold office at pleasure; but should they be removed, a statement of the reasons for so doing must be laid before both Houses of Parliament within fifteen

[1] *Can. Stat.*, 45 Vic. c. 4.
[2] *Ibid.*, 46 Vic. c. 7; *ibid.*, 47 Vic. c. 15.
[3] *Ibid.*, 48–9 Vic. c. 46.   [4] *Ibid.*, sections 8, 9.
[5] Section 29.   [6] Section 37.   [7] Section 33.
[8] Section 39.   [9] Sections 42–5.   [10] Section 46.

days of the opening of the next session.[1] In all other essentials the Act was the same as that of 1868.

The first impression on reading the Act is that a great step in advance had been made; but a more painstaking analysis shows that the statute was almost as unsatisfactory as the earlier one of 1868. The two reforms which the Royal Commission had advocated as fundamental—open competitive examination and promotion by merit—were not secured. Political patronage was as powerful as ever, except that the illiterate and hopeless incompetent were excluded. Before the passage of the Act a Minister could give offices to any of his supporters; after the Act he was limited to those who could pass an elementary test. Promotion, though it must take place after examination, could also be used as a means of dispensing favours, for a Minister could choose any one of the successful candidates to fill the vacancy. Mr. Casey, who saw in the statute merely a travesty of his reform proposals, said:

'It is then a perfect farce to say that these examinations are open to all comers, for although the examinations are open to all, only those who are favoured can get appointments; and it is not fair, under these circumstances, to say that the fact of having open examinations will be evidence that the appointments which may be made under this system will not be conferred on improper parties.'[2]

Sir Hector Langevin, Minister of Public Works, attempted to justify 'qualification examinations' on the old ground that the most suitable person might be chosen to fill a vacancy—a freedom which was not allowed under competition. He intimated that the Government still intended to use the power of appointment as a reward for party services, and added: 'I have no doubt there will always be politics connected with appointments made by any Government. I have yet to see a Government which will appoint its opponents to office.'[3] Such was the enthusiasm with which the Cabinet introduced the new system.

[1] Section 11.
[2] *Can. H. of C. Debates*, 11 Apr. 1882, p. 796.   [3] *Ibid.*, p. 795.

The suspicions of the Opposition were further aroused by the clause in the Act whereby the Board of Examiners, contrary to the recommendation of the Commission, were to hold office at pleasure. Mr. Casey thought they would be apt to use their powers to forward the cause of Government candidates.

'Who are these judicial individuals who are to decide as to the fitness or unfitness of those who enter the service? They are simply members of the civil service themselves; and are as much at the mercy of the government of the day, as are second or third class clerks in a department. . . . No doubt the examiners will be chosen from among political friends, and what examiners, dependent for their positions and salaries on the influence of the government of the day, will refuse to pass highly recommended individuals, if they happen to come anywhere near the standard which the government have chosen to set up.'[1]

Another fault of the Act was that it made no attempt to divide the service into two classes for intellectual and routine work. The counsel of the Royal Commission in this regard, as has been pointed out, was imperfect; but even such steps as they advised were ignored.[2] A decided improvement was made in the position of the deputy heads of the departments by compelling a statement of reasons to Parliament for their dismissal, and the clause was given additional importance from the fact that the deputy head had greater powers of discipline and administration than he had had before. The criticism of the Opposition, that it gave 'an illusory appearance of independent action on the part of an officer who, from his situation, must necessarily be in accord with the Minister who is his chief',[3] was not sound. The Act unquestionably gave the deputy head increased powers, and the clause regarding his removal both protected him in the exercise of those powers and gave him a tenure of office more independent of political changes.

The reason why the report of the Royal Commission was disregarded is not difficult to find. Public opinion was not

[1] *Ibid.*, pp. 796–97; cf. Edward Blake, *ibid.*, 25 Apr. 1882, p. 1122.
[2] Edward Blake, *ibid.*, 11 Apr. 1882, p. 791.
[3] Edward Blake, *ibid.*, 25 Apr. 1882, p. 1127.

sufficiently aware of the bad condition of the service, or, if it was informed, it was too indifferent or too sceptical as to the possibilities of change. The Commission had recognized this difficulty, and had given it some prominence in the report:

'We did not conceal from ourselves that there may be doubts as to whether the public opinion of the Dominion is even now fully alive to the importance of a thoroughly efficient civil service, or, on the other hand, has recognized rights on the part of the service, such as have long since been conceded in other countries. . . . While there exists in the public mind a very general belief that the civil service is defective and inefficient, and that the true remedy is the abolition of political patronage and personal favouritism in making appointments to public offices; there is on the other hand an impression that it is difficult and almost impracticable to apply the remedy and that those who possess the power of patronage will continue to exercise it at the sacrifice of an efficient and economical administration of public affairs. We believe this impression to be in the main erroneous.' [1]

A number of witnesses also had given their opinion that any attempts to abolish patronage in Canada would be rendered as futile as they had been in the past.[2] The same attitude was shown in the *Canadian Illustrated News*:

'It is somewhat naively intimated that this Board (i.e. the proposed Board of Civil Service Commissioners) would be as free from political influences as the judges. . . . There will be great doubt in the mind of any man who is not a mere tyro in political studies and experience, whether the substitution of a practically irresponsible bureaucracy of three, will be any improvement on the responsibility of Ministers to Parliament, which is always open to sharp criticism and check from the Opposition. . . . The reverse would be the case, and instead of progress we should have a decidedly retrograde step. We obtained our principle of responsibility of Ministers after a long and hard struggle. It has on the whole worked well; and it would be folly to sacrifice a very large and also essential portion of it to meet the views of a few *doctrinaires* who, however great may be their ability and experience in their own pursuits, are not men from whose hands one would be willing to take a change of this sort. Moreover, the supposition that such a bureau could be free from political influence is an

---

[1] *Can. Sess. Pap.*, 1880–1, § 113, pp. 12–13.
[2] *Ibid.*, pp. 265, 300.

absurdity. The bureau would probably find it more difficult to satisfy the party which did not appoint it, than the deputy heads of departments have done, at least in some cases, the parties who did not appoint them.'[1]

This lukewarm attitude on the part of the public found willing advocates in the Cabinet Ministers, who were anxious to keep the patronage in their own hands.[2] The avowed justification given in Parliament for the Act of 1882 was that the Government was hampered by the existing service and could not make the sweeping changes it desired.[3] While the apology may have contained a little truth, the chief of the proposed changes could not have interfered disastrously with the old membership or organization of the service. The cardinal reason for maintaining the old system was an administration hostile to reform, which saw no object in abandoning its appointing power so long as the public remained indifferent. Patronage, it was everywhere admitted, was a great trouble, but it was extremely useful at election time. A few minor reforms might be conceded to the clamant minority: these changes could not harm the service, and might even raise its efficiency, while at the same time members of Parliament could continue to exercise their influence almost as before.

[1] 19 Mar. 1881.

[2] A person, describing himself as 'Constant Reader', wrote to the *Toronto Globe* on 9 May 1882: 'Another mistake our leaders make is this—they seem to think that the people are pure. It is a great mistake. They are as corrupt as the Government that represents them at Ottawa. It has come to this in Canada: whoever commits the greatest deception and plays the best trick on his political opponent is the man that Canada delights to honour.' The *Globe* in an editorial dissented from this pessimistic view, but it seems to contain a large amount of truth.

[3] Sir Hector Langevin, *Can. H. of C. Debates*, 11 Apr. 1882, p. 793.

IV. THE PERIOD OF STAGNATION

1882–1908

'In serving writs I made such a name
That an articled clerk I soon became;
I wore clean collars and a brand-new suit
For the pass examination at the Institute.
    And that pass examination did so well for me,
    That now I am the Ruler of the Queen's Navee!'

H.M.S. Pinafore.

THE Board of Civil Service Examiners under the new Act was appointed in August 1882. It lost no time getting under way, and immediately issued its regulations, which were approved by the Governor in Council, in accordance with the Act. The regulations indicated the elementary character of the examinations that were to be introduced. The preliminary test was to be given on penmanship, spelling, the 'first four rules of arithmetic', reading print, and handwriting. The qualifying examinations were to include the following subjects: penmanship, spelling, arithmetic (to vulgar and decimal fractions), geography, outlines of British, French, and Canadian history, grammar, composition, English or French transcription.

The dark forebodings of the Opposition as to the personnel of the Board [1] proved to be quite unfounded when the appointments were announced. The members were John Thorburn, LL.D., A. D. DeCelles, and Peter LeSueur, all excellent men, the first being a man with wide educational experience, and the other two being civil servants of high standing. A poorer selection would have ruined the work at the start, for the relation of the Board to the Government held dangerous possibilities. The Board, if it were to be of any use whatever, had to be quite impartial and aloof from political bias; yet its members held office at pleasure, their salary depended on the whim of the administration, and two of them occupied other positions in the service. All these might have been used as levers by the Government to turn

[1] Cf. *supra*, p. 53.

the Board into an adjunct of the patronage committee, in which event the examination would have become a complete farce and the whole system brought into discredit. Even Mr. Casey, who had been most sceptical in 1882, was forced to admit eight years later that 'the gentlemen themselves are as respectable as any who could be named, but it is not to be expected that the public will believe them to be as independent as men who are not so subject to the control of the Government'.[1]

The last part of Mr. Casey's statement indicated the fundamental weakness of the Board in the eyes of the public. The members had not been given an independent status, and no matter how impartial they might be, they would not be given the credit for it. Favouritism and partisanship would be expected; and if not there, would be imagined. An independent body is, as a rule, in a much better position to command public confidence than one which is connected with the Government, even though this connexion may be largely nominal. It is a strange contradiction in modern democratic Government that a body free from the control of the people's representatives will often stand higher in popular esteem than one more intimately associated with Parliament. The very fact of independence creates a belief, usually justified, that the body occupying such a position will act from purer motives and with a wider vision than would one which is under Government control. The Board of Examiners was in fact almost entirely free from parliamentary interference; but it did not wear the raiment of an independent body, and as a result was expected by many people to favour the candidates of only one party. The Board referred to this attitude in one of its annual reports:

'In a large number of instances the applications for admissions to the examinations are accompanied by letters setting forth that the applicants have the support and interest of strong political friends, and the assurance of employment in the civil service if they can only make out to pass. And there seems to be an impression in the minds of many of the candidates that if they should come somewhat short at the examinations these influential

[1] *Can. H. of C. Debates*, 4 Feb. 1890, p. 218.

I

friends may be able to procure for them from the Board such measure of indulgence as may be necessary to get them through. And one of the most difficult duties devolving upon the Board consists in dealing with the aforesaid friends who occasionally, through misrepresentations on the part of the candidates, take exception to the decisions arrived at in respect of the performances of their protégés. To give weight to their remonstrances, they bring forward the opinions of outside parties (who can know nothing of the real facts) to the effect that the examiners have done them injustice in the valuation of the papers. This interference has always been a source of trouble, and it is hoped that, for the future, it will cease. The Board can have no possible motive for dealing unfairly, or even unkindly, with the candidates, ninety-nine per cent of whom, probably, are utterly unknown to them.'[1]

The Government did not meddle with the work of the Board for the simple reason that the latter's activities did not trouble it or interfere materially with its patronage. The Board's functions began and ended with the holding of examinations; it had no power of appointment, and the examinations tested only minimum qualifications. As a result, improvement in the civil service was scarcely perceptible. A few caustic comments from *The Week* will indicate that there was no great contrast between the period before 1882 and that of the next few years.

'Though we hear of "Civil Service Examinations" going on from time to time at Ottawa, they do not appear to have wrought much change as yet in the personnel of the service, or to have materially reduced the proportion of relatives of Cabinet Ministers and their favourites in Dominion offices.'[2]

'At all gatherings above the size of a family party there is sure to be some distinguished-looking man who turns out to be a member of the Civil Service. His wife is equally distinguished-looking, and always pretty. There are several such interesting pairs, and if you enquire through whose influence the capital has been thus enriched, the name of some Minister is the answer. There is hardly a Department where some promotions have not taken place, dictated by the social rather than administrative qualities of a Minister. Nor is it easy to condemn him. When he is seated at dinner near a pretty woman, and whispers a compli-

---

[1] *Can. Sess. Pap.*, 1892, § 16B, p. 6.
[2] *The Week*, 22 Nov. 1888, edit.

ment, she smiles bewitchingly and requests a place for her husband, or another step. . . . At Ottawa a fond wife with a pretty face and an enterprising disposition can accomplish great things for her husband, and sometimes for her friends.'[1]

The chief administrative difficulty of the Board in the first few years was that the number of candidates for entrance increased far beyond the vacancies to be filled. In the first year there were 392 candidates,[2] in 1884 the number rose to 1139,[3] and in the following years it rarely fell below a thousand. Two methods, both of them futile, were tried in order to reduce the number: the entrance examinations were held once a year instead of twice,[4] and the fees were raised.[5] In spite of these changes the candidates refused to be discouraged and came on as before,[6] apparently failing to realize that the bewildered Examiners had expected 'a superior class of aspirants' to appear as a result of the amendments. The obvious remedy was to raise the standard of examination, and thus lower the number of successful candidates, discourage the poor ones from writing at all, and increase the efficiency of the service. This solution was never mentioned in the Examiners' reports, probably because they realized that members of Parliament would not tolerate such a restriction on their power of appointment.

The *Civil Service Act* was frequently amended during the next decade, though no radical change was made in its provisions.[7] The general tendency of the amendments, however, was towards a relaxation of the original Act and the prevention of its provisions being strictly carried out.[8]

The total result of all the laws passed and the examinations held was meagre. Imbeciles and some undesirables were thereby excluded, but very few others who had the requisite political influence had any difficulty in obtaining admittance.[9]

---

[1] *Ibid.*, 10 Apr. 1884.
[2] *Can. Sess. Pap.*, 1883, § 13, p. 5.   [3] *Ibid.*, 1885, § 46A, p. 3.
[4] *Can. Stat.*, 51 Vic. c. 12, section 5.
[5] *Can. Sess. Pap.*, 1892, § 16B, pp. 5–6.   [6] *Ibid.*
[7] *Can. Stat.*, 46 Vic. c. 7 ; *ibid.*, 47 Vic. c. 15; *ibid.*, 48–9 Vic. c. 46 ; *ibid.*, 51 Vic. c. 12 ; *ibid.*, 52 Vic. c. 12.
[8] *Can. Sess. Pap.*, 1892, § 16C, p. xviii.
[9] *Can. H. of C. Debates*, 4 Feb. 1890, p. 218.

The examination system was but a garment of gauze which patronage had put on because some puritanical people had been shocked at its shamelessness. It was a concession to appearances, or, to use the simile of Professor Goldwin Smith, it was 'like the sugar tongs which the Frenchman held, in compliment to the habit of his English hosts, while he slipped his fingers between them to take up the sugar '.[1] A member of Parliament, addressing his constituents in 1889, indicated how slightly the examinations troubled him:

'I know very well I have not been able to satisfy all the applicants for employment in the Government, and I do not think it possible, with the number of applicants there are, for any man to obtain places for all in the Government. I am not aware of neglecting any of their requirements. I have endeavoured to do all I could for applicants for Government patronage.'[2]

The question of the disfranchisement of civil servants ceased to be an active one in England in 1867, when the franchise, which had been withheld by former Acts[3] from certain public officials, was restored.[4] In Canada, after the introduction of the ballot,[5] both Conservatives and Liberals expressed their disapproval of any law which would deprive the civil servant of his right to vote.[6] The legislatures of Nova Scotia and Quebec thought otherwise, and passed statutes excluding certain Dominion officials from the franchise.[7] Inasmuch as the provincial lists were at this time also used in the Dominion,[8] the laws had the additional effect of preventing these civil servants from voting at federal elections. The *Electoral Franchise Act* of 1885[9] destroyed this anomaly by creating a Dominion voting list quite separate from those in the pro-

---

[1] *Canada and the Canadian Question*, p. 185.

[2] *The Week*, 10 May 1889.

[3] *Brit. Stat.*, 7–8 Geo. III, c. 53, section 9; *ibid.*, 22 Geo. III, c. 41; *ibid.*, 43 Geo. III, c. 25.

[4] *Ibid.*, 31–2 Vic. c. 73.

[5] For old cases of disfranchisement cf. Doutre, J., *Constitution of Canada*, p. 112.

[6] Sir John A. Macdonald, *Can. H. of C. Debates*, 27 Apr. 1878, p. 2230; Edward Blake, *ibid.*, p. 2234.

[7] *N.S. Stat.*, 35 Vic. c. 15, section 1; *Quebec Stat.*, 38 Vic. c. 7, section 11.

[8] *Can. Stat.*, 37 Vic. c. 9, section 40.

[9] *Ibid.*, 48–49 Vic. c. 40; cf. Pope, J., *Sir John Macdonald*, ii, pp. 245–8.

vinces. With this Act the disfranchisement of civil servants passed outside the field of practical politics, though a statute of 1898 contained a clause that no person should be disqualified from voting in a Dominion or provincial election because he held office under the federal Government.[1]

In the summer of 1891 the Standing Committee on Public Accounts of the House of Commons disclosed a great number of scandals in the service.[2] Certain officials had been guilty of serious breaches of trust; some had altered accounts; others had accepted bribes; the Government had been defrauded in goods it had bought due to corrupt civil servants; clerks doing extra work had credited it to imaginary subordinates and then cashed the pay cheques; salaries had been drawn by absent clerks, one of whom had been away twelve months out of fifteen studying art and medicine. As a result of these revelations the Government was attacked in the Senate for the inefficiency of the service and the continued violations of the Act, and the Prime Minister was asked what proposals he had to put forward. Mr. Abbott replied that it was the intention of the Government to appoint a Royal Commission to make a thorough study of the whole system. His own opinion was that a permanent Civil Service Commission would be too expensive to maintain, and he was considering instead:

'The appointment of an official standing independent of party and of the government of the day, to a large extent very much as the present Auditor General does, who might be called the Comptroller, or Inspector . . . whose duty would be something analogous to that of the inspector of a bank. He would have the right to enter every department of the service when he chose, and investigate the conduct of employees and officials ; scrutinize the management of the finances of the department, as well as the way in which its work is done—in fact, look thoroughly from time to time into the mode in which the business of every department is conducted, and the mode in which the clerks and employees of that department are doing their duty, and report upon these subjects accordingly.'[3]

[1] *Can. Stat.*, 61 Vic. c. 14, section 6; cf. *ibid.*, 7–8 Edw. VII, c. 15, section 43.
[2] *Can. H. of C. Journals*, 1891, Appendix, § 2.
[3] *Can. Senate Debates*, 20 Aug. 1891, pp. 470–1.

This proposal, though vague, was an interesting one, but it never got any further than the speech in the Senate. Mr. Abbott evidently intended that the Inspector should confine himself to the business organization of the departments, while the Board of Examiners continued to exercise its functions in regard to entrance and promotion. But the scheme had this patent defect: it merely locked the door after the horse was stolen; it endeavoured to create efficiency in a system whose most crying fault was that it did not get efficient men to enter. It was folly to make appointments by party instead of merit, and expect a single Inspector to transform poor material into a competent organization. Bricks, as was discovered before 1891, could not be made without straw. Doubtless the Inspector could have done something to improve the internal arrangement of the service, but the main fault was the inefficiency of personnel, and that was to be left untouched.[1] If an Inspectorship of the kind suggested had been combined with a Civil Service Commission making appointments by open competitive examination or some other method apart from party politics, the service might have been improved beyond recognition.[2]

A Royal Commission in accordance with the promise of the Prime Minister was appointed on 14 November 1891, to inquire into the inefficiency and abuses of the Inside Service, and to make suggestions for reform.[3] It was composed of four members, one (the chairman) the general manager of a bank, one a judge of the Exchequer Court, one the deputy head of a department, and the fourth representing the general public. The aim of the Government was to obtain a survey of the service from the standpoint of a practical business concern, and to have general business principles applied to its organization. It is extremely doubtful whether the last object, desirable though it might be, was then or is now attainable. Political influence has no parallel in the ordinary firm, and administration under a Government must

[1] *The Week*, 28 Aug. 1891, edit.

[2] Twenty-eight years later a somewhat similar suggestion was made by the Leader of the Opposition, D. D. Mackenzie, *Can. H. of C. Debates*, 16 Apr. 1919, p. 1561.

[3] *Can. Sess. Pap.*, 1892, § 16c, pp. ix–xii.

of necessity be more complex and more formal than in commerce. It was nevertheless a good idea to turn the searchlight of the business mind on the service, and the recommendations of the Commission show in many places, particularly in matters of internal economy and organization, the benefit which resulted from this peculiarity in its membership.

The Commission held extensive hearings, and took over seven hundred pages of evidence. The witnesses were in substantial agreement on existing conditions, although different solutions were suggested for their betterment. Political influence was naturally blamed for most of the trouble, and politics was alleged to be behind nearly every appointment.[1] It brought many poor men into the service [2] and kept them there when they should have been discharged.[3] It pushed extra clerks into departments where they were not needed.[4] It tried to obtain increases in salary when they were not deserved.[5] A Treasury Minute of 1879 which forbad civil servants using political influence to gain promotion was everywhere ignored or found impracticable.[6] The usual way to dispose of a clerk who was hopelessly inefficient was to move him to another department, where he stayed until he was transferred a second time.[7] Even elections could not be run without civil servants; and a member of Parliament had been known to obtain leave of absence for a clerk in order to use him in the campaign.[8]

The Commission stated in its report that although the examinations for entrance and promotion had done some good, stricter regulations would have yielded much better results:

'Of these (entrance) examinations themselves it may be said that they have been of such a character that the ordinary High School boy could without difficulty pass them; and from the general trend of the evidence given before the Commission it will be observed that in the case of a considerable number of the

---

[1] *Ibid.*, pp. 18, 22, 100, 153, 262, 551, &c.
[2] *Ibid.*, pp. 9, 97, 164.
[3] *Ibid.*, pp. 123, 218, 551, 614.
[4] *Ibid.*, pp. 13, 91, 124, 514, 613, 628, &c.   [5] *Ibid.*, p. 131.
[6] *Ibid.*, pp. 10, 66, 98, 148, 195, 210, &c.
[7] *Ibid.*, pp. 124, 131, 264, 614.   [8] *Ibid.*, p. 132.

officials who have been appointed, a number of trials have been allowed before they finally passed.[1] This has led to considerable abuse, and is largely responsible for the employment for long and irregular intervals of so-called temporary clerks.'[2]

'Under the Canadian *Civil Service Act* a system of examinations for promotion exists which does not prevail in England, and your Commissioners find that although in regard to a few cases no examinations have been required, yet as a rule, promotions have not been made without such examinations. But in the holding of these there has been great disparity in the papers submitted by the several departments, for whilst in some instances the examinations have been thorough, entering exhaustively into the duties of the department, thereby testing the fitness of the candidates, in others the papers have been simple in the extreme. This system of examination for promotion has therefore been to a large extent ineffective and along with political pressure has led to the departments being generally overmanned in the higher offices. In fact promotions have taken place as a rule for other causes than the necessities of the service.'[3]

'Promotions too have not carried with them the full significance of the term, and officials have been advanced in salary from length of service alone, and not because the duties they had to perform were more important. This leads to continued apathy and a mechanical style of performing work, which finally results in more clerks being constantly employed than is necessary. There has been, the Commissioners fear, a tendency to make promotions for the benefit of officers who had reached the maximum salaries of their class, whether vacancies in the higher class existed or not, and for that purpose to create unnecessarily higher class clerkships.'[4]

A further cause of 'continued apathy' was undoubtedly the perfunctory method of granting increases in salary: they were not given as a reward, but were occasionally withheld as a punishment.[5] In the words of a witness, 'a respectable dullard' would as a rule get his increase the same as the most efficient clerk.[6] Furthermore, rapid promotion was almost impossible. A member of the Privy Council staff stated that 'under the present system a man serves from eight to twelve

[1] *Can. Sess. Pap.*, 1892, § 16c, pp. 32, 178, 528, 553, 617.
[2] *Ibid.*, p. xix.   [3] *Ibid.*, p. xix.   [4] *Ibid.*, p. xx.
[5] *Ibid.*, pp. 6, 24, 72, 159.   [6] *Ibid.*, p. 261.

years before reaching the maximum of the third class, and provided he is not stopped then, from sixteen to twenty years before reaching the maximum of the second'.[1] The Superintendent of the Post Office Savings Bank expressed his opinion with much less reserve than the majority of the witnesses:

'My experience demonstrates this, that the present classification of clerks into first, and second and third class, is simply an unqualified humbug. It rests on no defined principle, and has in practice been productive of the most absurd inconsistency and of much injustice to the service in the relative distribution of duties and salaries. The present class periods, too, are absurdly long; if they were strictly adhered to it would take forty and a-half years to reach the top. The remedy lies, in my opinion, in a classification of duties and responsibility with definite scales of minimum and maximum pay for each.'[2]

In this report the so-called 'temporary clerks' first appeared as a really serious problem. The Commission of 1868 had mentioned the existence of such a class and called attention to the anomalies in pay and status which it occasioned.[3] The evidence taken in 1880 had stated that there were a number of 'temporary' employees,[4] but the Commission said little about them in the report.[5] The probable reason was that as the examinations at that time had fallen into disuse, most appointments could be made to the permanent staff without much difficulty. But the Act of 1882 had reimposed restrictions on entrance which had weeded out the most inefficient, and temporary clerkships were again utilized to avoid the necessity of passing the barrier. By 1891 the problem had become one of the most important in the service. In that year there were 733 persons of all grades in the Inside Service under the Act, and no less than 370 others who did not come under its provisions and were known as 'temporary' employees—almost an exact ratio of two to one.[6] The Royal Commission reported:

---

[1] *Ibid.*, p. 14.
[2] *Ibid.*, p. 119.
[3] *Can. Sess. Pap.*, 1869, § 19, p. 8.
[4] *Ibid.*, 1880–1, § 113, pp. 108, 187, 200, 228, 287, 313.
[5] *Ibid.*, p. 28.
[6] *Ibid.*, 1892, § 16c, pp. xv–xvi.

K

'There are a considerable number of persons regularly engaged in the service of the government whose names are not in the list in question (i.e. the Civil Service List) at all. This large class is not embraced under the provisions of the *Civil Service Act*, although the duties, work, and responsibilities of the larger number of them are in no way to be distinguished from those of regular officers. The remuneration of this class of officials is at a certain rate per day or per month, which indicates that their position originally was temporary, by which name as a class they are still distinguished. They have, however, for the most part long ceased to be such, and practically are part of the permanent staff. . . . Some of them render services of a professional character, such as engineers, architects, &c., and are men of high education and experience, and generally their services are as valuable as those of permanent officers engaged in the same duties. . . . The salaries of this class of so-called "temporary" officers range from $4,500 per annum to $1 per day.'[1]

The recommendations of the Royal Commission were tinged throughout with the idea of compromise. The report concluded with the remark that 'it is possible that public sentiment in Canada may not as yet be ripe for open competition generally, and it may not be possible as yet to eliminate altogether the power of politics in making appointments',[2] and this feeling is shown in all the findings and proposals. The Commissioners looked constantly for what was practicable, and apparently thought that very few improvements could be effected. They unanimously agreed that open competition was highly advisable, and yet the draft Bill which they suggested placed appointments and promotions in the hands of the Ministry after pass examinations had been held.[3] A provision was inserted, however, whereby the entrance examinations could be made competitive by the Governor in Council.[4] The report advised that the service should be graded into two principal classes, those doing work of supervision and those doing routine work, and a new division of clerks was suggested in accordance with this plan.[5] The personnel of the Civil Service Board was to be a compromise

---

[1] *Can. Sess. Pap.*, 1892, § 16 c, p. xvi.
[2] *Ibid.*, p. xxviii.
[3] *Ibid.*, pp. xxiii, xxxvi–xli.
[4] *Ibid.*, p. xxxix.
[5] *Ibid.*, pp. xxiii, xxx, xciii.

between the one in existence and that proposed by the Commission of 1880. It was to be composed of five members, four of whom were to be deputy heads of departments, while the other member, the chairman, was to be permanent and hold office on the same tenure as the Auditor General.[1] The Board was to have two duties: to hold examinations, and to investigate the organization and administration of the departments and report thereon.[2]

Even such compromises as those proposed were not acceptable to the Government. The Commission had served the purpose for which it was appointed. The scandals in the service which had been disclosed by the House of Commons Committee had made a further investigation inevitable, and a dutiful ministry had hastened to comply with the demand by nominating the Commission. The inquiry having been held, the incident was closed: the ministers' sense of obligation was satisfied, and they turned to other affairs which held less embarrassing possibilities for their future. The thanks of the Government were extended to the Royal Commissioners, who derived a meagre consolation from the publication of a bulky report, neatly bound in half leather.

The next fifteen years was the most dreary period in civil service history. Conditions became gradually worse, and the Act of 1882 was still further relaxed by convention and by legal amendment. The Board of Examiners continued to give examinations on spelling and vulgar fractions, and entered respectful protests against violation and avoidance of the rules. They accomplished little. They had not sufficient power and their position was too uncertain for them to secure improvements, and their best efforts were unable to prevent the service slipping back. The Board had the privilege of calling the attention of Parliament to matters of importance, and they did so; but when Parliament ignored the report, there was nothing more to be said or done. The one function that the Board was expected to fulfil, the conducting of the

---

[1] The report proper and the draft Bill do not quite agree. The latter (p. xxxi) merely states tenure during good behaviour. The former (p. xxi) would imply also that there must be a joint address of the two Houses to remove; *Can. Stat.*, 141 Vic. c. 7, section 12.

[2] *Can. Sess. Pap.*, 1892, § 16C, pp. xxi–xxiii, xxxi.

examinations, was conscientiously carried out, though even in this the members may be blamed for their reluctance in advocating a higher standard.

The chief difficulty that the Board encountered, if one is to judge from its reports, was to keep the examinations for promotion an effective test of the candidates' ability. The rules called for obligatory examinations in writing, spelling, arithmetic, composition, and the duties of office, to which the deputy might add any or all of a number of optional subjects.[1] 'Efficiency', or the opinion of the deputy heads on the qualifications of their clerks, was another consideration in making promotions. This, however, was frequently of little significance, for while some deputies discriminated between candidates by giving high and low marks, others gave all applicants the maximum number in order to help them out.[2] In 1895, owing to a shortage of funds, it was decided by the Governor in Council that the promotion examination for that year should not be held.[3] In 1898 the Board reported that the number coming up for promotion examinations had decreased for the past few years, largely because the great bulk of the clerks had passed the test and were still awaiting promotion.[4] Attention was also called to a custom which had gradually grown up in regard to these examinations and which threatened to destroy a large part of their value:

'There is an "unwritten law" acted upon by the Treasury Board and by the Auditor General for some years past, which allows an employee to be promoted from one class to another on his first examination, provided the percentages obtained at that examination would be sufficient to qualify him for the rank to which it is proposed to advance him. As a result of this, it may, and does frequently, happen that employees come up for examination only once, instead of for each succeeding grade as was the case before the practice just indicated was adopted.

'It appears to the Board that the main objects of the promotion examination were first, that it should stimulate those who otherwise might feel disposed to do their work in a careless, perfunctory manner, trusting to outside influence to assist them in procuring

[1] *Can. Sess. Pap.*, 1893, § 16 B, p. 5.
[2] *Ibid.*, 1907–8, § 29 A, Evidence, p. 26.
[3] *Ibid.*, 1896, § 16 C, p. 7.   [4] *Ibid.*, 1899, § 16 C, p. 5.

their promotion, and second that it should be a means of encouraging those who are attentive to their duties, and who strive by study and persevering industry to become thoroughly familiar with all the details of the department in which they are employed. Suppose a candidate in undergoing the first promotion examination makes the necessary number of marks to qualify him for a chief clerkship, but let us suppose that no vacancy for the position occurs for say a dozen years, what guarantee would there be that meanwhile the candidate has been keeping himself *en rapport* with all the details of his official duties?'[1]

In 1904 an Order in Council was passed which allowed the departments to cut down the promotion examinations to 'duties of office' only, instead of the usual subjects mentioned above.[2] In the following year the Examiners deprecated the continual alteration and paring of the rules and advised that uniform regulations, better suited to the needs of the departments, should be adopted:

'The "regulations" so called have become a regular shifting sand, whereon no man may tell from one year to another how he may stand. As an example of how widely different are the views held regarding these examinations by heads of departments, it should be stated that, during the year with which this report deals, the regulations were amended, limiting the examination for all employees of the Post Office Department to the subjects of orthography and duties of office, and that in another department (Labour) the deputy head, exercising the privilege accorded him by the regulations, prescribed the following subjects in addition to the five prescribed in the regular curriculum, viz. grammar, history, geography, constitution, stenography, typewriting, and in the case of one candidate, translation from French into English and *vice versa*. . . . The Board's suggestion would be that each deputy head be called upon to report as to what he considers would be a proper set of subjects on which his officers should be examined, and with these expressions of opinion before them the Board would then be in a better position to arrange a system of examinations which would receive the support and co-operation of the deputy heads, and which would bring about results highly beneficial to the service as a whole.'[3]

---

[1] *Ibid.*, 1899, § 16c, pp. 5–6. Quoted in *ibid.*, 1900, § 16B, p. 6.
[2] *Ibid.*, 1905, § 31, p. iv; *ibid.*, 1907–8, § 29A, Evidence, p. 35.
[3] *Ibid.*, 1906, § 31, p. iv.

From this time on the promotion examinations became more and more lax, and were taken almost entirely from the control of the Board and placed in the hands of the deputies.[1] In the seven special promotion examinations held in 1905 the test was confined to the single subject of 'duties of office', given and examined by the deputy heads of the departments concerned.[2] In the next year the Board reported that the Finance Department had also availed itself of the new rule, and had examined its candidates for promotion on two subjects instead of the five originally used.[3]

The entrance examinations were given year after year with little change. They were of approximately the same standard as in 1882, and a schoolboy of thirteen would have been able to pass them.[4] One-fourth of those who failed wrote the examination a second time, and some came back again and again.[5] Unsuccessful candidates demanded that their papers should be re-examined, and 'under pressure from influential persons' the Board thought it wise to comply.[6] Political influence was also used in an endeavour to induce the Board to add a few marks to a failure, and threats were made that if the request were not granted the matter would be aired in the House of Commons. The Board, however, refused to stretch its conscience any further.[7]

In spite of this feeble record the Examiners were far from being discouraged. In 1899 they called attention to the small number of unsuccessful candidates and attributed this result to their own efforts. It was, they said:

'Undoubted proof that the Board, as was hoped at its inception, would by maintaining as high a standard as was practicable, act as a factor in stimulating the educational progress of the country. So true is this that many business colleges and other educational institutions keep up special classes for civil service work; and although it has not, of course, been possible for a majority of those who have obtained certificates from the Board to procure employment in the public service, still the improvement which the candi-

---

[1] *Can. Sess. Pap.*, 1907–8, § 29A, Evidence, pp. 9, 10, 26.
[2] *Ibid.*, 1906, § 31, p. v.   [3] *Ibid.*, 1906–7, § 31, p. 5.
[4] *Ibid.*, 1907–8, § 29A, Evidence, p. 32.
[5] *Ibid.*, pp. 2–3.   [6] *Ibid.*, 1906–7, § 31, p. 8.
[7] *Ibid.*, 1907–8, § 29A, Evidence, pp. 11–12.

dates have made in their educational equipment, and the habits of study acquired in the course of what is, to many of them, an arduous preparation, must, in the long run, be of great benefit both to themselves and to the community at large.' [1]

While it cannot be denied that the Examiners did their work fairly and honestly, it is difficult to take such enthusiasm without a smile. An examination, which was scarcely the equivalent of an entrance to High School, could not be expected to 'stimulate the educational progress of the country' to any appreciable extent. Cramming courses were most assuredly no evidence of such progress, and tended to defeat the purpose for which examinations were held. Still more exaggerated was the imaginary 'benefit in educational equipment and habits of study' derived by the candidates' 'arduous preparation' in penmanship, Magna Carta, and the capes of Nova Scotia. All this complacency on the part of the Board was called forth by the fact that a large number of candidates were successful, a phenomenon easily explained by the great advance made in the provincial elementary schools.

The success of the candidates in the examinations apparently induced the Board to commit itself still further. In 1905, after an existence of twenty-three years, the Board proposed for the first time that the standard of examination might conceivably be raised. [2] In the next report, finding that the expression of these radical tendencies did not lead to summary dismissal from office, the Examiners went a step further and suggested the possible use of competition as an aid in weeding out the worst candidates. They hastened to protect themselves by adding that public opinion might not be ripe for such an unexpected change. [3]

The *Civil Service Act* was amended many times in the fifteen years from 1892 to 1907. The old *Superannuation Act* was amended, [4] and later replaced by a *Retirement Act*. [5] Third

[1] *Ibid.*, 1900, § 16B, pp. 6-7.
[2] *Ibid.*, 1905, § 31, p. v-vi.   [3] *Ibid.*, 1906, § 31, p. vi.
[4] *Can. Stat.*, 60-1 Vic. c. 15; *ibid.*, 3 Edw. VII, c. 10.
[5] *Ibid.*, 61 Vic. c. 17; 2 Edw. VII, c. 6; 3 Edw. VII, c. 10; *Rev. Stat. Can.*, 1906, c. 17.

Class Clerks were abolished in 1895,[1] and restored in 1903.[2]
A new group of Junior Second Class Clerks was created in
1900,[3] and a Chief Clerkship, Grade A, placed above the
Chief Clerkship in 1903.[4] College graduates were allowed to
enter on their degrees as Junior Second Class Clerks, whilst
others had to write the examination and be admitted only
to the Third Class.[5] It was a partial approximation to the
English idea of taking in well educated men at a higher
standing than others who had entered through an easier
examination. An *Insurance Act* for the benefit of civil servants was passed in 1893,[6] and salaries were raised slightly in
1903.[7]

In 1896 the Conservative Government was defeated after
a continuous term of eighteen years. Immediately a large
number of civil servants were dismissed from office. In eight
departments between 13 July 1896, and 9 April 1897, 473
employees were dismissed, removed, or superannuated, and
of these 196 were stated to be for 'offensive political partisanship'.[8] This number increased greatly during the next few
years.[9] It is difficult to pronounce on the justice of dismissals
on such a scale, for the evidence is hopelessly conflicting, each
party accusing the other of unfairness and contenting itself
with a *tu quoque* as a defence.[10] There is, however, a strong
supposition that the majority of those dismissed because of
partisanship deserved their fate, for the long term of the
Conservatives in office and the nature of the appointments they had sanctioned tended to make many officials
violent supporters of the Government. In the debacle the

[1] *Can. Stat.*, 58–9 Vic. c. 15.

[2] *Ibid.*, 3 Edw. VII, c. 9, section 14.

[3] *Ibid.*, 63–4 Vic. c. 14.   [4] *Ibid.*, 3 Edw. VII, c. 9, section 8.

[5] *Ibid.*, 63–4 Vic. 14, section 7; *Rev. Stat. Can.*, 1906, c. 16, sections 72, 73.

[6] *Can. Stat.*, 56 Vic. c. 13.

[7] *Ibid.*, 3 Edw. VII, c. 9. Other minor amendments to the *Civil Service
Act* were: *ibid.*, 57–8 Vic. c. 18; 58–9 Vic. c. 14; 60–1 Vic. c. 14.

[8] In many of the other dismissals no cause was assigned, and a large proportion of these was undoubtedly for partisanship also. *Can. Sess. Pap.*,
1897, § 57 T; *ibid.*, 1898, § 31.

[9] *Ibid.*, 1900, § 64 B.

[10] *Can. H. of C. Debates*, 28 Aug. 1896, pp. 318–401; 1 Sept. 1896, pp.
484–545; 5 May 1897, pp. 1749–74; 6 May 1897, pp. 1836–98; 14 May 1897,
pp. 2301–407; 28 Apr. 1897, pp. 1377–95.

Outside Service suffered more than the Inside, because the
nominations to that branch were more openly political and
the opportunities for party activity at the elections were
more frequent and tempting.

The results of the election of 1896 showed that patronage
and the spoils still exercised their old sway over the service.
The new Liberal administration painstakingly carried out
the traditions of its predecessors and continued to regard
party services first and efficiency second in making appointments.

'Sir Wilfrid Laurier', writes one of his biographers, 'had a large
toleration for patronage. When eager civil service reformers confessed their desire to relieve him of the "incubus of patronage"
there crept into his eyes a look of humorous wisdom which would
have cooled their ardour if they had understood all its significance.
He believed there was far more of gain than of loss to governments
and parties through control over appointments to office and distribution of public contracts. He knew that "funds" were necessary to organize constituencies and carry elections and seldom
was anxious to discover the sources of the contributions. There
never was in Canada a more flagrant misuse of public works and
public appropriations to influence constituencies than in the
general election of 1908, but Laurier was acquiescent. He loved
power as dearly as ever did Sir John Macdonald, and one doubts
if in use of the means to hold power he was more scrupulous than
the Conservative leader of whose methods he had exact knowledge
and upon whose career his own, to a degree, was fashioned. But,
notwithstanding his general attitude towards patronage, the first
great step towards elimination of partisan considerations in
appointments to the civil service was taken under his last administration when the Inside Service was brought under the competitive system. It is true, also, that as he grew older he became less
tolerant of looseness in the departments and more concerned to
restrain the agencies of electoral corruption.'[1]

The doctrine that supporters must be supported was still
followed, and was openly paraphrased in 1904 by Sir William
Mulock, the Postmaster-General:

'As I understand it, the party system prevails in Canada and it
is the practice of the government of to-day to remember their sup-

[1] Willison, Sir John, *Sir Wilfrid Laurier*, pp. 468-9.

porters in distributing public patronage. That practice has obtained in days gone by and I hope it is in full force to-day. I should greatly deplore it if the Liberal party, in the exercise of its patronage on the Welland Canal or elsewhere, is neglectful of its friends and its own supporters.'[1]

The condition of the civil service from 1882 to 1908 was therefore one of stagnation, or, if there was any movement, it was in the wrong direction. The entrance examinations continued to be given with very little change, and the successful candidates, according to an official report, were probably of poorer quality in 1908 than in 1882.[2] The promotion examinations, as the reports of the Board showed, had lost what little virtue they had had through the hostility of the Ministry. The reduction in their number, combined with the rule allowing one test to do duty for two or three promotions, had made this part of the Act of 1882 practically inoperative and almost entirely useless. The Board of Examiners fought conscientiously for their scanty privileges, and the only reason they were not annihilated was that their battle was scarcely worthy fighting at all. Patronage merely smiled at their activity and continued its work almost oblivious of their presence. The general effect was that by 1908 'the public service . . . not only at Ottawa but elsewhere throughout the Dominion (had) fallen back during the last fifteen years'.[3]

In 1907 the Laurier Government appointed a Royal Commission of three men to report on the service. The Order in Council authorizing the Commission began with the amazing statement that 'the general principles of the Civil Service Act are regarded as satisfactory,' but it was considered 'advisable in the best interests of efficiency' to inquire into certain subjects arising under the Act.[4] The Commission made the most thorough investigation in the history of the service. It heard over two hundred officials in Ottawa, Montreal, Toronto, and Quebec, took nine months at the inquiry, and presented 1,900 pages in its report. It emphatically dis-

---

[1] *Can. H. of C. Debates*, 6 July 1904, p. 6114.
[2] *Can. Sess. Pap.*, 1907–8, § 29A, pp. 14, 21.
[3] *Ibid.*, p. 15.   [4] *Ibid.*, p. 7.

sented from the Government's view that the service was
'satisfactory', and recommended the complete repeal of the
existing Act.[1]

The evidence proved (if proof were needed) that political
patronage was still the dominant influence throughout the
public service, and that the Act of 1882 had done little to
curb it. Party connexion was just as important a qualification for office as before. Promotions were still affected by it,
as were salaries, dismissals, discipline, and purchases of supplies.[2] In some instances the Ministers endeavoured to exclude the office-seekers and prevent interference, but these
cases seem to have been rare.[3] Patronage was particularly
shameless in the Outside Service:

'In the outside service politics enter into every appointment,
and politicians on the spot interest themselves not only in the appointments but in subsequent promotions of officers. While at
Ottawa the departments generally are administered with a good
consideration for the public interest, yet in the outside service the
politics of the party is of greater importance in making appointments and promotions than the public interests of the Dominion.
Practically in no case is it possible to fill a vacancy in one locality
by a transfer from another. Each locality is separately guarded.
. . . In the outside service those who have the "political pull" use
it for all it is worth; they pass by their superior officers and bring
pressure to procure anything that may prove to their advantage.
To get over the difficulties which constantly arise and to circum-
vent the politicians, the higher officials, being in constant dread
of the latter, have evaded the terms of the Civil Service Act by
employing officials designated as labourers or examiners or some
other title, and have tried to get their several offices into good
working order. As a rule the officials in the outside service are
without hope, and the majority of them are in dire need.'[4]

The *Civil Service Act* was quite inadequate: it did not begin
to cover the whole of the employees, and many devices were
used to dodge its provisions. The Commission estimated that
only one-half of the members of the Inside Service and a 'very

[1] *Ibid.*, pp. 10, 13, 15.
[2] *Ibid.*, pp. 19, 20, 26, 29; cf. Evidence, pp. 128, 130, 155, 176, 379, 440–3,
586, 1077, 1240.
[3] *Ibid.*, Evidence, pp. 777, 781, 783.   [4] *Ibid.*, pp. 27–8

limited number' of the Outside came under the statute at all.[1]
Evasions of the Act were common. New classes of employees
were created in order that they would not come under the
schedule of civil service positions and be compelled to pass
examinations.[2] 'Temporary' clerks and officers were still
admitted and were graded as labourers, some having been in
the service for thirty and forty years.[3] It was also becoming
increasingly common to pass appropriations of an exceptional
nature with the clause appended 'notwithstanding anything
to the contrary in the *Civil Service Act*'.[4]

The Commissioners found that male employees, particularly in the lower grades, were much underpaid, and that
salaries, in spite of a diminished purchasing power, had remained almost stationary for thirty years.[5] The evidence
justified their conclusions. One man's salary increased from
$1,200 to $1,600 in twenty-six years, another's had remained
the same for twenty-one years, another's had been raised
$100 in twenty-nine years, a fourth's had 'jumped' $400 in
thirty-four years. One employee was endeavouring to keep a
wife and eight children on $2.25 a day. And there were
many others.[6] Salaries were also very unequal in similar
positions, and sometimes a man received more than his official
superior.[7]

One of the most serious conclusions reached by the Commissioners was that there was a decided decline in the quality
of new men entering the service. This they attributed to
the inadequacy of the salaries, the poor opportunities for
promotion, and the inducements in other fields due to the
rapid expansion of the country.[8] The report also deplored the
filling up of the lower grades by women, which, it argued,
seriously limited promotions from the ranks.[9] The abolition
of superannuation in 1898 was regarded by the Commis-

---

[1] *Can. Sess. Pap.*, 1907–8, § 29A, pp. 14–15.
[2] *Ibid.*, pp. 13, 29. Evidence, pp. 102–3.
[3] *Ibid.*, pp. 13, 18–19. Evidence, pp. 134, 158, 835.
[4] *Ibid.*, p. 13.   [5] *Ibid.*, pp. 17–18.
[6] *Ibid.*, Evidence, pp. 358, 360, 380, 511, 845, 846.
[7] *Ibid.*, Evidence, pp. 127, 414.
[8] *Ibid.*, pp. 14, 15–16, 21. Evidence, pp. 120, 155, 452, 843, 857, 1031.
[9] *Ibid.*, p. 14.

sioners as 'illogical, hasty, and inconsiderate', and they advised its immediate re-enactment.[1]

The Royal Commission recommended that appointments should be made only on merit after open competitive examinations, which were to be supervised by a permanent commission of three members. They made also the further suggestion that these examinations, instead of being of a general nature, should differ for each class or position in the service; instead of the examination being used to test general ability, it was to secure special qualifications; instead of relying upon experience to produce in time the required training, some of that training was to be obtained before entrance. The Commissioners were rather vague as to the extent and nature of these special examinations, and the examples which they quoted from the British service were all technical positions. It appears doubtful whether they would have applied such tests to ordinary clerkships in the Inside Service, which required little more than general ability. They remained silent on the important matter of promotion examinations, and simply suggested that greater opportunities should be given for the rapid advancement of young men with great talents. The Commissioners also considered that many salaries should be raised, probation should be rigidly enforced, and the examining body should be given the power of inspection and oversight of departmental administration.[2] They concluded with the following paragraph:

'It is a much more difficult proposition to preserve a uniformly high state of efficiency in a government staff than in the ordinary work of the world carried on by money-making organizations. This, your Commissioners think, is generally recognized, but to achieve any real success in either field the supreme necessity is character which above all means conscience. No government can ignore this and live. While demanding the highest character they should do everything possible to develop it, and one of the first things necessary is to see that its servants can at least live in a moderate degree of comfort, and, that after that a career be opened to every one in the service in which the rewards will be justly proportioned to the value of the service rendered.'[3]

[1] *Ibid.*, pp. 21-3.   [2] *Ibid.*, pp. 44-6.   [3] *Ibid.*, p. 46.

V. THE REFORM OF THE INSIDE SERVICE

1908–17

'Peers shall teem in Christendom,
And a duke's exalted station
Be attainable by com-
petitive examination.'
Iolanthe.

THE report of the Royal Commission of 1907 was well timed, for a number of circumstances combined to bring about reform in the direction it had indicated. In the first place, although the service was even worse than it had been in 1882, its needs were far more urgent. Canada was expanding at unprecedented speed, and it seemed very probable that the sanguine prophecy of her Prime Minister that 'the twentieth century is Canada's century' would be fulfilled. This phenomenal increase in population, coupled with a rapid extension of the sphere of governmental activity, necessitated large additions both to the number and variety of the civil servants. The technical branches and those calling for special skill and knowledge were growing in importance year by year. In the earlier days these consisted chiefly of engineers, architects, and surveyors; but later years had added statisticians, chemists, archivists, entomologists, physicians, immigration officers, and a host of others. Clearly, if the Government and administration were to occupy their proper places in the life of the young nation reform must come quickly, and an inefficient service was less tolerable at this stage of the country's development than at any time before.

Other forces also exerted pressure on the Government to impel it in the same direction. Public opinion was beginning to realize the extravagance and waste of patronage, and gradually threw its weight on the side of reform. Different public men had advocated the non-political service as the greatest need of the nation.[1] The Conservative party had taken up the matter and had inserted civil service reform in

[1] *Can. Annual Review*, 1905, pp. 188, 192; *ibid.*, 1907, p. 424.

its platform.[1] Finally, and most important of all, a general election was in sight, and the Government was not disposed to take any unnecessary hazards.

The outcome was the *Civil Service Amendment Act* of 1908,[2] which radically altered the Inside Service and provided that the Outside Service might also be brought under the same provisions by Order in Council.[3] It was the first genuine reform measure—thirty-three years after Mr. Casey had introduced his resolution in Parliament.

A permanent Civil Service Commission was authorized, which was to be composed of two members appointed by the Governor in Council and holding office during good behaviour, removable by the Governor-General on address of the Senate and House of Commons.[4] The Commission was to make investigations and reports on the operation of the Civil Service Acts, to exercise supervision over admissions and promotions, and to issue certificates of qualification to successful candidates.[5] The Inside Service was reclassified into three Divisions, each of which was separated into A and B Subdivisions. The Third Division was composed of clerks mainly concerned with routine and copying work.[6]

All appointments to the Inside Service, with a few exceptions, were to be made by open competitive examinations, which were to be 'of such a nature as will determine the qualifications of candidates for the particular positions to which they are to be appointed'.[7] Selections for vacancies were to be made by the Commission, and were to be, so far as practicable, in order of merit, but the Commission was empowered to select others who had shown special qualifications on a particular subject.[8] A probationary period was to follow appointment.[9] Whenever technical qualifications were desired competition might be dispensed with, and upon the Commission granting a certificate (by examination or otherwise) the Governor in Council might appoint such candidate to the vacancy.[10]

[1] *Ibid.*, 1907, p. 460.   [2] *Can. Stat.*, 7–8 Edw. VII, c. 15.
[3] *Ibid.*, section 4, subsection 3.
[4] Section 9.   [5] Section 10.   [6] Section 5.
[7] Section 13.   [8] Section 18.   [9] Sections 19, 20.
[10] Section 21.

Promotions were to be made for merit upon the recommendation of the head and deputy head of the Department and with a certificate of qualification from the Commission given with or without examination.[1] Third Division clerks might enter the open competitive examination for the Second Division after a term of service and upon other conditions determined by the Governor in Council on the recommendation of the Commission.[2] No person was to endeavour to influence a Commissioner with respect to any appointment or promotion or increase in salary, and if the person attempting to do so were a member of the service, he was to be refused any such request and was liable to immediate dismissal.[3] No civil servant was to engage in any partisan work in a Dominion or provincial election.[4]

The Act, although it affected in the main only the employees at Ottawa, made a number of very sweeping changes which altered the whole complexion of the service. It created a permanent Commission, independent of the Government, and holding office on the same tenure as the judges. It drew a sharp line of distinction between the officer and routine classes, and provided special competitive examinations for each. The entrance examination to the Third Division corresponded roughly to the old qualifying examination; that for admission to the Second Division was quite new and was much more difficult than any that had been given before. Promotion examinations were no longer to be compulsory, but used only when the Commission thought necessary. In short, the Act, so far as it went, was very satisfactory; its chief fault was that it left the Outside Service virtually the same as before.

The new Act came into operation on 1 September 1908, and the two Commissioners, both excellent men, were appointed a few days later. The work of organization proceeded rapidly, and apparently received the cordial co-operation of the Government. In 1911 the Commissioners were able to report:

'One of the most hopeful indications for the ultimate removal of

---

[1] Section 24. [2] Section 26.
[3] Section 42. [4] Section 43.

all appointments to the service from the sphere of political patronage has been the increasing extent to which positions of a technical or professional character, which might have been filled without open competition, have been voluntarily assigned to be filled by competitive methods, administered jointly by the Commission and the heads of the departments or branches of the service concerned with the duties to be performed.' [1]

The custom thus arose to fill many professional and technical positions by competition, though not necessarily by examination. Applications were confined to those holding degrees or diplomas from scientific or technical institutions of recognized standing, and the places assigned to those who had had the greatest success in positions outside the service.[2] The majority of the entrance examinations were given on academic subjects, unless the nature of the vacancy made a special test desirable. The Commission practically abandoned the system of promotion examinations which had been used since 1882, though a few continued to be held for members of the Third Division who were in the service prior to 1908—a special concession granted by the Act of that year.[3] With this exception, 'in the great majority of cases it has been deemed advisable that when the members of the service have once qualified to enter the Second Division, their subsequent promotion should depend upon their capacity and efficiency, as indicated by the services which they render and the manner in which they perform their duties.' [4]

A number of amending Acts were passed during the next few years, all of which, with one exception, were of little interest.[5] This exception authorized the appointment of a third Civil Service Commissioner, but no steps were taken to fill the position until 1917.[6]

The optimism of the Commission as to diminution of patronage must have suffered a severe shock after the defeat of the Liberal Government in 1911. No sooner had the Con-

[1] *Can. Sess. Pap.*, 1912, § 31, p. xi.   [2] *Ibid.*, p. xiii.
[3] *Can. Stat.*, 7–8 Edw. VII, c. 15, section 26.
[4] *Can. Sess. Pap.*, 1912, § 31, pp. xv–xvi.
[5] *Can. Stat.*, 8–9 Edw. VII, cc. 6, 7 ; 9–10 Edw. VII, c. 8 ; 2 Geo. V, cc. 10, 11, 12, 13, 14, 15, 16; 4–5 Geo. V, c. 21 ; 7–8 Geo. V, c. 9.
[6] *Ibid.*, 2 Geo. V, c. 10.

servatives assumed office than the heads of officials began
to fall. It is generally believed that the Conservatives in
1911 eclipsed the Liberals in 1896—no mean achievement—
though the way was probably made easier by the increase in
the number of employees. The Inside Service, which was
largely under the merit system, suffered very little. The Outside Service, however, being recruited by political methods,
still carried with it the privilege, on the part of a new Government, to dispense with officers whose loyalty was suspected
or who had been foolhardy enough to flaunt their political
opinions before vigilant opponents. Legal reform and popular belief in reform were but a recent growth, and the doctrine
that supporters must be supported died hard, particularly
when the supporters had been hungry for fifteen years. The
Canada Sessional Papers for 1913 [1] contain 363 separate
returns demanded in Parliament by the Opposition, all of
which concern dismissals by the new Government, and the
Hansard of that year is no less prolific in questions and debates on the same subject.[2] In less than four months 236
postmasters were dismissed from office, and in three years
almost 11,000 employees had resigned or had been removed.[3]
The reason for which the majority were turned out was the
old one of political partisanship, and little time was wasted
in inquiries or investigations. 'If a member', said the
Minister of Customs, 'states to me that he has personal knowledge or that he has evidence based on personal inquiries that
a man has been an active partisan I am satisfied to take his
word and dismiss the official.'[4]

In 1910 Mr. (later Sir) George E. Foster, when moving for
further reform of the service, had described its condition in
the following words:

'Until September, 1908, this was absolutely true, that no man
entered it, no man got preferment in it, no man felt safe within it,

[1] § 61; cf. *Can. Sess. Pap.*, 1914, § 44.
[2] *Can. H. of C. Debates*, 12 Jan. 1912, pp. 1076–1196; 26 Jan. 1912, pp.
2016–38; 16 Feb. 1912, pp. 3244–76; 27 Mar. 1912, pp. 6280–304; 29 Mar.
1912, pp. 6616–46. Cf. *Can. Annual Review*, 1911, p. 299.
[3] *Ibid.*, 29 Mar. 1912, pp. 6636–40; *ibid.*, 4 Mar. 1915, pp. 640–3.
[4] *Ibid.*, 12 Jan. 1912, p. 1088.

unless he either got the entrance by virtue of party influence or looked after his preferment and his permanent position by keeping on good terms with the party influence. . . . Since September, 1908, a measurable advance has been made, and a portion of the civil service has, to a certain extent, been cut loose and put into a more or less independent position in that respect. It still remains true that the vast mass of the civil service is in the position that I have just mentioned. . . . With the single exception of the civil service at Ottawa, it is absolutely true that no man enters into that employment unless he utters the party shibboleth, and no man remains in that employment unless he either keeps a mighty quiet tongue—if he happened to go to work before the existing government took office, whatever that government may be—and no man gets along unless he continues to utter the party shibboleth and keeps in touch and well within the good will of the party.'[1]

In less than two years after his speech was made, Mr. Foster's party was returned to office and he became a Cabinet Minister, whereupon he and his colleagues proceeded to prove that the words had been true. 'Party shibboleths' were made the test for admission to the Outside Service to a greater degree than for fifteen years. If any one had believed after 1908 that the civil service was sufficiently reformed they were fully disillusioned in 1911–12, and the desirability of further changes was made more apparent than ever.

The new Government, shortly after its accession to office, appointed a Royal Commission of three members to inquire into the state of the administration. The report which resulted [2] is notable for nothing except its mediocrity: the Commissioners made no recommendations, they unearthed no new information, and contributed not a single idea or suggestion on the subject of their inquiry. It is mentioned here simply to indicate its futility and uselessness, for it had no influence at that time or later.

In sharp contrast to the last-mentioned report is that of Sir George Murray,[3] who was appointed on 30 September 1912 to investigate the service. In the short space of two months, handicapped by the fact that he was dealing with material quite unfamiliar to him, Sir George Murray pre-

[1] *Ibid.*, 26 Jan. 1910, pp. 2436–8.
[2] *Can. Sess. Pap.*, 1913, § 57.   [3] *Ibid.*, 1913, § 57 A.

sented the most instructive report that has ever been made
on the Canadian service.

He called attention, in the first place, to the excessive
burden of detailed work that fell to the lot of the Canadian
Ministry as a whole and to the Ministers individually. The
remedies that were suggested were a more extensive division
of labour and a greater devolution of power. Functions which
had been performed by the Governor in Council were to be
delegated to individual Ministers or to small committees of
the Council. Matters of administrative and executive detail
which had absorbed a large part of the time of a Minister
were to be left to his subordinates, and the political head of
the Department was to confine himself in the main to questions of policy and those of major importance.[1]

Sir George strongly endorsed the idea of open competitive examinations for entrance, and approved the two-fold
examination standard—a strict one for the Second Division,
an easy one for the Third.

'We must, therefore, be content with such a measure of merit
as is evinced by success in a competitive examination in subjects
which indicate a previous education of a high standard; and we
must assume that the raw material so selected will, with suitable
training in the department, develop the required capacity for the
more advanced duties. The system of selection by open competition undoubtedly leaves much to be desired; but in this imperfect
world it is not the least perfect institution; at any rate nothing
better has yet, in my opinion, been suggested.'[2]

In order to procure young men of promise in the Second
Division he advised that the age limits for admission be
altered from 18 and 35 to 17 and 25. Temporary clerkships
should be discouraged as they generally were filled by men
with insufficient training. The need for such clerks could be
overcome to a large degree by shifting men from one branch
to another or even from one department to another. He
recommended that the Outside Service be brought under the
same rules as the Inside, as provided by the Act of 1908.[3]

Sir George Murray considered the interference of the Civil

---

[1] *Can. Sess. Pap.*, 1913, § 57 A, pp. 7–10.   [2] *Ibid.*, p. 13.
[3] *Ibid.*, pp. 12–17; *Can. Stat.*, 7–8 Edw. VII, c. 15, section 4, subsection 3.

Service Commission in matters of promotion as undesirable, but admitted the difficulty of getting the head and deputy head of a department to promote for merit alone. While not committing himself too decidedly on the question, he favoured promotion by the head and deputy head and the repeal of those sections of the Act which required a certificate from the Commission before a promotion could be made. A pension system along the lines of the old Act (repealed in 1898) was very desirable; but compulsory retirement should be added in order that inefficient officers might be dispensed with and the flow of promotion maintained.[1]

The report concluded with a general review of the method of conducting public business in the Dominion and further remarks on the classification of the service.[2] Sir George pointed out that although in the previous three years the total clerks increased 19·2 per cent., the increase in the First Division had been 52·6 per cent., and in the Second Division 19·6 per cent., while the number of Third Division clerks had diminished. He concluded from this that the classification of 1908 could not have been satisfactory, though it was probable that this influx to the higher divisions was due in part to the obliteration of the distinction between intellectual and routine work and the indiscriminate promotion of those doing the latter. A new classification should be drawn up, and the Department of Finance charged with the duty of seeing that it was adhered to.

Sir George Murray showed throughout the entire report a grasp of civil service organization and principles that has never been equalled by any other Commissioner in Canada. The reason for his success is apparent. He brought to his task an intimate knowledge and a long experience of the British service, and these were made the more valuable by a detached and unbiassed mind, devoid of all local prepossessions. Notwithstanding the excellence of the report, it produced no tangible results. The changes in the civil service, when they did come, were unfortunately made along quite different lines and were based on other principles than those which Sir George had advocated.

[1] *Can. Sess. Pap.*, 1913, § 57 A, pp. 17–19.   [2] *Ibid.*, pp. 20–7.

The reports of the Civil Service Commission for the next few years indicated that political pressure continued even at Ottawa, and that the Commission had not been given sufficient powers to deal effectively with some questions. It is instructive to note the difference in the demeanour of the old Board of Examiners and that of the new Commissioners: the former had always been afraid of angering the Government, whereas the latter did not hesitate to criticize and say quite frankly what they thought. The Commission pointed out a number of ways by which patronage continued to gain its ends in the Inside Service. Appointments to technical positions, under section 21 of the Act, did not have to be made under competition, but the Commission had to certify that the appointee had at least minimum qualifications. In many instances the Commission was completely satisfied with the candidates' knowledge, and even thought that they were better fitted than any others who might be induced to apply. In other cases, however, it was found that the candidates were less efficient than others who could be obtained if the post were thrown open to competition. In either event, the Commissioners could do nothing except make sure that the applicants possessed the bare minimum necessary for the position; if so, they granted the certificate; if not, they withheld it. The certificates, therefore, 'represented qualifications which ranged from the best available to the minimum tolerable', due in a large measure to the varying degree in which Ministers were influenced by partisan considerations.[1] Two years later the Commission reported some improvement in this respect:

'It is gratifying to be able to record that in cases of appointments to the higher and more technical positions in the Inside Service there is an increasing harmony and co-operation between the Commissioners and the majority of the departments with a notable reduction of the earlier evils of political patronage, and an unquestionable improvement in the technical and professional branches of the Inside Service.'[2]

Patronage also crept in through the old loop-hole of tem-

[1] *Can. Sess. Pap.*, 1914, § 31, pp. xiii–xiv.
[2] *Ibid.*, 1916, § 31, p. xiii.

porary appointments, resulting in much trouble for the Commission and inefficiency and inconvenience to the service.[1]

'Partly because of the inadequate number of duly qualified male clerks who are available for permanent appointment at the minimum salary offered; partly because inadequate provision is made in the estimates of several large departments for the appointment of permanent clerks in the Third Division; and partly because of the opportunities afforded for the exercise of a considerable number of political and personal patronage, much of the regular and permanent work of the Third Division in certain departments is being performed by temporary clerks.'[2]

The Commission also called attention to the practice of making a temporary clerk a temporary sorter, who received the same salary and could be kept on indefinitely, though discharging the same duties in his new capacity as he did when a clerk. The Commission confessed that they were powerless to prevent this and similar evasions of the law. During the year 1913, 480 temporary clerks were appointed to the Third Division, 211 of whom were re-employed for a second time, and only 88 qualified later for regular appointment, despite the fact that almost the entire number were engaged on work of a permanent character. During the same period only 186 clerks were appointed permanently to the Third Division.[3]

The following year, 1914, saw a still further increase in the number of temporary employees.[4] The lower grade examination in the Inside Service, e.g. that for messengers, sorters, packers, &c., was still non-competitive, and this grade came under much the same conditions of patronage as the Outside Service. Persons were selected for employment before the examination, and so few were chosen from the general lists that the Commission discontinued holding two semi-annual examinations for this grade.[5]

Friction between the Commission and certain of the Ministers inevitably arose: the former endeavouring strictly

[1] *Ibid.*, 1914, § 31, p. xiv.   [2] *Ibid.*, p. xv.
[3] *Ibid.*, p. xvi.   [4] *Ibid.*, 1915, § 31, p. xiv.
[5] *Ibid.*, p. xii; cf. *The Civilian* (*Canada*), 18 Apr. 1913, p. 635; 11 July 1913, p. 141.

to observe the law, the latter doing their best to evade it.[1] In one instance a musician, whose grandfather had been a good Conservative, was promised a position if that party were returned to power. No sooner was the election of 1911 over than he sold his apartment and appeared in Ottawa as a candidate for a vacancy on the geological survey. He readily obtained the recommendation of the Minister and came before the Commission. The latter discovered that he had no qualifications whatsoever, but that he wanted the position in order to have time to practise his music—almost an exact illustration of the epigram of Beaumarchais: 'The post required a mathematician; it was given to a dancing master.' There is little cause for wonder that the Commission looked with suspicion upon such candidates and upon the Ministers who were sufficiently devoid of conscience to recommend them.

The barriers for entrance to the service were even more effectively lowered by the war than they had been by the pressure of unscrupulous ministers, although the latter continued with unabated vigour. The effects of the war began to be perceptible in 1915. Although the numbers of temporary clerks under the Act were slightly diminished, there was a large increase in such clerks who did not come under the Act but were paid directly out of war appropriations. These clerks were relieved from any qualifying examination whatever, and there were no restrictions as to salary, time of employment, &c., as would have been the case had they been under civil service rules. The *War Measures Act*, 1914,[2] stated that the places of employees who had enlisted might be filled by others who were to be paid out of war appropriations, and by an Order in Council these were also exempted from the regulations of the *Civil Service Act*.[3] 'The practical effect of this measure was to apply to various positions in the Inside Service the usual conditions of appointment which prevail in the Outside Service.'[4] These amendments and the exigencies of war largely nullified the restrictions for entrance; and the following years saw a still greater

[1] *The Civilian (Canada)*, 21 Feb. 1913, p. 543.
[2] *Can. Stat.*, 5 Geo. V, c. 2.
[3] *Can. Sess. Pap.*, 1916, § 31, p. xiv.   [4] *Ibid.*

influx of those who were not under the Act, and of temporary clerks who came under the Act only to a limited degree.[1] In the five years of war the number of civil servants increased from 37,000 to over 60,000.[2]

The condition of the service in 1917 was discouraging. Reform, which had begun so confidently in 1908, had suffered many blows after the election of 1911 and the outbreak of war. The Outside Service was run under almost unrestrained patronage, and was in a worse condition than in 1890. The Government controlled all appointments, there was no fixed standard of qualifications, promotions and increases in salary were given for political orthodoxy. The Inside Service was fast deteriorating as a result of the war, and the Act was deliberately dodged in order to satisfy party supporters. Classifications were changed, temporary clerkships were freely created, special votes were passed in war appropriations, and merit almost ceased to be a qualification for entrance. Against all these infringements in the letter and spirit of the law the Civil Service Commission protested vigorously, and the chairman finally resigned in disgust. ' The *Civil Service Act*', said the Secretary of the Commission a number of years later, 'was practically a dead letter. All the departments were taking on, during the period of the war, employees in great numbers, without any reference to the provisions of the *Civil Service Act*.' [3]

[1] *Can. Sess. Pap.*, 1917, § 31, p. xv; *ibid.*, 1918, § 31, pp. xii, xiii.
[2] *Can. H. of C. Journals*, 1923, Appendix, § 5, p. 1043; *Can. H. of C. Debates*, 31 Mar. 1922, pp. 555–6.
[3] *Can. H. of C. Journals*, 1923, Appendix, § 5, p. 181.

VI. THE FLOW AND EBB OF REFORM

1917–1928

'This stern decree, you'll understand,
Caused great dismay throughout the land:
    For young and old
    And shy and bold
Were equally affected.'

The Mikado.

THE year 1917 began a remarkable change in the civil service. The war had adversely affected its personnel by opening the doors of entrance and waiving the usual requirement of examinations. But the war had also an indirect effect no less important and much more beneficial: it caused the formation of the Union Government in 1917. This coalition party gave two distinct pledges before it dissolved Parliament and went to the country: to reinforce the overseas army and prosecute the war with vigour; to abolish patronage and reform the civil service.[1] The appeal was successful, and the party was returned at the polls with a large majority. It is likely that the Government, following a recommendation made earlier in the year by a conference of deputy ministers and the Civil Service Commission,[2] wished to extend reform gradually rather than bring the entire service under the Commission at one stroke of the pen. This was made almost impossible by the Government's own action. Immediately after the election it appointed two high officials for reasons so at variance with the party's promise that a general outcry was raised by the country.[3] The Cabinet, apparently somewhat amazed to find that the people expected an immediate fulfilment of its pledges, did not wait for Parliament to meet, but hastily passed an Order in Council on 13 February 1918 making reform immediately effective throughout the entire service. This Order stated that, pending legislation, all future ap-

[1] *Can. Sess. Pap.*, 1919, § 31, pp. 9–10.
[2] *Can. H. of C. Journals*, 1923, Appendix, § 5, pp. 892–4.
[3] *The Civilian (Canada)*, 15 Feb. 1918, p. 455; *ibid.*, 15 Mar. 1918, p. 505; *Can. Annual Review*, 1918, p. 449.

pointments to the Outside Service (except on Government
ships and railways) should be made only upon the recommendation and with the approval of the Civil Service Commission, the latter's opinion being determined wherever possible by the results of competitive examinations. Technical
appointments in the Inside Service were to be made by the
Commission and deputy heads of departments, instead of by
the Governor in Council and the deputies as heretofore. The
Commission was also to approve all transfers from the Outside to the Inside Service, to recommend (with the co-operation of the deputy heads) all promotions, and to authorize all
temporary employment in the Outside Service. Finally, the
Order provided that all persons who had been honourably
discharged after active service overseas and had passed the
examinations should be placed, irrespective of the marks
obtained, above all other successful candidates in the order of
merit.[1]

This new state of affairs was briefly mentioned in a notice
issued by the Commission on 27 February 1918, calling for
candidates for competitive examinations in the Outside
Service:

'As all positions in the Public Service in every part of Canada
(excepting those on Government Railways and in the Royal
Navy) have now been placed on a competitive basis and are filled
by the Civil Service Commission by means of examinations held
from time to time at various centres throughout the Dominion,
it is absolutely necessary that any person desiring a position
should avail himself of the first opportunity to present himself as a
candidate at one of these examinations.'[2]

Another Order in Council of 15 March 1918 provided
temporary regulations until legislation could be passed.[3]
Three days later the Government, intent upon making a
thorough house-cleaning, approved of a third Order. This
stated that the power to dismiss public officials on the
grounds of political partisanship should be sparingly exer-

---

[1] 1918, P.C., § 358, *Can. Gazette*, 1918, pp. 2947–8. This was made more
explicit on 28 Feb. 1918, by P.C., § 491 ; *Can. H. of C. Debates*, 19 Mar. 1918,
p. 31 ; *ibid.*, 12 Apr. 1918, pp. 695–7.
[2] *Can. Gazette*, 1918, p. 2957.   [3] *Ibid.*, p. 3215.

cised, and that, so far as the last election was concerned, no dismissal should be made for such a cause except after inquiry by and approval of the Civil Service Commission. In deciding such a case, the Commission was to regard solely the question of the public interest and the official's efficiency and length of service.[1]

Later in the year a new *Civil Service Act*[2] was passed to establish beyond doubt the provisions enacted in the Order in Council of 13 February.[3] In addition to bringing the Outside Service under the jurisdiction of the Commission, the Act gave other powers to the latter body which had been vested before in the Governor in Council.[4] It also reclassified the Inside Service into three divisions in addition to the deputy heads, who were considered a separate class. The Third Division included porters, messengers, sorters, &c.; the Second (with subdivisions A, B, and C), the routine clerks; and the First (with subdivisions A to F) comprised the higher executive, technical and administrative officers.[5] Entrance to each division was to be by competitive examinations of varying degrees of difficulty;[6] but these might be omitted for certain professional and technical positions.[7] The provision of the Order in Council regarding returned soldiers was confirmed.[8] Finally, the Commission was empowered to undertake a classification of the Outside Service.[9]

The Act virtually eliminated political patronage by substituting the Civil Service Commission for the Cabinet Ministers and the members of Parliament. Later events, it is true, proved that party influence in the service was not entirely dead, but it received in this statute a blow from which it has never recovered. Ever since the beginning of Canadian political history patronage had been the accepted rule of all Governments; henceforth it was to be the exception. The war had done one good thing: it had quickened men's con-

---

[1] *The Civilian* (Canada), 29 Mar. 1918, p. 537; *Can. Sess. Pap.*, 1919, § 31, p. 31.

[2] *Can. Stat.*, 8–9 Geo. V, c. 12.

[3] *Can. H. of C. Debates*, Apr. 12, 1918, pp. 695–7.

[4] *Can. Stat.*, 8–9 Geo. V, c. 12, sections 4, 15, 16, 17.

[5] Section 42.   [6] Section 38.   [7] Section 15.

[8] Section 39.   [9] Section 52.

sciences, and the response came with surprising speed. The members of Parliament, who had been tolerant for so many years, were amongst the first to discover the evils of the system they had countenanced. 'Patronage in this country', said a member, 'is one of the worst things that exist to-day in civil government. It is bad because it lends itself to a system of corruption. It is one of the most corrupt methods of canvassing for votes, going and promising half a dozen men an office.'[1] One can only wish that the great discovery had been made half a century earlier.

The corruption of the electorate was one side of the evil, the other was the inefficiency of the service itself. It is inconceivable that any one could have needed further proof as to the ineptness of party appointments, but more evidence was forthcoming in the year following reform. A report on the printing department, 6 March 1919, disclosed such inefficiency, overmanning, extravagance, and lack of co-operation that even the most hardened politicians professed to be shocked. No blame was attached to the officers of the printing bureau, but to 'a system built up by political patronage and influence'. The following are excerpts from the report:[2]

'The conditions . . . viewed from the standpoint of commercial efficiency may be briefly described as shocking. Under any but Government ownership the sheriff would long ago have closed the doors of the plant. . . . The system has placed each class of employees on a dead level, and made it uncomfortable for anyone to attempt to distinguish himself amongst his fellows.'

'To maintain a man in idleness for two months in order that he may work one is obviously bad business practice. . . . The art of doing nothing and making it appear like real labour has been highly developed.'

'An appointment to the Bureau staff has, through practice, apparently become a life engagement. Only the most serious and persistent failures endanger continuity of employment. The mere fact that there is no work for the employee to perform has no longer any bearings on his retention.'

'Largely the difficulty at the Bureau can be explained by the

---

[1] Can. H. of C. Debates, 12 Apr. 1918, p. 710.
[2] Ottawa Citizen, 7 Mar. 1919.

statement that the employees have been engaged through political influence or patronage, and that owing to this it has been impossible to have developed or maintained efficiency, or to have dismissed inefficient or unqualified help when in the judgement of the management this should have been done. With the idea on the part of the individual that his money has been sure without any consideration of the return he has had to give for it, and that it was sure for all time, the incentive for effort has been entirely removed. The management have been powerless to correct the difficulty owing to the influence brought to bear at various times on behalf of some of the employees.'

'The proof-reading department', said the report, 'appears to have been used as a dumping ground for people who could not otherwise be placed.' School teachers, lawyers, notaries, a doctor, a machinist, a musician, a baker, and a dry goods clerk all found refuge as proof-readers within the hospitable walls of the bureau. In the same branch four people were found on the pay roll who were receiving regular weekly wages, but were not required to attend the plant or to do any work, and had done nothing for at least a year.

The attempt of the Act of 1918 to include under its rules almost the entire service proved too sanguine. As has been already stated, it was deemed advisable from the first to exempt the employees on Government ships and railways. In 1919 the Department of Soldiers' Civil Re-establishment was also exempted because the numbers were increasing so rapidly that the Commission, with its new organization yet undeveloped, could not properly certify as to their qualifications.[1] The Income Tax Department, the Soldiers' Settlement Board, and the Census employees did not come under the Act on the theory that these branches were temporary and not part of the permanent service.[2] It is needless to add that the Income Tax Department has as yet shown no signs of confirming so pleasing a supposition.

The abolition of patronage and the sudden inclusion of about 45,000 extra employees under the Act made the task of the Commissioners almost impossible. They were confronted

[1] Can. Stat., 10 Geo. V, c. 29.
[2] Can. H. of C. Journals, 1923, Appendix, § 5, pp. 32, 179–81.

with two imperative problems—how was the Outside Service to be organized, and how were appointments in it to be made ? The natural answer to both questions was that the Outside should follow the example of the Inside Service. It was felt, however, that the positions in the former varied so enormously, and their conditions, qualifications, salaries, &c., were so different that a concise classification like that of the Inside Service, comprising only a few general divisions, was not practicable. With some misgivings [1] the Commission decided to place every position and office which possessed any distinctive features whatsoever into a category of its own, and to classify both Inside and Outside Services on this plan. The work, which by the Act had been entrusted to the Commission, was given by them to Messrs. Arthur Young and Company, a Chicago firm of experts, who had had some experience in state and municipal civil services in the United States.

Sixteen distinct steps were found to be necessary in order to classify each employee in the service—making a grand total of about 800,000 operations.[2] Cards were sent to all civil servants asking for information about their positions, and rashly adding that if there were not sufficient room on the card to describe their duties another sheet might be attached. Many availed themselves of this unexpected opportunity for showing their value to the nation. It was intended that these modest accounts would be checked for accuracy by the superior officers, especially by the deputies, but the latter were for the most part out of sympathy with the whole idea, and found themselves too preoccupied to revise a couple of thousand answers apiece. From the accurate data thus obtained, aided by occasional conferences with the departments and the Commission, the experts drew up what was known officially as *The Classification of the Civil Service of Canada*. Others not so charitable dubbed it 'the joke book', 'the yellow book', 'the best book of short stories in the English language '.

The instant the *Classification* was published the whole service was in uproar. Appeals poured in by the thousand. Some were heard by the Commission, others by the Commis-

---

[1] *Ibid.*, 1923, p. 897.   [2] *Ibid.*, p. 901.

sion and deputy heads of departments, others by a special Board of Hearing and Recommendation composed of representatives of the departments, the Civil Service Federation, and the Commission. In spite of the protests of Arthur Young and Company the *Classification* was altered and made workable by the various appellate bodies,[1] and an amended schedule published. This revised *Classification*, together with the experts' recommendations, known as *The Report of Transmission*, were submitted to Parliament in the autumn of 1919. They were accepted, and the Act amended accordingly.[2]

The general principle of this new scheme was that positions having similar duties and responsibilities were brought together to form a class, each being given a title, a definition of duties, a statement of qualifications, a line of promotion, and a range of salary. In this way 1729 standard classes were formed, which were further grouped into thirty-four occupational services. This reclassification carried with it an entire alteration in the fundamental principles which had hitherto governed the Canadian service. The civil servant was no longer admitted by means of an academic examination which was supposed to test his general proficiency and possibilities, but was examined on special subjects, more or less technical in nature. Promotions presumably took place from the lowest to the highest positions, and no distinction was drawn between intellectual and routine work. The promotion examination was restored in all its futility. In short, the whole aspect of the service was changed, and those principles which for years had been looked upon as fundamental were abandoned by a complacent Parliament with scarcely a murmur.

In glancing over the debates at this time [3] one is struck by the fact that not a member of the House of Commons seemed to be aware of the alterations that the new Act was to make. Hon. A. K. MacLean, the prime mover in the reclassification, while contending that the Act of 1918 was 'truly revolutionary', thought that the Act of 1919 wrought few changes, and the majority of the members of Parliament

---

[1] *Can. H. of C. Journals*, 1923, Appendix, § 5, pp. 224–30, 901.
[2] *Can. Stat.*, 10 Geo. V, c. 10.
[3] *Can. H. of C. Debates*, 2 Oct. 1919, pp. 748–84; 10 Oct. 1919, pp. 957–77.

were equally superficial in their judgement. As a matter of fact the 'revolutionary' Act was the later one; that of 1918 was but the old Act of 1908 improved and extended to the Outside Service.[1]

The Commission, desirous as it was to suppress patronage and encourage reform, found after very short experience that it was wellnigh impossible to control all appointments to the service. Many of them, such as day labourers and the lowest grade of rural postmasters, were so unimportant and were such a great distance from Ottawa, that the Commission found it both advisable and necessary to delegate much of its power to departmental inspectors and other similar officials.

'The appointments', said one of the Commissioners, 'were of such a trifling character that we were practically rubber stamping the acts of people over whom we had no control, and we reached the conclusion that in order to have time to apply ourselves to the really important business of the Commission, appointments to the professional, technical, administrative and clerical services, we would have to dispense with these classes of positions over which we could not properly exercise any control, or to which we could not apply any regular test.'[2]

The Commission therefore proposed that all positions paying $200 a year and less should be filled by the departments concerned, and this was approved by the Governor in Council, 14 August 1919.[3] About 10,000 positions were exempted under this Order.[4] Many of them, however, notably the rural post offices, were still filled nominally by the Commission, as some of the departments insisted that the Order was impracticable and inconvenient because it contained a clause stating that the appointment must be made 'without reference to personal or political considerations'.[5]

The next step towards further exemptions was taken in Parliament. On 28 April 1921 a Bill (known as the Spinney Bill) was introduced into the House of Commons providing for the removal of all rural postmasters, manual labourers,

---

[1] A fuller discussion of these changes appears in the second part of this book.
[2] *Can. H. of C. Journals*, 1923, Appendix, § 5, pp. 907–8.
[3] P.C., § 1694; cf. *ibid.*, pp. 910–11.
[4] *Ibid.*, p. 829.   [5] *Ibid.*, p. 911.

and professional, scientific, and technical officers from the operation of the Act.[1] The inspiration behind this move was undoubtedly a sinister one; some members of Parliament and their constituents had begun to repent of their haste and enthusiasm in 1918, and desired a partial return to the old patronage system. The Bill was referred to a Special Committee of the House, which reported that it was inadvisable to attempt to make any exemptions by statute.[2] The Committee pointed out that the Commission had power to exempt from its jurisdiction certain classes to which it was not practicable to apply the provisions of the Act, and suggested that the Commission's powers in this regard should be made more explicit.[3] The Committee further recommended that the Commission, in consultation with the deputy heads, should 'undertake a careful review of the entire service with a view to determining what further classes of employees should be exempted'.[4]

Pursuant to the suggestion of the Committee, the Commission in the summer of 1921 sent a circular to the departments asking them to specify what further classes they desired to have exempted from the provisions of the Act. The deputies complied joyfully; and submitted a huge list comprising classes from beekeepers, housemaids, and hatchery spawntakers to medical officers and the Gentleman Usher of the Black Rod.[5] One deputy justified his contribution to the list by contending that he was better fitted than the Commission to make the selection, and that it would be cheaper to appoint through the departments,[6]—an attitude which appears to have been fairly representative of the views of the others.

The list submitted by the deputies was, of course, too inclusive for the Commissioners, particularly in regard to many

[1] *Can. H. of C. Journals*, 1921, pp. 239, 371.

[2] *Ibid.*, pp. 372–3.

[3] *Can. Stat.*, 11–12 Geo. V, c. 22, carried this out, reading 'where the Commission decides that it is not practicable nor in the public interest' to apply the Act to any position, the Commission with the Governor in Council may grant exemption.

[4] *Can. H. of C. Journals*, 1921, p. 372; cf. pp. 368–73; *ibid.*, Appendix, § 3.

[5] *Ibid.*, 1923, Appendix, § 5, pp. 973–8.

[6] *Ibid.*, p. 684.

technical and professional offices, and they prepared a reduced list of minor positions for the Governor in Council, which was approved on 21 September 1921.[1] This Order in Council differed from that of 14 August 1919, in that it omitted to state that the exempted positions were to be filled irrespective of political and personal considerations, the reason being given that its insertion would have made many appointments impracticable.[2] In 1922 the Commission on its own initiative recommended the exemption of a further group of employees, which was approved on 29 June 1922.[3] This also omitted the 'political' clause, the Commission not wishing to force the departments to assume work which they did not feel could be effectively carried out. The Order also included all the class exemptions up to that time—affecting in all about 13,000 employees.[4]

The Civil Service Commission was completely free from any imputation of party motives in recommending these different exemptions. Its position was always quite logical. It contended that it should have jurisdiction only over those positions which lent themselves to a competition of skill or education, or those which could be filled by a regular and orderly procedure. The Commission rightly insisted that if it were to issue certificates it must be convinced of their essential correctness and justice; in a word, the Commissioners would not make appointments they could not control.[5]

Whatever the motives of the Commission in countenancing and even encouraging exemptions, the results were unfortunate in one respect. Political patronage in the minor offices came back to where it was in 1917. An applicant who wants one of these positions to-day (1928) must secure the endorsement of the member of Parliament, the defeated candidate, the local party association or patronage committee. The following account, for example, appeared in the columns of the *Ottawa Citizen* in 1922:

'A couple of weeks ago the local Liberal Association took over the patronage of Ottawa, such as it is. Two patronage committees

---

[1] P.C., § 3518; *ibid.*, pp. 982–4.   [2] *Ibid.*, p. 911.
[3] P.C., § 1053; *ibid.*, pp. 984–9.   [4] *Ibid.*, p. 829.
[5] *Ibid.*, pp. 903–4, 913.

were appointed. One committee consisted of the Liberal chairman of each ward in the city and two others from the ward, and this acts in a sort of advisory capacity and collects the applications for jobs. The other smaller super-committee consists of Messrs. George Higgerty, A. E. Provost, and E. P. McGrath. These, it is understood, sort out the thousands of local applications and decide which of the individuals are to get the few jobs available. It is stated that for every 200 applications there are about three jobs available.

'The patronage committees meet three times a week, every Monday, Wednesday, and Friday evening. The work takes two or three hours each of these nights. It is understood that when the proposal was made that Ottawa patronage would be handled by a committee instead of by the members of parliament for Ottawa both Mr. McGiverin and Mr. Chevrier (the members) accepted joyously.' [1]

The evidence given before the Committee of the House of Commons a year later showed that the same condition existed in all exempted positions not only at Ottawa but also throughout the country:

'*Committee:* You could not get an explanation from the department now in the exempted classes?

'*Witness:* This is the sort of an explanation we do get, letters that come to our association (the Great War Veterans' Association) to our secretary at Winnipeg, Mr. Bowler, in reply to an inquiry regarding some appointment:

"I wish to advise you that his application was referred to the Liberal Association at Selkirk, and I am now advised by the Secretary of the Association that another party has been recommended for this position.

Yours truly,"

'*Committee:* That is the reply you got from the department?
'*Witness:* Yes.' [2]

'*Committee:* I am afraid you did not catch my point. What I meant to say was that the inference was made, as I understand it, that this patronage committee worked in conjunction with the department?

[1] *Ottawa Citizen*, 20 July 1922.
[2] *Can. H. of C. Journals*, 1923, Appendix, § 5, p. 562.

'*Witness:* No, Sir.

'*Committee:* In regard to appointments?

'*Witness:* No. I do not see that there is any use beating about the bush about the workings of these Committees. The thing must be run in an open-handed way. Why should it not be that the Government in power be expected to make appointments from their following, to vacant positions; that is only human nature. That has always been the case, whether there has been a Liberal, a Conservative, or a Progressive Government in Ontario.

'*Committee:* They do not appoint their opponents?

'*Witness:* No, sir; certainly not.

'*Committee:* Why do you confine it to Ontario?

'*Witness:* I am not referring to any particular political party that may be in power.

'*Committee:* So with the Civil Service Commission the patronage system is still in existence, to a certain extent?

'*Witness:* Yes, in that way.

'*Committee:* For positions not under the control of the Commission?

'*Witness:* Yes.

'*Committee:* The members for the constituencies are consulted?

'*Witness:* Yes. It is a time-honoured practice.

'*Committee:* Let us take a constituency not represented by a Liberal member; where do you get the recommendation from?

'*Witness:* I suppose, in fact I know, that our engineer or our architect goes to the representative of the Government in that constituency. He may be a defeated candidate or he may not be. He goes to whoever has the confidence of the minister and consults with him.' [1]

In occasional instances party pressure has had its effect even in those positions which are supposedly under the merit system. The Commission wrote as follows in 1926:

'Section 4(b) of the *Civil Service Act* places upon the Commission the duty of reporting "upon the violation of any of the provisions of this Act, or of any of the regulations made thereunder". The Commissioners have pleasure in reporting that there has been a steady improvement in the observance of the law and the regulations and a marked development in the co-operation existing between the Commission and the several departments. The Commission, however, regards it as a duty to call attention to the

---

[1] *Ibid.*, pp. 638–9; cf. *ibid.*, pp. 578–9, 602–4, 704–5, 951–2, 955.

following instances in which, in the opinion of the Commissioners, the spirit and principle of the *Civil Service Act* have not been as fully upheld as might be possible.

' In certain cases the persons who have been selected and certified by the Commission in accordance with the provisions of the Act for appointment to vacant positions, have not been installed in these positions by the departments, without what appears to the Commissioners to be undue delay. In some cases, no steps have yet been taken to install in office the candidates who have for months past been certified therefor, but persons placed in office by a department have been retained, for whose employment no legal authority exists. . . .

' The Commissioners have found upon receiving requisitions for the filling of many positions, both by promotion from within the service, and by open competition from without, that the positions in question have sometimes for months been occupied by incumbents who have been placed therein by the department in an acting capacity. Subsequently this temporary appointee has an unfair advantage over other competitors for the promotion or permanent appointment. . . .

' The Commissioners have been in receipt of many complaints from members of the service and others regarding the delay which takes place in connection with promotional competitions in certain departments. In the great majority of such cases it has been found that the delay occasioned has been due to the failure of the department interested to supply the Commission, with reasonable expedition, with the necessary reports upon the qualifications, efficiency, and fitness of the candidates concerned.' [1]

The election of 1921 resulted in a change of Government; and the exemptions of that year and the year following gave the new administration an opportunity to square the dismissal account of 1911. The Order in Council of 18 March 1918, providing that removals for partisanship should take place only after investigation by the Civil Service Commission [2] was unfortunately not renewed; although the power of dismissal was exercised much more sparingly than ever before. The procedure was explained by the Prime Minister:

' The practice the government has adopted with respect to any

[1] *Report of the Civil Service Commission,* 1925, pp. ix–x; cf. *ibid.,* 1926, pp. vii–viii.
[2] Cf. *supra,* pp. 91–2.

charges of political partisanship against members of the civil service has been to proceed very guardedly, taking care to see that the charge is proved in a manner to which no exception can be taken, before permitting dismissal of the person offending. The government has followed the precedent adopted by previous governments of appointing commissioners to investigate such charges where there appear to be substantial reasons for believing that they are well founded. . . . Where an hon. member has been prepared to state to the House that of his own knowledge an offence contravening the provisions of the Civil Service Act respecting political partisanship has been committed, the government has acted under the provisions of the Civil Service Act, which provide that a civil servant guilty of political partisanship shall not be retained in the service.' [1]

This temperate attitude on the part of the Government was undoubtedly made easier by the fact that the great number of appointments had been taken out of the hands of the party. It is probable also that the civil servants themselves were beginning to realize that conditions had greatly changed and that a party no longer expected them to push its interests in the constituencies. Whatever the reason, the dismissals in 1921 and succeeding years were far fewer than in 1911,[2] and there seems to be every prospect that they will grow still less in the future.

The Civil Service Commission has had to use a number of different methods in making appointments under its control. Low grade employees are not capable of writing examinations, and are appointed largely on ratings supplied by the departmental inspectors. The latter advertise the position, make inquiries about the candidates, interview them, compare their qualifications, and make the recommendation independent of political or personal factors.[3] Clerkships and other examinable positions are filled by written or practical tests which aim at discovering the special aptitudes of the candi-

[1] *Can. H. of C. Debates*, 15 Feb. 1923, p. 286.
[2] e.g. after the election of 1911 more than 800 postmasters were dismissed for partisanship, and after the election of 1921 over an equal period of time only 62 were dismissed, the majority of these having had a public investigation; *ibid.*, 28 May 1923, p. 3138.
[3] *Can. H. of C. Journals*, 1923, Appendix, § 5, pp. 7–11, 16–18, 22–30, 34–5, 990–2.

dates. Lists of eligibility are kept by the Commission, and the positions given to those who stand highest in the competition, subject to the preference given for overseas service.[1] The procedure in making a technical or professional appointment is more complex. The Commission advertises the position, and chooses an Advisory Board to conduct the investigation into the candidates' qualifications. The Board is made up partly of men nationally known in the profession concerned and partly of expert representatives from the department to which the appointment is to be made. For vacancies in the lower grades of the technical service the Board will set and examine written papers; for higher positions it will scrutinize the college degrees, past record, letters of recommendation, experience, and general reputation of each candidate, and perhaps hold a number of interviews. In all cases the Board submits to the Commission a list in order of merit of those found desirable, and the Commission thereupon makes the appointment.[2]

One other function has been assumed by the Civil Service Commission since 1919, that of reorganizing different branches of the Government service. Working in co-operation with the branches concerned, the staff of the Commission have developed considerable skill in improving the organization of the departments, in eliminating superfluous employees, and in reducing costs generally.[3]

During many years of its history the civil service could truthfully complain that it was ignored and neglected; but the last decade has been strewn with investigations and Acts of Parliament designed for its improvement. The beginning was made in the reform of 1918–19 by Order in Council and Statute, followed by the Arthur Young reclassification.[4] In 1919 three inquiries were held. The printing bureau was investigated;[5] a Special Committee of the Senate reported on the possibility of bettering the machinery of government;[6]

---

[1] *Can. H. of C. Journals*, 1923, Appendix, § 5, pp. 36–40, 88.

[2] *Ibid.*, pp. 43–4, 92–7, 160–5, 239, 265–71, 845.

[3] *Can. Sess. Pap.*, 1923, § 24, pp. vii–viii; *ibid.*, 1924, § 24, pp. v–vi; *ibid.*, 1925, § 24, pp. vi–vii.

[4] Cf. *supra*, pp. 90–2, 95.   [5] Cf. *supra*, pp. 93–4.

[6] *Can. Senate Journals*, 1919, pp. 340–74.

and a Special Committee of the House of Commons reported
on the possible reduction and rearrangement of the whole
service.[1] In 1920, partly as a result of this last report, the
Public Service Retirement Act (commonly known as the
Calder Act) was passed,[2] providing for the retirement of
many old, superfluous, or inefficient employees who had been
retained in order to relieve the war-time scarcity of labour.
The following year saw the Spinney Bill and the Commons'
Special Committee noted above.[3] On 30 June 1922 a committee of deputy ministers was appointed 'to consider matters affecting the civil service'. The deputies sent in a very
emphatic and disquieting report. They suggested that technical positions should be filled on their recommendation, that
they should advise the Governor in Council on further exemptions, that they should have the chief voice in promotions,
and that the existing classification should be abolished.[4]
This was followed on 16 February 1923 by a motion in the
House that the Civil Service Acts of 1918 and 1919 should be
repealed because of their failure to meet the needs of the
country.[5] Such an arraignment of the Act clearly pointed to
further investigation; and a Special Committee of the House
was appointed.[6] This Committee did not agree with the
deputies' report or with the maker of the motion in the Commons, and found the general condition of the service satisfactory. It made, however, a number of minor recommendations, the chief of which was for a scheme of superannuation.[7]
Later in the same year a general retirement and superannuation system was established by Act of Parliament.[8] Finally,
the Senate appointed in 1924 a Special Committee to inquire
into the operation of the *Civil Service Act*, but its report
added nothing to the information already available.[9]

[1] *Can. H. of C. Journals*, 1919, pp. 517–19. Appendix, § 6.
[2] *Can. Stat.*, 10–11 Geo. V, c. 67 ; cf. *Can. Sess. Pap.*, 1922, § 32, pp. xii–
xiii ; *ibid.*, 1923, § 24, pp. xiii–xiv ; *ibid.*, 1924, § 24, p. vii.
[3] Cf. *supra*, pp. 97–8.
[4] *Can. H. of C. Journals*, 1923, Appendix, § 5, pp. 1038–42.
[5] *Can. H. of C. Debates*, 16 Feb. 1923, pp. 345–82 ; 22 Feb. 1923, pp. 519–
71 ; *Can. H. of C. Journals*, 1923, p. 71.   [6] *Ibid.*, pp. 109–10, 171.
[7] *Ibid.*, pp. 547–58 ; cf. *ibid.*, Appendix, § 5.
[8] *Can. Stat.*, 14–15 Geo. V, c. 69.
[9] *Report of the Special Committee on the Civil Service (Senate)* 1924.

Such has been the troubled history of the Canadian civil service. Beginning with a handful of partly political, partly civil employees in colonial days, the service gradually enlarged its numbers and its scope until to-day it comprises forty to fifty thousand engaged in a bewildering variety of work. Its history has been largely a fight against the spoilsman and party patronage, and although that fight has not entirely ceased, it has lost much of its importance. One thing emerges as a result of the last few years' experience: it is not enough to try to improve the service by the negative means of checking indiscriminate admissions, there must also be a positive effort to stimulate and encourage the new civil servant in his work. Many people thought that the abolition of patronage would solve the problems of the service; it is now clear that there is no such short cut to efficiency. What looked like the City of Salvation proves on achievement to be only the first stage of the journey, though it is probable that the Slough of Despond has now been crossed. It is the purpose of the remainder of this book to indicate some of the present problems of the service, and to outline a few of the ideas and principles that may aid in producing a sound civil service organization.

PART II
PRINCIPLES OF CIVIL SERVICE ORGANIZATION

VII. THE PLACE OF THE CIVIL SERVICE IN GOVERNMENT

'Things are seldom what they seem:
Skim milk masquerades as cream;
Highlows pass as patent leathers;
Jackdaws strut in peacocks' feathers.
Storks turn out to be but logs;
Bulls are but inflated frogs.
Drops the wind and stops the mill;
Turbot is ambitious rill;
Gild the farthing if you will,
But it is a farthing still.'
H.M.S. Pinafore.

THE Government of Canada, in common with other parliamentary forms, may appear to many a sad and costly failure. The franchise is given away with reckless hand; the people vote for the candidates who make the most successful appeal to their pockets or to their emotions; the representatives thus chosen meet and talk without stint or apparent purpose, expending the greater part of their energy in violent internal bickerings and parades in and out of the division lobbies. This seeming incompetence is even more apparent in the method used to administer the Government departments. A Parliament, composed of butchers, bakers, and candlestick makers, chooses some of its members from the same motley occupations to supervise the important divisions of the country's business. A butcher becomes Minister of Militia, a baker assumes control of the Finance Department, while the candlestick maker supervises the erection of lighthouses, the propagation of fish, and the placing of a new gas buoy on the St. Lawrence. In short, the task of running a Government is entrusted to amateurs whose special knowledge, if it exists, lies in quite different fields. It is difficult to imagine the survival of a bank or railway whose president is chosen because of his knowledge of agriculture or electricity, but such irrelevant qualifications frequently govern the choice of Cabinet Ministers. An ability to speak fluently, to argue convincingly, to be re-elected without defeats, to come from a particular province—these are the virtues which are often rewarded with high office. Superficially it would seem as though there was a deliberate effort to secure men who know almost nothing about the work of their departments.

The apparent follies of responsible government go still further. Not content with placing novices in charge of the administration, it needs must change them from time to time. No sooner does the head of a department begin to feel at home and obtain a semblance of familiarity with his work and his subordinates, than he is compelled to leave. A re-shuffling of Cabinet offices or a disastrous election ejects him from his ministry, and places in his stead another amateur, as unfamiliar with the details of office as he had been a year or two before. Ministerial mortality is high; each time a change occurs the hard-won experience is lost and there is a presumptive alteration in departmental policy. To the cynic it may well appear that democracy has perpetrated on itself a joke so vast and so preposterous that even Rabelais would admit he was outdone.

In spite of the cynic, however, the administration of the Dominion is conducted with moderate efficiency, but this is due in large measure to the non-political and expert part of the Government—the civil service. The permanent officials include specialists in virtually all branches of human knowledge, and they are constantly at the side of the Cabinet Minister, advising and helping him in every act and decision. It is their shoulders which bear the weight of the administration, their heads which pore over columns of figures, their brains which supply the Minister with answers to embarrassing questions, their resourcefulness which devises new expedients for departmental difficulties. The old belief that any well-meaning person could fill a Government position acceptably has given way to the idea that only specialists and officials skilled by a lifetime of experience can do efficient work.

Perhaps here lurks another Rabelaisian joke. It may be that responsible government is not inefficient, for the excellent reason that it is not responsible at all. Democracy succeeds simply because democratic control does not exist: the people think they govern through their representatives in Parliament, but in reality they are being ruled by a trained and skilled bureaucracy accountable to no one. The butcher in the House of Commons states that the safety of the country depends on his getting ten million dollars for a new kind of rifle, and a complaisant House grants the money. In reality, the demand probably originated with a fussy general in the Department of Militia who was obsessed with the idea of a yellow peril. When the baker rises in his place to introduce the budget and discourses for two hours and a half on the state of the nation's finances, his mastery of detail and breadth of view are applauded throughout the Dominion. But his facts have been marshalled for him by expert accountants, and the reduction in the income tax which he proposes has its inspiration with the assistant deputy minister, who finds living in Ottawa with three children and a mother-in-law a trifle expensive. The candlestick maker, who earnestly urges the appropriation for a gas buoy, has possibly lived all his life on the prairie, and is completely ignorant as to why the buoy should be placed at that particular spot in the St. Lawrence. He, like the others, speaks not for himself, but for his nominal subordinates: the voice is Jacob's voice, but the hands are those of the bureaucratic Esau.

Responsible government appears caught between the two alternatives: an experienced civil service or an untrained ministry, efficient bureaucracy on the one hand, inefficient democracy on the other. If the professional official is given control, then popular government becomes a myth; if the civil servant is not to rule, then the amateur Minister is dealing with affairs about which he knows very little. Fortunately no such choice has to be made. This is one of the rare instances where it is possible both to eat the cake and have it. Responsible government can be worked in such a way as to use the best and avoid the worst features of both alternatives.

First, it is clear that government to-day must be subject to popular control. The people must elect whom they please, and under a parliamentary form these in turn must choose

their leaders. This necessarily involves changing ministries
and inexperience in the Cabinet officers. It is equally true
that modern conditions make it imperative that the civil
service should be skilled and highly trained. The great
political discovery made by England in the last century was
that these two things could be combined: the minister could
continue to be representative in character, and yet have his
inexperience and other faults remedied by the expert knowledge of his subordinates; while the civil service, on the other
hand, could be efficient, yet have its bureaucratic tendencies
checked by the supervision of the Cabinet and Parliament.
'Success', said Bagehot, 'depends on a due mixture of special
and non-special minds—of minds which attend to the means,
and of minds which attend to the end.' The civil service is
one part, the ministers the other—together they compose an
efficient whole. Earl Grey had this idea in mind, in his dispatch to Nova Scotia in 1847, when he distinguished between
those officers who were political and changing, and those who
were non-political and permanent.[2]

There are certain peculiar bureaucratic sins which appear
with monotonous regularity in any large group of public
officials.[3] The most notorious is the love of red tape. While
a certain methodical exactness is necessary and proper in the
conduct of governmental business, this is apt to be given an
emphasis out of all proportion to its importance. Office
routine ceases to be a means and becomes an end in itself.
Changes in this routine are regarded with profound distrust,
and, as a result, antiquated and circuitous methods persist
long after their usefulness has passed. Each civil servant
becomes so engrossed in his little job that he forgets he is
only a small part of the whole. He fusses busily over his
correspondence, writes a lordly little 'memo' about some
trifling matter, and rebukes a subordinate for daring to have
an opinion contrary to his own. He equally becomes the
victim of what Walter Lippman calls 'the panacea habit
of mind'.

[1] Bagehot, W., *The English Constitution*, chapter vii, p. 265.
[2] Cf. *supra*, pp. 11–13.
[3] Cf. Muir, R., *Peers and Bureaucrats*, pp. 48–53.

'You find engineers who don't see why you can't build society on the analogy of a steam engine; you find lawyers . . . who see in the courts an intimation of heaven; sanitation experts who wish to treat the whole world as one vast sanitorium; lovers who wish to treat it as one vast happy family; education enthusiasts who wish to treat it as one vast nursery. No one who undertook to be the Balzac of reform by writing its Human Comedy could afford to miss the way in which the reformer in each profession tends to make his speciality an analogy for the whole of life.' [1]

Another well-known vice of the bureaucrat is an indifference and insolence towards the general public. He knows that his office is secure and will not be taken from him except on grave provocation. He is not working under any strain of competition, and has little to fear from losing any popularity. In the reflected glory of his Government position he begins to feel superior to the rest of mankind, and thinks that the ignorant public can know nothing of his great work and the many responsibilities which he must bear. All these induce in him an irritability and an intolerance of interference and criticism. The civil servant is also apt to lose contact with the facts of life and be overcome by figures and black letters on white paper. Much of his work is necessarily done by correspondence, and many of his contacts with what is going on is at best third- or fourth-hand. The shuffling about of blue and yellow filing cards and the joining of one paper to another with little pins and comments attached are obviously artificial ways of getting things done; and although these methods cannot be avoided, they have a deadening influence on the mind of those using them.

Finally, a bureaucracy will probably lack incentive. The permanent tenure discourages intense effort in many men, for it is well known that laziness will not be severely punished. The rewards of the service are few, promotion may come slowly, and seniority is frequently the ground for advancement. The absence of drastic penalties for inefficiency and the lack of speedy recognition of merit can have but one result. This tendency is often accentuated by a tradition that great zeal or activity is very bad form—an idea closely

[1] Lippman, W., *Drift and Mastery*, p. 185.

allied to the comforting Oxford belief that the climate of the Thames valley makes strenuous intellectual effort impossible. Unfortunately, a civil service policy of ca'canny may be believed in by the country at large, and the employees frequently see to it that the public is not disappointed.

Many of these bureaucratic tendencies in the civil service can be overcome by internal organization and effort; but the executive and parliament supply further protection. It is here that the non-technical Minister finds his justification. He brings to the department a fresh mind, a distrust of superfluous red tape, a disposition to question anything and everything which the bureaucrat may hold sacred. He makes embarrassing inquiries into long-accepted matters of routine, he demands to know why a certain expenditure is being asked for in the budget, he suggests that other departments be consulted so that economies may be effected through greater co-operation.

'He can say to the permanent chief, skilled in the forms and pompous with the memories of his office, "Will you, Sir, explain to me how this regulation conduces to the end in view? According to the natural view of things, the applicant should state the whole of his wishes to one clerk on one paper; you make him say it to five clerks on five papers." Or again, "Does it not appear to you, Sir, that the reason of this formality is extinct? When we were building wood ships, it was quite right to have such precautions against fire; but now that we are building iron ships" &c., &c. If a junior clerk asked these questions, he would be "pooh-poohed!" It is only the head of an office that can get them answered. It is he, and he only, that brings the rubbish of office to the burning-glass of sense.'[1]

Bagehot added that 'the use of a fresh mind applied to the official mind is not only a corrective use, it is an animating use'.[2] The Minister not only points out errors, but he stimulates and spurs the civil servants into activity. The inherent sluggishness of a public department is quickened by an energetic chief. The latter may not change anything of importance and may approve of all the suggestions placed before him; but his presence alone shakes the official loose from his

[1] Bagehot, W., *The English Constitution*, chapter vii, p. 267.
[2] *Ibid.*, p. 268.

red tape and complacency. The mere knowledge that a proposal will be scrutinized by a lay superior produces a more
carefully considered proposal. Even a change of Ministers,
provided it does not take place too often, is usually beneficial.
The Minister, like anyone else, may become so accustomed to
his departmental routine and methods of business that he may
lose the freshness of mind and originality of approach that
are his chief qualifications for being there. A shake-up in the
Cabinet, therefore, is sometimes not only politically necessary
but desirable for effective administration.

It must also be remembered that the chief of a department
is a member of the Cabinet as well. His task is to oversee the
work under his control and at the same time make that work
fit in with the general ideas of his colleagues. He shares in
the building up and carrying out of those plans which are
known collectively as the Government's policy. Each Minister is a co-ordinating officer, and he is bound to give some
heed to the work of the others. Each is a constant reminder
to his department that it does not stand alone, but is only one
part in a much more important whole.

The task of a new Minister, who assumes charge of a
department and yet knows nothing about it, may appear
colossal. But if he possess the proper qualifications—a broad
outlook on his work, a mind trained to search out essentials,
a willingness to trust his helpers, the ability to distinguish
between sound and unsound advice—he will settle down in
his position with surprising ease. The way in which the new
minister spends the first morning in his office, and the speed
with which he can gather in his hands the strings to the department's activities, has been admirably described in *Lord
Raingo*:

'Already he felt as if he had been in the Ministry for weeks. He
had had practically no previous experience of administration
except the administration of his own private affairs. For,
although he had bought and sold vast undertakings, he had
learnt little about any of them beyond what might emerge from
a ruthless, critical examination of their books of account; and he
knew that one might even for a brief period preside over the destinies of an industrial enterprise as Chairman of the Board and still

remain ignorant of the daily human realities which were the material of its success. Nevertheless he considered that he had begun to get the hang of the Ministry, to envisage it as an entire organism and understand its mode of functioning.

'He had selected a secretary, an assistant-secretary, and a nice, soothing, plump stenographer. He had mastered the system of "Minutes" which circulated from section to section, adding to themselves marginal notes in black and marginal notes in red, and which stood for all times as a record of what a particular official had decided or suggested on a particular question at a particular moment. He had dictated minutes; he had dictated a letter. He had surveyed the diary of the conferences which apparently formed a large share of the activities of the Ministry. He had carefully read through the brilliant roll of the staff and had a chat with one popular novelist and with the austere, precise poet who was in charge of "cables". Various other persons, male and female, had been presented to him, and he had had encounters in corridors. He knew what the interiors of the offices looked like; he was acquiring the vocabulary and idiom of the place; he was separating in his mind the cheerful from the grumblers, the willing from the unwilling, and those who could think straight from those who could not. A full morning, at the end of which he was saying to himself, as he reached the Embankment:

"*No!* New brooms must *not* sweep clean. *No!* New brooms must *not* sweep clean."

'He saw the delicacy and the difficulties of his task. He saw that he must moderate the eagerness of his ambition. He had supreme power, but there was no such thing as supreme power, and indeed all his wariness and force would be needed to prevent the nominal master from becoming the slave of the Ministry.' [1]

Parliament also has a share in the control of the civil service. In the first place, the House of Commons makes and unmakes the Ministry, and thereby exerts an indirect influence over the permanent staff. When the party in power goes out and the other one comes in, the administrative officials are faced with the necessity of justifying their suggestions to a new body of men animated by somewhat different ideas. It may even be that the entire policy of some departments may be changed; and although this is not of itself

---

[1] Bennett, Arnold, *Lord Raingo*, pp. 123-4.

desirable, yet the effect of the re-adjustment on the civil service is excellent.

In the second place, as Bagehot said, 'there is no limit to the curiosity of Parliament', and it takes great joy in poking at the work of the departments. The question-hour teems with inquiries of all kinds, some made with a genuine desire to obtain information, others from less laudable motives. Every one snipes at the Government; and there is always the hope that a lucky shot may prove very disconcerting indeed. 'Why did John Macdonald of Ecum Secum not obtain a rebate on his income tax?' 'Why did the lighthouse keeper at Rimouski lose his job?' 'Why did the Post Office authorize brown instead of magenta as the colour for the new sixteen-cent stamp?' 'Is the Minister aware that certain officials in the Inland Revenue Department took an extra holiday after Christmas?' Day after day the interrogation goes on. Parliament becomes a huge nursery of curious children asking the interminable questions that drive the parents almost to madness. But the Ministers must give polite replies to all inquiries, which is only another way of saying that the civil service supplies the bulk of the information. The custom is a ceaseless bother; but it is invaluable as a check on arbitrary action and inefficiency.

Finally, Parliament, in passing Supply, exercises a further control. Every cent that is to be spent must be accounted for, and the occasion is used for more meticulous questioning. The Opposition seizes on every opportunity for causing embarrassment, and an expenditure of $58·25 may receive ten times the attention given to one of $300,000. The most intimate details of the administration are subject to parliamentary scrutiny, and the departments must justify every act that involves any payment of public money.

Thus far the discussion has centred on the faults of the service and their amelioration by the Cabinet and Parliament. But the amateur Minister also brings to his work sins which are peculiar to himself. The outstanding one is lack of knowledge. He is, compared to his assistants, almost if not quite ignorant of a large part of the work of his department. He knows what he wants to have done, but is at loss to suggest the way in which to do it. He frequently finds that what he desires has been tried before and found unsatisfactory, or that unsuspected conditions exist which make even a trial unprofitable. He comes down to his office in the morning full of enthusiasm for a newly concocted plan of reform or reorganization, only to discover, after twenty-five minutes' conversation with his deputy, that his scheme has neglected to consider many awkward facts and cannot be made to embrace certain very important branches of the service. He reads somewhere or has suggested to him that a technical problem on fish propagation demands investigation, and he decides that his department should give the lead and conduct the research; but he is apt to find on inquiry that his officials have already done the work and can produce the results from a file three years old. Similar instances might be multiplied almost indefinitely.

Inexperienced Ministers, or those who possess only mediocre ability, frequently get into trouble through rash election commitments or an uncontrollable desire to acquire votes. A Minister of this type is usually over-conscious of his vulnerability at the polls, and that consciousness may lead him to propose measures which, though popular, are ill-considered, or unduly expensive, or scarcely workable at all. Promises are recklessly made at election time due to an excess of political emotionalism, the excitement of the campaign, and the overmastering fear of defeat. Frequently the Minister has but the vaguest idea as to the manner of carrying these promises into practice, and he is compelled to fall back on his civil servants to extricate him from his difficulty. Some measures will be quietly abandoned or indefinitely postponed, some completely altered, and a few carried out somewhat as the Minister had envisaged them. But it is not the Minister who has proved equal to the emergency of his own creation; it is the deputy and his assistants who have done the worrying, who have devised the schemes, and who have invented the mechanism which gave the Minister's airy castle substance.

The failings of the Minister are thus compensated for in large measure by the civil servants, although it is almost impossible to define with exactness the extent of their influence.

The permanent officials undoubtedly wield a great deal of power, though most of it is exercised so unostentatiously that its significance is often overlooked. They make themselves felt in four ways—in forming executive policy; in giving a continuity to Government work; in initiating legislation; and in pure administration.

The old idea was that the political head decided questions of policy, while the permanent chiefs carried the policy into effect, gave general advice, and tried to protect the Minister from making mistakes. In recent years, however, the civil servant has begun to play a more important role, as indicated by the following quotation from a distinguished British official:

'If specialists are to be mainly employed as advisers I consider that there are certain conditions which they are entitled to demand. In the first place they have a right to demand that their advice should be sought. I have known cases in which administrative officers have come to decisions on technical questions without ever consulting the technical advisers of the department. That is clearly indefensible and may lead to serious mistakes being made. But if specialists are entitled to be consulted are they also entitled to claim that their advice must be taken and acted upon? Here I think we must distinguish between two different classes of problems. A specialist may recommend that a particular policy should be adopted by his department. In such a case he is not entitled to claim that his advice must be taken. Wider considerations than the intrinsic merits of the proposal have to be weighed, and it may be found that what is desirable is not expedient, and that consequently the advice of the specialist must be rejected. For instance, . . . we may suppose that, in order to check the spread of wart disease in potatoes . . . a proposal is made by one of our technical advisers that an order should be made prohibiting the import of seed potatoes of susceptible varieties from Scotland. It might be true that such an order would be the only effective means of absolutely preventing the introduction of disease, but, on the other hand, such an order might irretrievably damage the potato-growing industry of some parts of England to an extent far greater than would be caused by the possible introduction of disease. In such a case the final decision must be made by the administrative authorities of the department, subject to the Minister's approval, and the specialist will have no reasonable ground for complaint if his proposal is rejected.

'The other class of case is where a policy has been decided on, and a question arises as to the best method of carrying it out. If such a question raises technical issues the specialist advisers of the department must be consulted, and in such a case their advice ought, save in very exceptional circumstances, to be taken. . . . Suppose that it was decided on purely financial grounds to abandon the policy of slaughter in cases of foot-and-mouth disease, and to adopt instead the policy of isolation, treatment, and cure. In such a case the decision as to the period of isolation, the methods of treatment, and the specifics used should be taken without question on the advice of the technical veterinary officers of the department, and they would have very reasonable cause for complaint if their advice was overruled by a lay administrator. Similarly, in the numerous cases which arise in every Government department when reference has to be made to the legal adviser of the department for an opinion as to the interpretation of an Act of Parliament or as to the legality of a course proposed to be taken, I cannot imagine any sane administrative officer doing anything but accept as final the opinion given.' [1]

Even this statement does not go far enough in emphasizing the increasingly important part taken by the modern civil servant in the formulation of policy. His influence is brought to bear in a number of ways.[2] He is asked to forecast the probable results of a suggested change or a new experiment, and his answers will probably determine the fate of the proposal. His co-operation in matters of policy is almost invariably sought if for no other reason than that the Minister must rely on his ability to invent the means for carrying any idea into practice. His is the more difficult task of 'putting policies into working clothes, instead of the taking finery in which they are persuasively arrayed when presented, without full responsibility, to an unthinking public'.[3] The deputy minister does not necessarily have to wait for an invitation to express an opinion; it is his frequent duty to suggest a

[1] Floud, Sir Francis L. C., 'The Sphere of the Specialist in Public Administration', *Journal of Public Administration*, 1923, pp. 122–3. Cf. also Gibbon, I. G., 'The Official and his Authority', *ibid.*, 1926, pp. 81–94.

[2] Hore, Sir Adair, 'Officials and Policy', *Public Administration*, 1927, pp. 461–70; Gibbon, I. G., 'Framework of Public Administration', *ibid.*, 1927, pp. 235–43.

[3] *Ibid.*, p. 237.

policy without being asked, for the conditions in the department which demand change may be quite unknown to the
Minister himself. The exceptional knowledge of the deputy
will bespeak for any of his proposals a very careful consideration by his superior.

It is conceivable and even probable that this extension of
the official's activity is not entirely welcomed by some Ministers or by the public; but modern specialization, the need of
expertise, and the complexity and size of the government
departments are making such increased participation more
and more inevitable. The permanent officials alone possess
the necessary information, they alone have a real knowledge
of the foundations on which new measures must be built, they
alone can bring scientific and dispassionate minds to the
study of half-considered proposals, to the analysis of past
experience, and to a co-ordination and comparison of both.

Although the influence of the permanent officials on policy
is very great, it must never be forgotten that the ultimate
responsibility rests on the Minister. He may, and sometimes
does, embark on a new policy, or so definitely commit himself
that there is no turning back, without seeking the advice of
his officials at all; but it is a risky proceeding and is becoming
less frequent. The Minister may also ask for advice and,
having received it, act in exactly the opposite way. But the
civil servants have this enormous strategic advantage over
a Minister: what is new and strange to him has been familiar
to them for years. They are able to make suggestions and
criticize alternatives with a vast background of detailed
knowledge, while his contribution is confined to a few vague
principles re-enforced by a practical ability to veto any proposal he dislikes. The *expertise* of the civil servant may even
serve on occasion to indicate to the Cabinet the course of
action which it should pursue, and help it to sort out its own
ideas. This somewhat unusual side of the official's activity
was described by Lord Milner a few years ago:

'I remember not a few ministerial discussions in which I took
part myself which followed something like this course. We met
together to discuss some rather urgent and burning question of
policy. We were perhaps fairly agreed when we met about the

R

direction in which we wished to go, but as the discussion proceeded first one difficulty and then another cropped up on points of detail. On these we differed a good deal from one another, and then the debate often got off on to side issues, and after an hour and a half or two hours of it we were all in a muddle, and we were getting very tired, and everybody's hair—if he had any hair—was ruffled, and the prospect of arriving at a clear conclusion was gloomy. Then the attendant civil servant would quietly slip into the hands of the chairman an insignificant little piece of paper with a few tidy resolutions which pulled the whole thing together, and omitting what was immaterial or impracticable, so to speak explained us to ourselves, and embodied the greatest common measure of agreement between us. Those resolutions were readily adopted, and we went away having after all done something.' [1]

In helping to form executive policy, the civil servants supply not only the expert and experienced part but the permanent element as well. Ministers may come and go, ministerial ideas may change with the Governments, but the departmental chiefs will remain almost from decade to decade. Plans which have been formed under one Minister are carried out under another, and amended and improved under a third. There thus emerges a departmental policy as distinguished from the policy of a particular Minister, and the vast majority of changes which any individual Minister may make are amendments to old schemes and not new ventures of his own. The thread of continuity is supplied largely by the deputy heads, who endeavour to ensure that the department shall in most matters follow a fairly straight and consistent course.

'I worked fairly hard (while cabinet minister)', said Lord Haldane, 'but did not succeed in accomplishing nearly all of what I set out to do. I left my work with a strong sense of the undone vast. There was much that required the method of gradual evolution, and in consequence time. For it is not the want of knowledge that is the chief difficulty. Knowledge can be attained pretty rapidly. What is needed in addition is the continuity in policy which requires above all a common faith in agreed-on ideals. This is difficult of attainment in so far as Ministers change

[1] Milner, Lord, 'The Aims of the Institute of Public Administration', *Journal of Public Administration*, 1923, p. 89.

periodically. The result is that for continuity in the application of administrative principles we have to look elsewhere. We cannot reckon on it with ever-altering ministries. Public opinion as it is to-day has too little both of knowledge and interest to be able to insist on it. We come back, therefore, in last resort to the Civil Service itself and notably to its permanent chiefs.' [1]

The civil service also exercises a very unobtrusive but powerful influence on legislation—not so much on the controversial measures, but on those which deal with administrative reforms.

'The great majority of legislative proposals have no interest for most members of parliament, and the public hears nothing about them until it sees a list of them at the end of the session. Many of these are purely departmental in character. . . . These are the bills . . . which go through all their stages with the greatest ease, attracting no attention. Often enough they affect the daily life of the citizen far more intimately than the measures over which controversy rages. They are nominally the work of Parliament; but really the work of the bureaucracy.' [2]

Finally, the execution of departmental policies and the issuing of administrative orders lies for the most part with the permanent service. The Minister lacks the expert knowledge to decide many technical questions, he is unable to master all the intricacies of detail associated with the work of the department, and he is quite unequal to the task of overseeing in person an entomological experiment in Manitoba or a geological survey in British Columbia. There is, therefore, a large area of independent action permitted to the civil servant within which he may move with almost entire freedom. The area is great or small, vague or clear, important or negligible, according to the nature of the office. In some positions his decisions will be virtually final. In others his opinion will be constantly sought, and usually honoured by being accepted. In other positions the area of independent action may include only matters of routine. The tendency in all purely administrative matters is to give the official a free

[1] Haldane, Lord, 'An Organized Civil Service', *Journal of Public Administration*, 1923, p. 8.
[2] Muir, Ramsay, *Peers and Bureaucrats*, p. 18.

hand and to trust to his judgement and knowledge of local
or peculiar conditions.

It is evident that the secret of administrative success lies in
alert, though unspecialized, Ministers acting in co-operation
with experienced and expert permanent officials—both being
subject to the criticism and investigation of Parliament. The
old conception of the relationship, that the Minister, who
receives his mandate from Parliament or from the people,
outlines the policy while the service carries it into effect,[1] is
daily becoming less accurate; though it still contains a good
deal of truth. Nothing, however, has occurred to alter the
appropriateness of the often-quoted summary of Sir George
Cornewall Lewis: 'It is not the business of a Cabinet Minister
to work his department; his business is to see that it is properly worked.' An inquisitive, arrogant Minister, who insists
on knowing everything and who demands that he be consulted about minutiae, is already a failure. He must learn to
delegate authority, to trust his subordinates, and to accept,
or at least to consider with great care, the advice tendered
him. At the same time, however, if the Minister wishes to
disregard the advice or overrule any of the decisions of his
subordinates, he is at perfect liberty to do so; for he is politically responsible for the work of the department and he
alone will be blamed if anything should go wrong. Responsible government demands of its civil servants honest, fear-
less, expert advice, a mastery of detail, and an ability in
administration. It expects the political heads to give the
lead in most matters of policy, to jar the permanent staff out
of its lethargy, and to accept all praise or all blame for the
consequences of any projects any branch of the Government
may undertake.

The importance of the civil service has been much enhanced
by recent developments in the political life of the country.
The sphere of government has been enormously extended at
unusual speed, with the result that the civil servants have
grown in number and their work has become more and more
technical and specialized. Every new activity has created
a demand for a new species of public official, and old depart-

---

[1] e.g. the above quotation from Bagehot, *supra*, p. 112.

ments have been enlarged and new ones created to supply the need. There is scarcely a profession or trade which has not scores of representatives in the government employ, and the most casual examination of the service list reveals a multitude of strangely named officers performing the most varied functions. District live stock promoter, buoy foreman, Indian farming instructor, junior wage investigator and mediator, rainfall observer, hatchery cook, assistant chief traffic officer, statistician, lawyer, chaplain, current observer, dynamo tender, oakum spinner, grain scooper, rigger foreman, senior clerk, chief clerk, head clerk, messenger clerk, file clerk, clerk —these are but a few of the motley collection. The work of government has become so enormous and so technical that it can be accomplished only by a large, expert staff, elaborately organized and controlled.

With the increased importance and complexity of the service has come a greater public dependence on it. It can no longer be ignored as a vague power functioning in a far-off city in Ontario, and only remotely connected with the ordinary life of the citizen. It has ceased to be the especial care of the politician and has become of real concern to every one. Amateur officials, changing with each Government, are not apt to be tolerated because they do little harm save run up the expenses of the country. The citizen's comfort and pocket-book are affected too intimately. He is beginning to regard an inefficient service as a personal grievance—it may be the cause of ruining his potato crop, of delaying his mail, of adding to his taxes. He is becoming increasingly conscious of the fact that the state is an invaluable assistant in his work, and that an untrained staff may be not merely an inconvenience but an obstacle to his success.   ·

> The farmer strolling round his paddock,
> The fisherman in quest of haddock,
> Unite to sing with grateful glee
> The praises of their Ministry.
> Rude simple souls, they lack that store
> Of expert scientific lore
> On which alone success depends,
> And this their kind Department sends.

For, if calamities befall
The men who till, the men who trawl—
If beasts contract the foot-and-mouth,
If blizzards blow from north or south,
If prices slump and credit fails,
If nets are rent by sportive whales,
The Staff is ready in a trice
To help them with its best advice,
On land or sea, in drought or storm,
Sent free of charge in pamphlet form.[1]

Clearly, this change in emphasis has necessarily altered the popular conception of what a civil servant is and what may be expected of him. In pre-Confederation days the direction of government business was a fairly easy matter: the work to be done was simple, and the Family Compact and their henchmen were quite able to perform the labours imposed upon them. This was equally true when responsible government was established, and the birth of the Dominion made no radical change. The tasks of government were extended, but they were still essentially those which amateurs could manage with fair success. Patronage could be tolerated, because alterations in personnel could be made without startling inefficiency. But as the Dominion enlarged, as the Government at the same time spread slowly over more and more of the country's activities, as the work grew increasingly technical, political favouritism became inadequate as a recruiting expedient. The day of the untrained amateur was over; and it was necessary to adopt new methods to supply the expert assistance which the growth and difficulty of the administration demanded. This has been accomplished by the reforms of the last twenty years, which have transformed the service in a manner much more in accordance with its new requirements.

All of these facts emphasize the exceeding importance of the civil service, and indicate the necessity for a careful consideration of its fundamental principles. The decline of individualism, the growth of state interference, and the expansion of the country have substituted an army for the old

---

[1] *Punch*, 20 Apr. 1927.

corporal's guard. The handful of amateurs has been replaced by the host of specialists. While it is essential that the political control should be maintained, it is no less necessary that the service should be as highly trained as possible and that this skill should be given every opportunity to make itself felt. This can be accomplished by a great variety of expedients—by securing good men, by giving them a secure tenure, by paying a fair salary, by promoting for merit, by encouraging initiative, by building up an *esprit de corps*. It is to these factors that attention will be directed in the following chapters.

VIII. SELECTION

'I've information vegetable, animal, and mineral;
I know the kings of England, and I quote the fights historical
From Marathon to Waterloo, in order categorical;
I'm very well acquainted, too, with matters mathematical;
I understand equations, both the simple and quadratical;
About binomial theorem I'm teeming with a lot of news,
With many cheerful facts about the square of the hypotenuse.'
The Pirates of Penzance.

THE problem of creating a good civil service may be stated
in very simple terms: it is to secure the best possible men, to
retain them, and to give them every encouragement to use
their ability to advantage. All questions of selection, tenure,
personnel, management, &c., must be determined by the
manner in which they help or hinder the attainment of such
ends. On this there is general agreement. The moment, however, one attempts to decide which of the means is the most
suitable to win this objective, conflicting opinions appear and
the real problem turns out to be a very difficult one indeed.
This is accentuated by the nature of the civil service itself.
The host of employees on which a modern democracy must
depend for the proper conduct of its business is so vast and
heterogeneous that no one solution can be applied to all. Some
are professional men, others are day labourers, some administrators, others routine clerks; one man is a technical expert,
another a stenographer, a third a policeman. They are alike
in only one respect: they have a common employer. As a
consequence of this great diversity, the regulations and
expedients to be used must vary with the different officials—
no one solution can be found equally applicable to all. This
is particularly true of the process of selection.

One generalization on selecting officials, however, can be
made with little hesitation, viz., the old method of appointment by party leaders has proved hopelessly inadequate and
inefficient. The history of the Canadian service as outlined
in the preceding chapters should establish this beyond any
possibility of doubt. The baneful influence of patronage
caused inefficient and uneducated men to be put in office, it

ruined discipline, it discouraged merit, it destroyed promotion, it created indifference, it nursed party activity, it demoralized the entire work and spirit of the service. The simple truth is that the political part of the Government cannot be trusted with the duty of making civil service appointments; it acts in almost every instance from personal or party motives. A typical incident was supplied by Lord Palmerston, who was asked by a political supporter to give an office of emolument to one of his friends. The request was accompanied by the statement that he asked no favours, but he desired that '*ceteris paribus*, my friend should get the job'. '*Ceteris paribus* be damned,' exclaimed Palmerston, 'your friend shall have it!' This lack of conscience, this deficiency in a sense of public duty, has invariably appeared hand in hand with political appointments, and the only adequate remedy is to remove the temptation entirely and choose the employees in some other way.

If political appointment is abolished some other method of selection must be discovered. The method chosen must not only do away with party jobbery but must be made so remote from politics that the members of Parliament cannot interfere with or influence the appointments. The bulwark must be strong enough to resist the constant pressure that will be brought against it. At the same time the method adopted must be suited to the primary end in view—the selection of the best men for all of the varied positions in the service. The political problem of abolishing patronage ought to be linked with the administrative problem of securing efficiency.

A workable solution has happily been found. The selecting power in the majority of cases is entrusted to independent, non-political commissioners, who apply various kinds of objective tests of ability to all candidates for positions. These tests will vary in nature and difficulty with the posts to be filled; but the person coming highest in the competition within his group is appointed to the vacancy. Merit is secured by allowing any one to enter the contest (which is widely advertised) and by giving the prize to the victor. In short, the test for admission is based only on fitness to discharge the duties, apart from any political prejudice, religious leanings, or other irrelevant qualifications.[1] This general principle has been adopted by the Canadian service, and in recent years four chief methods have been used: a competitive academic examination, a competitive special examination, a competitive test consisting of testimonials, past record, experience, &c., and (an exception to the rule) simple appointment without any open competition or examination. The merits of each of these will be discussed in turn, followed by a brief statement of their present position in Canada.

The general academic examination, i.e., one on subjects commonly taught at school or college, may be used to test fitness for administrative and clerical positions. It may be of varying degrees of difficulty according to the importance and requirements of the office to be filled, but the idea governing it in all cases is the same: it endeavours to discover natural aptitude and general ability, on the assumption that training and special knowledge will be acquired after admission to the service. In order to indicate more clearly the merits of the academic examination, the following discussion will be confined to those of the highest grade, viz., those which endeavour to appeal to the college student or graduate. Rarely has a device been so maligned, partly because of a deliberate intention of discrediting civil service reform, partly because of a genuine misunderstanding of the purpose for which the examination has been held. Rarely, however, has any device been so lucidly explained from the time of its birth, for one of the godfathers at the christening was Thomas Babington Macaulay. Speaking in the House of Commons in 1833, he described in brilliant fashion the fundamental idea of the academic examination:

'It is said, I know, that examinations in Latin, in Greek, and in mathematics are no tests of what men will prove to be in life. I am perfectly aware that they are not infallible tests, but that they are tests I confidently maintain. Look at every walk of life, at this House, at the other House, at the Bar, at the Bench, at the Church, and see whether it be not true that those who

---

[1] It is here assumed that the commissioners supervising these tests will be impartial and independent of politics. The means used to secure these traits will be discussed in Chapter XI.

attain high distinction in the world are generally men who were distinguished in their academic career. . . . Education would be a mere useless torture if at two or three and twenty a man who has neglected his studies were exactly on a par with a man who has applied himself to them, exactly as likely to perform all the offices of public life with credit to himself and with advantage to society. Whether the English system of education be good or bad is not now the question. Perhaps I may think that too much time is given to the ancient languages and to the abstract sciences. But what then? Whatever be the languages, whatever be the sciences, which it is in any age or country the fashion to teach, those who become the greatest proficients in those languages and those sciences will generally be the flower of the youth, the most acute, the most industrious, the most ambitious of honourable distinctions. If the Ptolemaic system were taught at Cambridge instead of the Newtonian, the senior wrangler would nevertheless be in general a superior man to the wooden spoon. If, instead of learning Greek we learned the Cherokee, the man who understood the Cherokee best, who made the most correct and melodious Cherokee verses, who comprehended most accurately the effect of the Cherokee particles, would generally be a superior man to him who was destitute of these accomplishments. If astrology were taught at our universities, the young man who cast nativities best would generally turn out a superior man.' [1]

Macaulay's description leaves no uncertainty as to the chief purpose of the academic examination. The test is based on what the candidate knows, but it goes much further than that. It tries to discover what are the capabilities, what are the potentialities, what will be the future career of the candidate. It reads the future by revealing the past; it uses acquired knowledge merely as an index of what knowledge may be acquired twenty years hence. Although a mastery of Greek history may help the work of the young civil servant very little, it nevertheless forms the base of the square on which his future accomplishment will be plotted: the length

[1] *British H. of C. Debates*, 10 July 1833, pp. 525–6. The American Telephone and Telegraph Company has recently investigated the relation of college scholarship to success in the Company, with results which corroborate Macaulay's theory in business as well as professional life. Gifford, W. S., 'Does Business Want Scholars?' *Harper's Magazine*, May 1928, pp. 669–74.

of the one will determine the area of the other. The aim is to select the best of a group of young unproven students; and it is difficult to imagine a more reliable test than one dealing with the work which has been engaging their minds during the preceding four or five years. Being untried and inexperienced, their ability must be gauged by what they know and not by what they ought to know. The odds are all in favour of the supposition that the few who emerge at the top of such a competition are the most capable of the candidates, and that their intellectual superiority will be continued in later life.

It must be remembered that these candidates are to receive their special training through practical experience in the service. Hence the object sought by the entrance test is not premature technical knowledge but rather inherent natural ability. The exact shape of the stone is unimportant compared to its quality and the way in which it has taken the preliminary polish. A breadth of mind, a quick initiative, a culture, a mental discipline, a reliable judgement, these are the qualities which an administration must discover if it is to live, and these characteristics are found most frequently in the leaders of educated men of good intelligence. 'Experience shows', said a British Royal Commission, 'that as a rule the best university training ripens natural ability and develops administrative capacity.'[1] Education combined with academic training produces the kind of young man desired as an entrant, and the service can then give him the experience and practical knowledge which he must have as a skilled official. The emphasis of the test, therefore, is not really so much on the knowledge of the candidates, as on the characteristics and training of which the knowledge is a sign and a prophecy.

'I have myself often observed', said Lord Haldane, 'the advantage which the years spent at the university give. Not in all cases, for the best student there may possess little aptitude for business and practical affairs. But in the majority of cases there is a great difference between highly educated men and women and those who are not so educated. The outlook, power and quickness in comprehension, the gift of dealing with people, the readiness to take the initiative and to assume responsibility, are

[1] *Fourth Report of the Commissioners*, 1914, Cd. 7338, p. 39.

all in the main more highly developed when the business to be transacted is seen by the civil servant against a background of other knowledge of the type through which the mind has become enlarged. It is only the exceptionally gifted who possess a substitute for this background.'[1]

'Knowledge is an entirety. There is no phase in it which does not bear closely on every other. That is because of the freedom of outlook which the highly-trained mind possesses. Whether the training has been in the humanities, in literature or history or economics, or in mathematics or science, it comes back to the same thing. What gives new power and new capacity for freedom and penetration is the discipline to which the mind has been subjected. The higher and more strenuous and concentrated such training has been the greater is likely to be the development of mental power and the ability to take the larger point of view. And only the higher forms of training, such as we associate with university standards, can fully help to this.'[2]

Such is the general idea and purpose of the highest academic examination. It presupposes a certain division of the service into classes concerned with supervision and classes devoted largely to routine and clerical work—a theory which will be discussed in detail later.[3] The highest administrative posts can best be filled by officials with a certain mental training and background. How can they be obtained? They are not produced as a rule after a lifetime of drudgery in minor service positions which tend to deaden the very faculties desired. They cannot be secured from outside the service, for the special knowledge of administration can be adequately learned only by experience. The solution is to pick out bright, promising, eager young men, place them in minor administrative positions, and train them for the future.

The academic examination, in spite of many attacks, remains the best test yet devised for securing promising material for administrative work. But it must be used intelligently with a full appreciation of its purpose and of its limitations. Like a powerful engine in a motor car, it is inefficient and even harmful unless the other parts are brought into

[1] Haldane, Lord, 'An Organized Civil Service', *Journal of Public Administration*, 1923, p. 11.
[2] *Ibid.*, p. 16.   [3] Cf. *infra*, pp. 156–8.

harmony with it. The examination is only an expedient to accomplish certain ends; and the whole scheme must be watched, altered to meet changing conditions, the limitations noted, and various safeguards used to secure greater effectiveness.

In the first place, it is not enough merely to have the examination open to all of a required age who wish to compete. The subjects on which the test is given must be of such a kind as will make the widest possible appeal to those candidates who are desired in the service, viz., the college graduates. The papers given should therefore correspond with the work of the universities of the country. This requirement has changed a great deal since Macaulay's day, when courses in the classics and mathematics were virtually the only ones studied. To meet the altered conditions, examinations should be offered in all branches of the arts and sciences, a scheme which necessitates very extensive options and a balancing of marks obtained in one branch against those obtained in another.[1] The age limit should be fairly narrow, and should correspond with the graduating age of the college students, approximately 20 to 25. The examinees thus come up fresh from their training, and the successful ones enter on their work with their minds active and eager to respond to new ideas and suggestions.

Further, the subjects chosen should be those which would be studied by the majority of ambitious students in their usual college course. They must not be blind-alley subjects, those taken with the sole intention of entering the service and good for very little else. A limitation of such a kind would narrow the candidates to men who had picked out government employment as their goal early in their college career, and would exclude many who might be considering the service as a possible alternative to another profession. Few would be induced to prejudice their future in this fashion, for a failure to receive an appointment would leave them unprepared for other employment. In short, the papers should be, for the most part, on general cultural subjects, which would attract

---

[1] For a full discussion of this problem cf. *Report on the Class I Examination (Great Britain)* 1917, Cd. 8657, pp. 9–14, 19–26.

the greatest number of possible candidates, and the test must be made to fit in with the commonly accepted scheme of education, rather than encourage the creation of special college courses to fit the examination. Too great a specialization should be discouraged for another reason, viz., that natural talent is more easily detected over a wide range of subjects than in one or two. Greater diversity makes a better test of initiative, resourcefulness, alertness, acute observation, and general knowledge. Moreover, a second-rate man well versed in one subject is not as valuable to the Government as a man of natural ability who has not mastered any subject in particular. The recent suggestions of the Committee on the Class I Examination in Great Britain [1] endeavoured to meet this difficulty by altering somewhat the examination scheme. They proposed that in addition to the section of specialized knowledge, in which the subjects were optional and on an approximate equality, there should be another section which would be compulsory, and which would aim at discovering alertness of mind and powers of observation. This latter section was to include an essay, a paper on English, one language, a paper on social, political, and economic subjects, a paper on general science, and a viva voce. The intention was that although the honour students would be examined in their particular fields, the cleverest of them would be able to make themselves felt (and acquire marks) in a proportionally greater degree on the section on general knowledge. It is probable, however, that a number of these tests would actually defeat the object desired, for they would be likely to encourage cramming and the acquisition of superficial information. But the retention of the essay, the paper on English, and the viva voce, and an adding to the weights given them in the marking, would almost certainly help to eliminate the second-class specialist.

The subjects of examination should be qualified still further. Certain branches of knowledge are admittedly of greater educative value in a civil servant than others—not in a technical but in a cultural sense. Cherokee, while perhaps a suitable test of natural ability, is of little cultural value,

[1] *Ibid.*, pp. 14–17, 19, 27–32.

and will not help the official as an administrator—unless he should get a position in the Department of the Interior. Such subjects, however, as history, English and (in Canada) French literature, law, economics and political science, are as valuable tests of ability and furnish as appropriate a training for the professions as do other academic subjects, while they give the future civil servant a knowledge, insight, and breadth of view, which the classics and sciences cannot rival. Provided, then, that the number of candidates is not appreciably diminished, it is better to take the future administrators from those with a suitable cultural background. The manner in which this may be done is not to confine the examination to the preferred subjects, but merely to ensure that they are given as much weight (or even a little more weight) in the marking system, and trust that this slight pressure will have the desired effect.

Many criticisms of the academic examination are based on the assertion that they are mere memory tests and that anyone can pass them with distinction after a few weeks' 'cramming'. When the Royal Commission of 1880 on the Canadian service reported in favour of competitive examinations,[1] the minority wrote:

'There is no need of very deep or labourious thinking to perceive that in the process of competitive examination, if anything, only the mnemonic acquirements of the candidate on the day of examination can be shown; the discerning faculties, the aptitudes, the temperament, and general fitness for any given task, remain quite in the dark. There is but one mode of ascertaining the moral, intellectual and physical fitness of men, brought in connection with certain circumstances, labours, and duties; that is probation or trial at the work of the kind required.'[2]

The truth of such criticism depends entirely on the nature of the examination. A question which asks for the enumeration of the capes of Nova Scotia is obviously undesirable both as to difficulty and type, unless it is given to the entrants in a low grade of the service. Easy questions discover no geniuses, nor do those which demand nothing more than a recital of

[1] Cf. *supra*, pp. 44–50.
[2] *Can. Sess. Pap.*, 1882, § 32 a, p. 87.

facts. The papers must require of the candidates their utmost efforts, and must give them scope to use their own minds and express their own ideas and criticisms. The minority on the Commission of 1880 had probably never taken a severe examination in their lives, and therefore had little conception of what a difficult test could do. Such objections might be answered also by an inspection of some of the papers actually used in the Canadian service. Take, for example, the following question, set in 1914 for entrance to Subdivision B of the Second Division:

'Write a paper on the *Sphere of the State*, indicating and discussing the chief theories as to what the State ought and ought not to do, and illustrate your answer by contrasting the policies adopted at different epochs: give your opinion, supported by facts, as to the prevailing tendencies of the present day in regard to State interference.' [1]

Questions of this type undoubtedly call for qualities other than those purely 'mnemonic'; for although any one might attempt to answer them, a brilliant student has enough latitude to indicate of what he is capable. A 'smattering' knowledge of many subjects can easily be penalized by the British system of deducting one-fifth of the maximum from the candidate's mark on each paper, and adding to the result one-fourth of the remainder. Thus, if he made 100, he would be credited with 80 (100–20) plus 20, or 100; if his original mark were 52, he would receive 32 (52–20) plus 8, or 40. In this way, any one who hoped to amass a large aggregate by using a superficial knowledge on many subjects would be at a disadvantage compared to one who attempted a smaller number which he had mastered thoroughly.

A more serious charge against the academic examination is that 'it encourages the merely assimilative, unreflective, unoriginal type of mind at the expense of more honest, more searching, more critical and creative types. It penalises those who feel the difficulties of difficult themes, and puts a premium upon jaunty and self-satisfied dogmatism.' [2] There is a good deal of truth in this objection, though it is applicable

[1] *Ibid.*, 1915, § 31, p. 110.
[2] Muir, R., *Peers and Bureaucrats*, p. 44.

T

to all examinations, academic or otherwise. The fault cannot be entirely eliminated; but it can be reduced to small proportions by combining with the usual examinations other tests of a more varied nature. Most of these have been briefly indicated above. First, the academic examination itself must be of such a nature and difficulty that the original and reflective student is encouraged to express his ideas. A supplementary test may take the form of an essay on one of a number of assigned subjects in his major field, these being carefully chosen to stimulate individual effort. It is possible that theses might be required, though their use is necessarily limited and the difficulty of assigning and grading them almost insuperable. The viva voce is undoubtedly the best check on the plodding, unimaginative student, and it can be used with comparative ease. With this as a weapon an examining board should not take long to discover if a candidate had an 'unreflective, unoriginal type of mind' or the opposite. The objection that a nervous examinee will not be able to do himself justice in such a test is not a serious one. Such a lack of control is probably in itself a defect in a prospective civil servant, and an ability to keep cool and retain his presence of mind is an undoubted merit.[1] Furthermore, many candidates are able to put their ideas more clearly and succinctly in an oral test than in a written one, and consequently a viva voce will, in some cases at least, remedy this possible injustice of the written examination. The moderate use of an intelligence test will act as another corrective, for it is particularly valuable as an aid in measuring mental alertness and capabilities.

Finally, the objection is sometimes raised that the examination stresses unduly the scholastic attainments of the candidates and ignores their moral qualities. A partial reply is furnished by the rule which requires testimonials on character, though these are too frequently superficial and perfunctory. A further check is furnished by the examination itself. 'University experience abundantly shows', wrote the Master of Balliol in 1854, 'that in more than nineteen cases out of twenty, men of attainments are also men of character.

[1] *Report on the Class I Examination (Great Britain)* 1917, Cd. 8657, p. 17.

The perseverance and self-discipline necessary for the acquirement of any considerable amount of knowledge are a great security that a young man has not led a dissolute life.' [1]

Such are the arguments for the academic examination, and they are, as a whole, unanswerable. The system has had years of trial in Great Britain, and has been largely instrumental in producing a type of civil servant second to none in the world. To what extent has the device been tried in Canada? The pass examination, which was the only kind used before 1908, was hopelessly ineffective. It was coupled with political nomination, it was not competitive, and it made few pretensions at being difficult.[2] It succeeded in keeping nothing out of the service except extreme ignorance. From 1908 to 1918 the examinations, where given, were more useful; for competition was introduced and the quality raised. But even during these years the chief result was the elimination of the hopelessly unfit and the admission of those candidates who were slightly better educated than the others. The only academic examinations which ever approached a high standard were those instituted in 1918 for Grade F of the First Division.[3] These covered all the important sciences and languages, and roughly corresponded to the educational system of the Canadian universities. But they lacked many of the safeguards which the academic examination must have if it is to be successful. They were not severe enough to be an effective test; the candidates were given insufficient opportunity to show their initiative and resource; there were no essays given; no viva voce was held. The result was that usually only minimum qualifications were judged: the system often obtained good men, but there was no assurance or even likelihood that it would single out the best. Nevertheless, the examinations of 1918 were pointing in the right direction, and had they been given any real trial, they would probably have developed into a valuable recruiting system. They were abolished, however, a year after their establishment.

The classification of 1919 has relegated the academic examination to the historical text-books. The theory that the

[1] Letter to Sir Charles Trevelyan, *Can. Sess. Pap.* 1880–1, § 113, p. 404.
[2] Cf. *supra*, pp. 40–1, 63–4, 70.   [3] Cf. *supra*, p. 92.

service should be replenished by young men of ability, receiving their training in the government departments after
admission, has been displaced by the theory that all positions
are special in character, and that the entrance examination
must discover the peculiar requirements necessary for an
individual office. Each of the two thousand classified positions demands particular qualifications, each is in a separate
compartment, each has a specially built door through which
one must enter. The change in principle is fundamental, and
it is certainly no improvement. The special examination is
not only advisable but necessary for admission to many
positions which require knowledge in a limited field; but for
general administration the best qualifications are natural
talent, education, and an ability to learn readily through
experience and training. The present system does not
emphasize these qualities, but rather tries to measure a
momentary ability to write shorthand or to balance a ledger.
There is no deliberate effort to ascertain what the candidates
are capable of doing in the future: the secondary qualifications are stressed, the primary ones virtually ignored. In
addition to a misplaced emphasis, the special examination
for administrative positions has other faults. It limits
severely the number of subjects and thereby narrows the
field of recruiting; competition becomes less keen; the quality
of the candidates is lowered. Furthermore, as all the offices
paying a respectable salary are supposed to be filled by promotion, these special tests apply only to the lowest clerical
positions, which necessitates in turn easy examinations and
an educational standard below that of a good high school.

The life of the academic examination in Canada was thus
brought to an abrupt and premature close, and the saddest
feature of the affair was that the murder was committed
under a misapprehension. Had the examination lived it
might have been approaching to-day its period of greatest
usefulness; but its purposes and motives were wrongly interpreted and it was punished for the interpretation. The
superficial saw in the whole examination idea a method to
check patronage and only incidentally a criterion of merit.
If it was to be used to test merit at all, so the argument ran,

it must test those parts of the candidate's knowledge which would be immediately useful to him in his position. He should be able to sit down at his desk in the department and solve the same problems which had troubled him in his examination five days before. Judged by this logic and on these postulates the academic examination was futility writ large, for an acquaintance with the binomial theorem and the law of diminishing return would have no sudden or visible effect on a civil servant's efficiency. In short, the prophetic element in the academic examination was completely overlooked, though it was by far the most important part, and the entire emphasis was placed on a knowledge of facts and special ability of a quasi-technical kind. The *Report of Transmission* of 1919 has only to be quoted to indicate the shallowness of the reasoning used:

'When selections were made for the Inside Service only, consisting in the main of clerical employees, academic tests met with some degree of success, though very frequently eligibles whó had taken the general tests found upon appointment that *they lacked some essential qualification such as proficiency in mathematical computations, ability to operate a typewriter, knowledge of filing systems, ability to handle correspondence, or knowledge of modern office practice.*' [1]

The second important method of selection is the competitive special examination. The academic test, as has been indicated, is suited for the most part to administrative and clerical positions, which, although very important, comprise a comparatively small number of those in the service. There are a great many posts which demand some training before entrance or which do not require those qualities of mind which the academic test endeavours to detect. Such positions are those of excise and customs officials, draughtsmen, lower grade clerks, typists, plumbers, &c., and those other ranks of the service where only minimum qualifications are required as messengers, packers, porters. The uselessness of choosing these employees by questions on geography or Latin is evident, and for these offices the special examination should be invariably used. This method endeavours to gauge a

[1] p. 43. The italics are my own.

candidate's fitness for a particular post, his knowledge of one or two kinds of work, his mental or physical qualifications of a special kind. The subjects on which he is examined are therefore not usually academic, but are chosen with the work of the office constantly in view. The greater part of the competition will be on character, experience, and the ability to do the peculiar tasks required.

In the selection of these men the practical test is frequently of much more importance than the written paper. A prospective stenographer, for example, may be asked to type several letters from dictation, a plumber may be required to solder a pipe, a mechanic may be expected to show his skill at repairing a machine. Theodore Roosevelt, while a Civil Service Commissioner, examined a customs inspector in Texas on saddling and riding an unbroken mustang, shooting at the gallop, reading cattle-brands, classifying live stock, speaking a little Spanish, and proving his courage and endurance by testimonials.

There has always been some recognition in Canada of the necessity for special competitive examinations,[1] and the reform Act of 1908 stated that the entrance tests were to be 'of such a nature as will determine the qualifications of candidates for the particular positions to which they are to be appointed'.[2] But inasmuch as the Act covered only the Inside Service and as the great majority of these positions were of a clerical nature, very few special tests were given. It was not until 1918, when the Outside Service came under the Commission's control, that special examinations became imperative. The new conditions were met by such Orders in Council as the following:

'In all cases where an examination is provided for under any statute for any special position (such as Lay Inspectors, Veterinary Inspectors, Egg Inspectors, Grain Inspectors, Steamship Inspectors, Cullers, Public Analysts, Inspectors and Assistant Inspectors of Electricity) such examinations shall be held under the direction of the Civil Service Commission, and successful candidates appointed in order of merit. These special competi-

---

[1] e.g., *Can. Sess. Pap.*, 1880–1, § 113, p. 23; *ibid.*, 1907–8, § 29 A, p. 45.
[2] *Can. Stat.*, 7–8 Edw. VII, c. 15, section 13.

tions shall include such academic subjects, technical papers or practical tests as may be agreed upon between the departments and the Commission.'[1]

The classification of 1919 emphasized still more the importance of the special examination, which was extended to cover nearly all the offices in the service. In addition to character, general education, and experience, all of which are judged by references, the applicant is examined for one or more of the following qualifications, which are supposed to indicate his special ability to perform the duties of the position:

(a) Knowledge of the duties of the office desired, his ability to carry them out, and his judgement, discretion, organizing ability, as shown by written tests.

(b) Proficiency, tested by the actual performance of the kind of work which will be required of him in the position.

(c) Physical condition, strength, agility, as shown by a medical examination.

(d) Personality, manner, mental qualities, determined by a personal interview.

(e) In some cases, education, judged by academic tests.[2]

This method is admirably suited for examining candidates for many positions like those mentioned above, and one of the outstanding merits of the 1919 classification was that it applied special examinations to posts which needed them badly. But the classification made at the same time a very serious blunder—it assumed that some form of special examination would do duty for all kinds of offices in the service. No matter what the nature of the position might be, irrespective of the ease or difficulty of the test given, the aim under the classification is the same—to discover by examination the exact knowledge and skill possessed by the candidate at the moment of entrance. It definitely rules out academic subjects except in very rare instances, and uses tests on such things as office practice, stenography, book-keeping, filing systems, &c., while neglecting those subjects which will give prophetic results. The future advantage of

---

[1] 21 Dec. 1918, *Can. Stat.*, 1919, p. cxviii.
[2] *Report of Transmission*, 1919, p. 41.

having a well-educated, first-class man is sacrificed to obtain a temporary present advantage of obtaining some one of third- or fourth-rate intelligence who knows how a department should conduct its correspondence. The Civil Service Commission has taken great pains to clear up any doubts that might have arisen in this respect:

'The endeavour of the Commission has been to make its examinations of a practical character, so that employees may be selected by virtue of their capacity to perform the work required, rather than because of their scholastic or academic qualifications alone. It is, of course, recognized that employees must possess sufficient education to make a satisfactory groundwork on which to build for future advancement, but, after satisfying itself as to the presence of this educational groundwork, the Commission has mainly sought to build up an examination system which will select the type of employees who can most satisfactorily perform the duties to which they will be assigned.' [1]

'The examinations of the Commission are, as far as possible, eminently practical tests designed to bring out the ability and qualifications of the candidates for the type of position for which they are applicants. . . . Civil service examinations have come to mean, not red tape and academic impracticabilities, but the application to the public service of employment methods used more and more successfully and more and more extensively in private business.' [2]

In contrast to this may be placed the testimony of Sir Francis Floud, Permanent Secretary to the Ministry of Agriculture and Fisheries in Great Britain:

'It might be thought that, in a Department like the Ministry (of Agriculture and Fisheries), which is responsible for much work of a technical character, it would be preferable to recruit the staff specially rather than to draw them from the examinations which are common to the Civil Service as a whole. It has been found, however, that to enlist men who have received a good general education in the schools and universities, and to give them a thorough training in the routine of a Government Department, produces a type of administrator who is adaptable to many different branches of work, and acquires a capacity to deal effectively with

---

[1] *Can. Sess. Pap.*, 1922, § 32, p. viii.
[2] *Ibid.*, 1923, § 24, p. ix.

all the ordinary functions of Government. Such work as the administration of Acts of Parliament, the handling of Local Authorities, the preparation of statistical or economic reports, financial control, the management of staff and office organization is as a rule better performed by men who have grown up and been trained in the machinery of Government than by men who have been trained for a different career and enter a Government Department in middle age. Nothing would be gained and much would be lost by staffing the Ministry of Agriculture and Fisheries with nothing but practical farmers and fishermen. They would have little or no opportunity of making use of their practical knowledge, for the Ministry does not farm or fish, except to a very limited extent, and the bulk of the work of the Department calls for qualities which the practical farmer or fisherman would have had no opportunity of acquiring. A little knowledge is a dangerous thing, and in dealing with the men who are practically engaged in the industries which the Ministry exists to serve, it is far better that the ordinary staff of the Department should make no pretensions to be experts. The important thing is that they should have open and adaptable minds, and the capacity to exercise a sound judgement on the advice or proposals, often divergent and contradictory, which come before them from the experts and the practical men of the industry. There is a distinct technique of administration which must be learnt, and it must be combined with a sense of proportion and a recognition of political, financial and practical limitations with which the specialist is often impatient. In order to develop these qualities of adaptability and sound judgement, it is the practice of the Ministry to regard its administrative and clerical staff as interchangeable between the different Branches of the Department, so that they may acquire as far as possible a good general knowledge of the work of the Department as a whole, and give them a wider outlook than if the whole of their careers were spent on the same duties. At the same time, as has already been stated, the work of the Ministry could not be carried out without the employment of a large number of specialist officers, whose work, though different in character, is just as important as that of the administrative and clerical staff. This specialist staff has, however, to be recruited in a different manner.' [1]

The important thing to be remembered in studying the

[1] Floud, Sir Francis L. C., *The Ministry of Agriculture and Fisheries,* pp. 49–51.

U

problem is that the kind of ability desired for some offices is different in quality from that desired in others. Superficially, the classification scheme may appear to admit the complexity of the problem by the multiplicity of the tests; but in reality they are all of the same type, though of varying degrees of difficulty. All of the special examinations aim at discovering present qualifications and premature technical knowledge which, while excellent for many positions, are inadequate for many others. Such offices as those of an administrative and clerical nature may be filled far more successfully by the academic test, which probes more deeply, forecasts more accurately, and secures on the whole a much higher type of employee.

A third class of offices in the service are those which are commonly described as professional or technical. Such positions require special attainments of a high order and can usually be recruited only from college graduates or men of mature age. They resemble the offices last discussed, inasmuch as they demand peculiar attainments in a particular department, but their qualifications place them much higher in the aristocracy of the service. They are to be distinguished also from the administrative and clerical group, the members of which may be selected because of their general knowledge and ability and are qualified to enter any one of a number of departments. In short, the professional and technical offices form a small important class, chosen for their expert knowledge in a very limited field.

It is obvious that a general academic examination would be of little use as a selecting process for these positions, nor would the ordinary form of the special examination be very much better. The aim is still, of course, the same—to obtain the men of the greatest capacity; but a test must be devised which offers a reasonable chance of success. Written examinations of any kind are, as a rule, ill suited to discover the highly specialized acquirements which these positions demand. The qualities needed are not readily found by means of written question and answer: they are highly technical, and much depends on the ability to apply expert knowledge to practical problems arising in the course of the work of the department. In many instances, the man desired is of middle age, whose earlier professional skill has been matured by years of experience, and whose real ability can be adequately judged only by the success he has attained in practice. It is as unreasonable as it is unnecessary to ask a man who has completed a difficult section of a transcontinental railway to pass a written examination, as it would be to expect a Prime Minister to answer questions on parliamentary practice and party management.

Another important fact to be considered is that men over thirty years of age cannot do themselves justice in an examination. They have ceased studying text-books, and their knowledge is no longer pigeon-holed with a view to rapid reproduction. Their minds have lost a certain elasticity and rapid adaptability which the good examinee must possess. They have forgotten the art of window-dressing—to put their most attractive goods in the foreground and drape their weaknesses with a skilfully ambiguous phrase. Easy questions that many younger men might answer glibly would puzzle them. Theory has been lost in practice or is used almost subconsciously. Finally, the majority of professional and technical men (and particularly the best of them) cannot be induced to write examinations at all, and if this method were used the competition would be reduced in numbers and quality. Many look upon written tests as a school-boy idea, and are unwilling to pore over text-books and study things which they have forgotten in order to enter a competition from which they may emerge only second best. Many think it is unprofessional and involves a loss of prestige and dignity, that it is a confession that they have failed in their ordinary work. In short, it is a bother and an effort, with no assurance of success and with little hope that a just verdict will be obtained.

Technical and professional officials can be best selected by an elaborate form of the special examination—one which has been adapted to their more exacting needs and has been euphemized so as to sustain and appeal to their professional dignity. Where the plumber was examined by watching him solder a pipe, the engineer is tested by finding out what kind of a bridge he has built ; where the stenographer was asked to write a letter from dictation, the chemist is asked to submit a piece of research. All kinds of expedients may be used to discover the merits of candidates, such as testimonials from previous employers, confidential information from men in the same field, past record and reputation of the candidate, his definite achievements in his science or profession, interviews between him and the selecting body, in short, anything which will furnish the material for reaching a fair judgement. In filling less important positions of the same nature, the applicants will probably be younger and more inexperienced and will have a professional career too brief to be very significant. These may be asked to write examinations on their special subjects or to submit their college records as proof of their ability. In every case there must be a flexibility in using these tests, a willingness to try all methods which promise to reveal the candidate's qualifications. Any reliable source of information, any past work of the candidate, any instrument which will bring to light his talents and capacities—thesis, experiment or record, whatever it may be—should be utilized.

This leads to the question as to who should conduct the inquiry and weigh the evidence. It is clear that the ordinary examining officers of the Civil Service Commission are quite unfitted to do it. First, they have not the expert knowledge to pass on technical or professional qualifications, for in most cases the candidates would be intellectually their superiors. Nor would it be at all possible to staff the examining board with men of such diverse training as would be necessary to conduct even a moderately simple investigation. Further, the applicants would resent any judgement by men who were not at least as well qualified within the professional field as they were themselves, and as a result few candidates would apply. Finally, even with technically trained examiners there is always a danger that they would become stale and lose touch with the more recent developments in their science. The best plan seems to be the appointment of special boards (advisory to the Civil Service Commission) composed of men, some outside the service, some in the department or branch which has the vacancy—all of undoubted ability and prominence in their profession—who would conduct the test, examine the credentials, &c., and report their judgement to the Commissioners. The latter would then be able to utilize this expert advice in making their decision.

The Canadian practice for many years was to treat professional and technical positions as a separate class, and vest the appointments in the Governor and Council without any reference to the Board of Examiners.[1] This procedure was adopted possibly because of the inability of the Board to judge professional qualifications, but more probably because of the reluctance of the politicians to abandon the best of their patronage. After the Act of 1908 these positions were still filled by the Governor in Council, but those appointed were required to secure a certificate from the Commission stating that they possessed the minimum qualifications for the offices concerned.[2] This plan worked well in some cases and badly in others. A conscientious Minister would either make excellent appointments himself, or allow the Commission to advertise and obtain the men without the intervention of the department. Other members of the Cabinet, however, were not so scrupulous, and nominations proposed by them were frequently held up by the Commission.[3] The Act of 1918 took all technical and professional appointments from the Governor in Council and gave them to the Commission, 'provided they are satisfied, either with or without competitive examination as is determined by the regulations of the Commission, that he possesses the requisite knowledge and ability and health, character and habits'.[4] The classification of 1919 left this condition unchanged, save that technical and professional positions were abolished as a separate and distinct category.[5]

Ever since the Commission has had complete control of these appointments it has been aided by advisory boards in making selections. Some members of these boards are high

---

[1] *Rev. Stat. Can.* (1906), c. 16, section 37.

[2] *Can. Stat.*, 7–8 Edw. VII, c. 15, section 21 ; cf. *supra*, pp. 79–81.

[3] Cf. *supra*, p. 86 ; *Can. H. of C. Journals*, 1923, Appendix, § 5, pp. 725–6, 854.

[4] *Can. Stat.*, 8–9 Geo. V, c. 12, section 15.

[5] *Ibid.*, 10 Geo. V, c. 10.

officers in the department concerned, some represent a well-known professional organization, and some are chosen for their particular knowledge of the work of the vacant position. The Commission has given numerous examples of such cases. In 1918 three skilled accountants were desired, and a board was appointed consisting of two chartered accountants outside the service and the head of the Accountants Branch in the department. When an assistant to the Board of Historical Publications was required, the body to which applications were referred was composed of two professors of history and the Dominion Archivist. In both cases the Commission accepted the recommendation of the board without question. It is an interesting case of delegation of function. Parliament (or more exactly, the Privy Council) divests itself of the power of appointment in order to secure the impartiality and judicial sense of the Commission, while the latter, lacking the knowledge to make a sound judgement, must appoint a board to investigate and report its findings.

The system has worked excellently, and is now well established. The impartiality of the boards, the high character and qualifications of their members, the uniform soundness of the recommendations made, have won the appreciation of the Commission and of the greater part of the service. The chief opposition has come from the deputy heads of departments, some of whom feel that they alone should be allowed to make appointments of a professional and technical nature. In their memorandum of 30 June 1922,[1] the deputy heads urged that such positions be filled only on their recommendation, because they could appreciate better than any one else the exact kind of specialized knowledge required. The objection to this proposal is, of course, not that the deputies lack the necessary information (which they undoubtedly possess in most cases), but that they are frequently exposed to party or personal influence by the political head of their department, an influence which on account of their position it might be difficult to resist. One deputy admitted in evidence that 'the question of political patronage might come in if the protection or the control of the Civil Service Commission were

[1] Cf. *supra*, p. 105.

removed. I have no reason to say that it would, but it might'.[1]
The Professional Institute of the Civil Service of Canada, a
body which is most intimately concerned with appointments
of this kind, has given its endorsement to the present system:

'We are unreservedly opposed to the introduction of patronage
in any form in dealing with positions in the civil service. We are
not all of us entirely satisfied with the present method of making
appointments, but we unquestionably prefer to have the technical
service remain under the Civil Service Commission and we would
rather have the present system continue without change than to
have the service again exposed to that enemy of efficiency—patronage. . . . We should prefer to see the closest co-operation between
the Civil Service Commission and the government departments,
so that the deputy minister's intimate knowledge of his department might be utilized most completely, and very particularly so
that appointments and promotions might be dealt with more
rapidly.'[2]

The last group of offices are those which are filled without
any examination or competitive test of any kind and are not
under the control of the Civil Service Commission. They fall
into three unrelated subdivisions, each of which has been
made an exception to the general rule for a special reason.
The largest of these subdivisions is composed of unimportant
and part-time positions paying less than $200 a year, all of
which are now filled by the department in which the vacancy
occurs. They were all placed under the Commission in 1918,
but owing to a number of causes were removed from its control by a series of Orders in Council.[3] In many cases this has
meant a reversion to patronage. The deputy heads of departments comprise another group. They are appointed by the
Governor in Council, and, although they hold office at pleasure,
reasons for their removal must be tabled within fifteen days of
the earliest session of Parliament. In effect, therefore, their
tenure is especially protected. The reasons for their unique
position, both as to appointment and tenure, is not difficult
to find. The Minister must have the final decision when so

[1] *Can. H. of C. Journals*, 1923, Appendix, § 5, p. 661.
[2] *Ibid.*, p. 264; cf. also pp. 264–78.
[3] Cf. *supra*, pp. 97–9.

vitally important a post becomes vacant, while on the other hand, changes must be as few as possible in order to secure continuity of work. A third subdivision is that of private secretaries to Cabinet Ministers. These are appointed by the Ministers themselves, and are paid salaries under special parliamentary appropriation or, if they are already in the service, $600 in addition to the amount they have been receiving. When the Minister goes out of office the secretary goes with him; and if he has not been in the service before, he leaves the Government employ entirely.[1] It is obvious that these secretaries are rightly treated as exceptions to the rule, for the Minister must have as his assistant a person in whom he has implicit confidence. The same reason which dictates freedom of choice in appointment also demands that the secretary should leave with his principal, so that the succeeding Minister shall not be hampered by an unknown and perhaps hostile assistant.

In spite of all these methods of selection, however, some poor men will slip into the service, and a term of probation is used as a final check on the inefficient. During this period (usually six months or a year) the deputy head has the power of rejecting any successful candidate who has been placed in his department, and the appointment is never made permanent until the time has expired. A clause to this effect has always been found in Canadian Civil Service Acts, although the different departments have not used it to the same extent. In 1892, for example, it was stated that the privilege of rejection was little used.[2] In 1907 the evidence showed that the Post Office rejected inefficient employees without hesitation, but that the Department of Inland Revenue kept all men, good or bad.[3] The Minister of Finance was apparently nearest to the truth when he said that once a man was taken on probation it was almost impossible to get rid of him.[4] The same difficulty was mentioned by the Civil Service Commission in its report for 1921:

'Too frequently it appears to be the feeling of both employees

[1] *Can. H. of C. Journals*, 1923, Appendix, § 5, pp. 652–3, 925–6.
[2] *Can. Sess. Pap.*, 1892, § 16 c, pp. 259, 545.
[3] *Ibid.*, 1907–8, § 29 A, pp. 280, 776.   [4] *Ibid.*, p. 184.

and employers in government departments that "once in the
service, always in the service". While the Commission feels that the
great majority of persons appointed under the merit system make
highly satisfactory employees, it believes that greater consideration should be given by supervisory departmental officers to the
probationary period, which would obviate the possibility of retaining in the service persons unsuited therefor.'[1]

The deputy heads of departments frequently complain that
the competitive tests have failed; but on being asked why
the inefficient men are not turned out after probation they
reply that the clause in the Act is a dead letter. Yet they are
the ones who make it so; although the Commission has lately
been accused of questioning the right of the deputy to discharge without cause assigned.[2] If the selective processes
are to be used with the greatest possible success, they must be
combined with a system of probation which will be ruthless
enough to discard all prospective employees of even doubtful
merit.

[1] *Ibid.*, 1922, § 32, p. xi; cf. *ibid.*, 1923, § 24, p. xii.
[2] *Can. H. of C. Journals*, 1923, Appendix, § 5, pp. 783–6.

IX. GRADATION: PROMOTION: SALARY

'As office boy I made such a mark
That they gave me the post of a junior clerk.
I served the writs with a smile so bland,
And I copied all the letters in a big round hand—
I copied all the letters in a hand so free,
That now I am the Ruler of the Queen's Navee!'
H.M.S. Pinafore.

IN spite of the great diversity in the work of the civil service, there exists, or should exist, a fairly definite connexion between the low and high offices. This organized plan of positions and their relationship to each other is commonly known as gradation: it is an elaborate scheme of division of labour wherein each officer performs his particular duties as one part of the whole. Gradation affects, therefore, the place of a civil servant in the official hierarchy, the position he can occupy at entrance, his relationships with his fellow employees, and the possibilities of his advancement. It is linked up with the selective process on the one side and with promotion on the other: it determines the nature of his original appointment and also his potential future. The general scheme of positions is thus of very great importance; for it must necessarily play a large part in determining the nature of a young appointee's work, in stimulating or discouraging departmental activity, in appealing to those who might possibly join the service, and in retaining those who have already entered.

The Canadian service has had three general schemes of gradation since 1867. The first one was very incomplete, and grew up bit by bit without much thought or purpose. The next was a half-hearted copy of the English model, with little real appreciation of what that model actually implied. The last, which derived its immediate inspiration from the United States, was an attempt to carry out some of the ideas which had been vaguely considered in the first of the three schemes.

The earliest of these plans of organization was scarcely a plan at all, although it appeared attractive on paper. The service was divided into different grades, entrance was sup-

posedly effected through only the lowest positions, and a theoretical promotion took place from the bottom to the top.[1] This ideal, however, was never even approximately realized. When a vacancy occurred it was filled by promotion, if convenient; but should a member of Parliament desire the patronage (as he usually did) his nominee received the job. A man frequently remained for years in the same position to which he had been appointed, while the prizes of the service were distributed amongst outsiders. In some instances, a proper display of party enthusiasm would bring a moderate advancement, in others, efficiency and merit would receive a deserving, though unexpected, promotion. In short, there was no rule or principle underlying the organization. A young man entered the service at one of the lowest positions, and in twenty years he might still be there or might perhaps have become head of the department. No one could tell which was likely to happen, for it depended upon circumstances in which the efficiency of the employee and the theoretical gradation of the service counted for little. There was an official hierarchy, but for the most part it made its order of precedence as it went along. This, of course, the civil servants knew, and it had the natural effect on the type of entrants and the ardour with which they later pursued their work.

The second plan of gradation slowly grew out of the first, and was a lukewarm attempt to copy the British scheme. It recognized different types of work within a certain field, and tried to recruit men of corresponding education for each type, instead of having them all enter on an equal footing in the lowest ranks. The first legal evidence of the change was in 1900 when college graduates were admitted directly to second-class clerkships, and the same idea was extended by the Acts of 1908 and 1918.[2] This new plan gradually emerged from the chaos into which the earlier system had degenerated chiefly because some improvement in the organization was urgently needed, and the British service presented a convenient solution. But the adoption of the scheme resembled in many ways the adoption of the academic examination with which it was closely related. Both were derived from

[1] Cf. *supra*, pp. 19–20.   [2] Cf. *supra*, pp. 72, 79–80, 92.

the same source, both lacked adequate appreciation of their possibilities, both were accepted with too many changes, and both were finally rejected without a fair or adequate trial.

The extent to which this second plan of gradation was insufficient can best be seen by a closer study of the British model, particularly as it is found in the clerical and administrative positions.[1] It forms one of the outstanding characteristics of the British service, and fits in with the plan of academic entrance examinations which has been studied above. The service is divided horizontally into two chief classes—one concerned almost entirely with routine and minor supervisory work, the other, a much higher type, doing work of an executive nature which demands initiative, resource, excellent education, and training. Entrance to each class is through open, competitive, and (in the clerical and administrative service) academic examinations—an easy one for the routine class, an extremely difficult one for the officer or executive class. Promotion is supposed to take place within each class from the bottom to the top, this being based on merit as displayed by the employee's actual achievements in the department.

The justification of this scheme has been partly given in the preceding chapter. All entrants cannot be officers, nor can the service afford to train every one of them in order to discover who possesses the desired qualifications. It is therefore necessary to separate the most likely candidates, train only these in the manner desired, and choose the leaders from the most successful. The first part of this selective process is carried out by the academic examination; the second and third parts by experience and promotion. The examination eliminates the unfit and indicates the most promising of the young college men who desire to enter, while the subsequent life in the service will lead to the acquisition of expert knowledge and the advancement of those who have proved their worth as practical administrators. The horizontal two-fold division into officer and routine classes is based on a theory of mental development. It is considered that a civil servant who spends years at low-grade work will not increase his powers of

[1] Cf. Northcote-Trevelyan Report, *supra*, pp. 36–7.

initiative and resource, but will have them largely destroyed by contact with the deadening monotony of routine. The corollary follows that promotions from the lower classes to the high executive posts should be made very sparingly; indeed, they should be exceptional. This distinction between officer and routine classes was noted by Sir George Murray in his report on the Canadian service in 1912, and he strongly urged its continuance and greater development:

'It is in my opinion of great importance that this distinction between the work of the two divisions should be preserved. The essential difference between them is that the work of the two higher divisions requires the exercise of discretion and the possession of altogether higher qualifications, whether professional, technical, or administrative, than that of the third.

'For routine work, under direct supervision, all that is required is punctuality, accuracy, and precision. The copying of accounts, the compilation of statistics, the filling up of forms, and even the drafting of simple letters, are all matters in which there is no room for the exercise of discretion. The qualifications required for the work of the higher classes are essentially different from those required for the routine duties of the lower classes; and are not usually developed from them. There will always be a large number of persons who, while quite capable of routine work, will never be able to rise to duties of a higher character requiring a higher standard of education and the higher qualities required for successful administration.'[1]

Sir George Murray, however, somewhat overstated an otherwise good case by his disparagement of the lower division. Even routine work, such as the 'drafting of simple letters', may call for some discretion and may reveal at the same time natural ability of an unusual kind. The horizontal dividing strip, therefore, should not be too impermeable; promotion from the lower class to the upper should be allowed in exceptional cases, but the chief source of supply from which the officer class will be drawn should be the higher division. The two-fold system originated in England partly because of the social and educational distinction between the two grades of clerks—conditions which do not exist in

[1] *Can. Sess. Pap.*, 1913, § 57A, pp. 20–21.

Canada in any marked degree—but the fundamental need in the two countries remains the same. Men of education and talent must be secured if the service is to do its work well; these cannot be induced to enter the lowest positions nor can they receive there an adequate training; and the best way out of the difficulty is to admit them by different examinations and to promote them within their particular class.

The most careless inspection of the Canadian service from 1900 to 1918 will indicate how inadequately the British conception of the two divisions was realized. The feeble attempts to hold difficult academic examinations have been described in earlier chapters, and without a very high standard of entrance the whole scheme inevitably fell to the ground. The difficulty was that the distinction between the two sets of examinations was so slight that it lost its whole value as a selective process, and the type of man admitted under the one test was not materially different from the type admitted under the other. Furthermore, the work of the upper division was only vaguely marked off from that of the lower, and promotion occurred at all points from one to the other. The upper division not being definitely recruited from superior material, its duties not clearly executive and supervisory and not marked out from the routine and mechanical work of the second division, it being in no sense of the word exclusive, and promotion to it from the lower grade being an everyday occurrence, there is no cause for wonder that the so-called British scheme of gradation was a failure. There were, however, possibilities of development; but these possibilities, like those of the academic examination, were never comprehended by the legislature. Finding the Canadian adaptation of the British plan unsuccessful, Parliament decided to try another one—the 'classification of 1919.'

This third plan, while based immediately on American state and municipal precedents,[1] was nothing more nor less than a reversion to the principles supposedly underlying the earliest Canadian scheme of gradation above mentioned. It was a conscientious attempt to carry out ideas which before

[1] An improved form of the same plan was later adopted by the American Federal Government.

had been very inadequately realized due to the distracting influences of party politics. In other words, the gradation of 1919 was largely the same as that of 1867, except that merit had displaced patronage as a controlling factor, and a more elaborate classification had to be added due to the enormous growth and complication of civil service positions. The fundamental idea of both schemes was an organization composed of many different types of positions, recruiting its staff through the lowest offices, and promoting these step by step to the top. But whereas the service of 1867 and later years was content to allow this scheme of recruitment and promotion to remain only an ideal and permitted patronage to rob it of all efficacy, the classification of 1919 aimed at enforcing the rules and carrying them out in practice.

The lines of cleavage under the classification of 1919 are therefore vertical and not horizontal. The service is split into large occupational groups, which do not necessarily correspond with departmental divisions but are determined by the profession, trade, or kind of work involved. Each group contains all those engaged in the same or allied occupations, from the highest officer to the most humble member of his staff. All entrants are supposed to come in at the lowest positions and work themselves upwards by efficiency and general merit. The high offices are thus to be filled by promotion, which is almost invariably vertical and rarely crosswise. If the latter should take place, the employee immediately enters an entirely different occupational group and has before him different lines of promotion.

This scheme has necessitated a most involved tabulation of positions known as the *Classification Schedule*,[1] each kind of office being therein described and its place fixed in the whole organization. The following information is given for each of the 2,000 [2] classes in the *Schedule:* (a) *Title.* Each office or class has a title which is supposed to indicate briefly the nature of the position, e.g. Senior Customs Clerk,

[1] Cf. *supra*, pp. 95–6.
[2] This number varies from year to year. It began in 1919 at 1729, reached 2536 a few years later, and is now (1928) between 1900 and 2,000. *Can. Sess. Pap.*, 1922, § 32, p. v.; *Report of Civil Service Commission*, 1925, p. vii.

Hatchery Cook, Grain Scooper. (b) *Definition of Class*. This is a statement of the duties which are normally performed by members of this class, with supplementary information, where needed, as to the seasonable nature of the work, part or full time, supervisory or mechanical, &c. (c) *Examples of Duties*. Specific examples are frequently added to illustrate the type of work to be done, e.g. the duties of an Able Seaman are supposedly made clearer by adding that he is to wash down decks, polish bright metal work, chip and paint hull and decks, generally to keep the vessel clean and orderly, overhaul and stow gear and tackle, take a turn at the wheel, stand on watch as lookout at sea, and man a lifeboat.[1] (d) *Statement of Qualifications*. This is a short paragraph giving the minimum requirements for entrance to the class, including education, experience, technical knowledge, special skill or aptitude, physical condition, age, &c. (e) *Lines of Promotion*. Two things are included under this head: the class or classes from which employees for the described position would logically be chosen, and the class or classes to which the employee in the described position would naturally be promoted. (f) *Range of Salary*. The last item in the description is the minimum and maximum salary paid in that class, together with increases in remuneration over a period of years.[2]

The following is one example from the *Classification Schedule:*

ARCHITECTURAL ESTIMATOR [3]

Definition of Class:

To prepare, under supervision, from plans prepared in the Dominion Architect's offices estimates of cost and bills of quantities of materials required in various proposed buildings; and to perform other related work as assigned.

---

[1] *Classification of the Civil Service of Canada*, 1919, p. 5. The examples are intended to be neither inclusive nor exclusive, but, as one member of Parliament remarked, the tendency is that 'if an Able Seaman is asked to take a scuttle of coal out of the hold in order to warm up the captain's cabin, he will turn up the book and tell you that that is not in the book and consequently that is not his job'. *Can. H. of C. Debates*, 10 Oct. 1919, p. 975.

[2] *Report of Transmission*, pp. 8–11, 27–30.

[3] *Classification of the Civil Service of Canada*, 1919, p. 17.

Examples: Checking estimates submitted by inspectors, district clerks of works, and district architects of alterations and additions to public buildings; checking tenders submitted on different contract works in order to arrive at unit prices for comparison.

Qualifications:

Education equivalent to high school graduation; either a course of two years in architecture in a school of applied science of recognized standing with one year of subsequent experience in an architect's office, or three years of experience in an architect's office; ability to read and use architectural plans to obtain the quantities of the various materials shown on plans.

Lines of Promotion:

Promotions may be made according to law from such other classes with lower maximum salaries, and to such other classes with higher maximum salaries, in the same or related services, as may be specified by the Civil Service Commission. Examples:

From: Junior Architectural Draftsman.

To: Architectural Specification Writer, Junior Architect.

Compensation:

Monthly:	$ 105	110	115	120	125	130
Annual:	1260	1320	1380	1440	1500	1560

The purpose of all these elaborate descriptions was to place both the Inside and Outside Services under one regular system, and supply the Commission with information to aid it in filling any vacancies. At the same time the classification endeavoured to secure a greater certainty of promotion and uniform compensation for the same work. Every position is named, and employees doing similar work in different departments bear similar labels. The Commission, once the classification has been drawn up, has only to refer to the book to find out the required personnel of any branch in any department. Thus 'it could say that the branch should comprise, say, 1 Chief Clerk, 1 Principal Clerk, 14 Junior Clerks, 3 Junior Statistical Clerks, 1 Junior Departmental Librarian, 1 Messenger Clerk, 2 Statistical Clerks, 2 Clerk Stenographers, 1 Clerk Typist, 1 Junior Law Clerk, 2 Draftsmen, and 1 Mechanical Engineer. Each of these designations would have a meaning uniformly accepted throughout the service by all departments, and each class of position thus designated would carry a recognized scale of compensation and call for certain well understood qualifications.'[1] By the same token, should the Chief Clerk resign, the Commission would look at the 'line of promotion' indicated in the schedule, and would raise the Principal Clerk to the vacancy, provided he could meet the qualifications demanded. The 'line of promotion' of the Principal Clerk would next be consulted, and one of the fourteen Junior Clerks or one of the two Statistical Clerks would probably be advanced to the higher grade.

The classification of 1919 has met with both praise and ridicule. It has done much to abolish inequalities in position and salary; it has emphasized merit in the making of appointments and promotions; it has convinced every one that whatever the faults may be, the motive behind the change has been the welfare of the service. The most conspicuous merit and the one most stressed has undoubtedly been the enormous decrease in patronage and political influence of all kinds, though in reality this is not attributable to the classification as such but to the Act of 1918. The changes which took place a year later merely implemented a reform already accepted in principle. The classification provided the details, which could conceivably have been supplied equally well, and probably better, by a further development of the scheme of gradation existing at the time the changes were made.

The general opinion of the civil servants themselves bears out this last statement. They regard the diminution of patronage and the establishment of open competition with unqualified approval, but the great majority criticize the classification itself. Some find fault with its exceeding rigidity, some insist that it is quite unnecessary, many others find it too complex to be efficient. The deputy ministers have been almost unanimously opposed to the new scheme. In one department the twelve classes under the earlier plan have been increased to 327, and in another eight have become 313, while both deputies complain that the resulting complexity has added to their difficulties in administration without giving any appreciable relief.[2] Another department has

---

[1] *Report of Transmission*, pp. 5-6.
[2] *Can. H. of C. Journals*, 1923, Appendix, § 5, pp. 634, 795.

twelve classes to cover stenographers of different kinds, and
the deputy stated that so far as he could ascertain the only
distinction between a Junior Clerk Typist and a Clerk Typist
was sixty dollars a year.[1] A fourth deputy describes the
classification as 'cumbersome and tedious, lacking in any
feature of elasticity and opposed generally to the principles
of expedition, efficiency and economy'.[2] The professional
civil servants, speaking through their organization, favour
a sweeping reduction in the number of classes, and this dis-
satisfaction is prevalent throughout the service.[3] The Under
Secretary of State summarized the whole matter in one
shrewd sentence: 'The mere matter of going around the
different clerks in the various departments and putting new
tags on them I do not think has brought about any very
great results at all.'[4]

One secondary result of the new scheme has been a colossal
waste of effort and time in administering it. The Deputy
Minister of the Interior kept a ten months' record of his Department's correspondence with the Civil Service Commission,
and found that the Commission wrote the Department 2,711
letters while the rest of the world wrote them but 2,398. In
the same period his Department sent the Commission 2,652
communications (to which were attached in many instances
certificates in duplicate), while it sent the rest of the world
a total of 4,242 letters of all kinds. The Deputy estimated
that 50 per cent. of the time of his staff, so far as correspondence was concerned, was taken up with the Commission.[5]

It may also be indicated that even the Civil Service Commission, at whose instigation the classification was made,
could not after four years' experience express any hearty
approval of the scheme, but could plead only for a more extended trial. One of the Commissioners in giving evidence
before the Special Committee of the House of Commons
made the following statement:

'There has been some agitation for the abolition of this classi-

---

[1] *Ibid.*, p. 674.   [2] *Ibid.*, p. 733.
[3] *Ibid.*, pp. 206, 281–4, 298–304, 469, 685, 1008–10.
[4] *Ibid.*, p. 625.   [5] *Ibid.*, p. 796.

fication, and going on to some other system. In this connexion, I just want to say this: after all that action has been taken, after the service has been in turmoil for five years, after this transfer of the service from the old Act to the new system has just been completed, the hearing of appeals has been concluded . . . the system is entitled to a fair and reasonable trial. The alternative, of course, is something different; additional hubbub in the service for whatever length of time it takes to apply the new system, another period of transition, additional public expenses, and after all I doubt very much whether we will be any nearer the millenium than we are to-day.' [1]

The most serious fault of the classification, however, is that it is fundamentally unsound in the making of appointments and promotions. The American 'experts' evidently thought that inasmuch as any natural born citizen might become president of the United States so any entrant to the civil service might become a Deputy Minister. But although one may heartily approve of equality of opportunity as a general principle, it is unwise to model either the government of the United States or the Canadian civil service with that objective solely in mind. It is better to remember that a genius will surmount all ordinary obstacles, and that the rank and file of citizens or civil servants will never reach the top of the ladder. The classification as drawn up by the 'experts' aims at promoting the humblest employee, but forgets that even if he should prove worthy of promotion, his years of drudgery and routine have seriously lessened his efficiency. Moreover, the system of promoting from the bottom to the top necessarily involves taking in poor material in the lowest offices, for unless advancement be extremely rapid or the initial salary disproportionately large a bright, well-educated man cannot be persuaded to enter at all. In a talk which the 'experts' had with the writer they conceded the force of this argument, and admitted that their scheme held out no inducements and made no provision for college men except in technical and professional positions. A further fact which may be reiterated here is that the entrance examinations under this system are special in nature, and fail to test natural aptitude or excep-

[1] *Can. H. of C. Journals*, 1923, Appendix, § 5, p. 901.

tional general ability, which, as has been indicated in the last
chapter, is in itself a very grave fault.

But even if one were able to disregard all these objections
and accept the fundamental principles of the classification,
a careful scrutiny will show that it must break down if
strictly applied. Promotion from the bottom of the service to
the top is usually inadvisable because of a lack of proper
training; it is usually impossible because of the educational
needs of the highest positions. As a result, the *Classification
Schedule* is compelled to refute the assumption on which the
whole scheme is built. Where the *Report of Transmission*
assumes that promotion can and will take place from the
lowest office to the highest, parts of the *Schedule* deny it.
Where the 'lines of promotion' indicated in the *Schedule*
assert equality of opportunity for all, the 'statement of qualifications' in the same book proves that such equality is
largely illusory. The tempting future held out by one paragraph is swept away by the grim demands of the next, and
even the paper hopes of promotion are destroyed. The
scheme denies that men of high educational qualifications
must be admitted directly to the better positions, yet it is
compelled to bring them in surreptitiously through the
back door.

This can be easily illustrated by choosing any office in the service, and tracing the career of the prospective Deputy Minister or head of a branch. A rural labourer, for example, is taken
on by the Department of Agriculture as a Farm Hand, and,
being very ambitious, he buys a copy of the *Schedule* and pro-
ceeds to trace his future course of promotion. He is delighted
to discover that after years spent in his country's service he
may become an Entomologist, or the Dominion Entomologist,
or the Deputy Minister of Agriculture, which is a fairly satisfactory end to a career begun with such scant equipment as (see
Schedule) 'ability to read and write and preferably a primary
school education'. But when the Farm Hand looks into the
manual more closely he begins to see why it has been called
the 'joke book'. He finds that although he is in immediate
line for promotion to the classified position known as Experi-

mental Farm Assistant, he is required before taking his step in rank to obtain in addition to his primary school education 'at least two years of training in an agricultural college of recognized standing' or its equivalent. From this position—if he should be able to qualify—he may theoretically be promoted to Junior Entomologist, though his requirements have again risen, and he must have obtained in the interval an education equal to university graduation with specialization in entomology and related subjects, with a general knowledge of agriculture and forestry. From this position he is supposed to be advanced to the rank of Assistant Entomologist, with an equivalent to graduation from a university 'of recognized standing' (any university was good enough before), special training in entomology and zoology, a knowledge of agriculture and forestry, and (though this should cause him no trouble) 'ability to rough it'. Finally, before the former Farm Hand, with his ability to spell and read, can reach his goal of Entomologist, he should fill the following demands of the *Schedule*: 'Graduation from a university of recognized standing with specialization in entomology, botany and zoology; at least five years of experience in entomological research work, at least three years of which shall have been spent in directing such work; familiarity with the insect problems of Canada; administrative ability; good address and ability in public speaking.'[1]

Such a scheme carries its own refutation, and similar examples can be found by the score. The young Clerk may become successively a Senior Clerk, Principal Clerk, Head Clerk, Chief Clerk, and Assistant Deputy Minister of Marine, provided he is able to acquire (after entering with the three R's) an education equivalent to a university graduation.[2] The Assistant Librarian must have a high school education and a full course in library work, and if he is to become a Librarian he must pick up in odd hours the equivalent of a university degree and a thorough command of both English and French. And so the joke book reveals its deep humour.

[1] *Classification of the Civil Service of Canada*, 1919, pp. 325, 322, 438, 47, 310.
[2] *Ibid.*, pp. 179, 623, 562, 371, 138, 35.

Any humble employee may be traced through a number of imaginary promotions—imaginary, because in almost every instance the educational barrier prevents advancement. It might be argued that the better educated candidates, trusting in rapid promotion, would enter the service in the minor positions, but it needs little reflection to answer that the college graduate who aspires to be an Assistant Entomologist will not be tempted by a job as a Farm Hand paying $2·50 a day, or as an Experimental Farm Assistant at $960 a year. It is true that some education might be picked up by night school work or even by leave of absence, but even that would be hopelessly inadequate in the majority of offices. The one conclusion which emerges is that the most vital idea of the classification proves unworkable even if it be judged on the basis of the *Schedule* itself. As a matter of fact, the 'experts' admitted to the writer that the 'lines of promotion' were in many instances suggestive only, and that the service would have to be continually replenished from the outside by better educated men. The Civil Service Commission also has found this to be true when administering the classification, and concedes that it is used to-day as a key to organization rather than to promotion. Such a concession, however, shows the whole scheme in its true colours.

The gradation introduced in 1919 is therefore inherently bad, and it works because there is a tacit admission that it is unworkable. No amount of patching will make it the equal of the earlier system, though a few of its good features could be added without difficulty to the English plan. The two great divisions into officer and routine classes and certain other important subdivisions could be used in conjunction with the *Classification Schedule*, each of the defined offices being placed clearly within one of the two great divisions. In the illustration cited, for instance, the Farm Hand and Experimental Farm Assistant would fall within the lower division, and the Junior Entomologist, Assistant Entomologist, and Entomologist, would be placed in the other. The educational line of cleavage is unmistakable. Offices could be filled in the different ways indicated in the last chapter, and promotions could take place within the limits of the division, with promotions from the second division to the first in very exceptional cases. This gradation would have many advantages not found in the present scheme, and the additional merit of being honest and holding out no illusory promises.

The recent classification made a further change in promotions, though it did not form an essential part of the reorganization. Promotions before 1918 were supposed to have been made throughout the entire service for merit only, but this, particularly in the Outside Service, was the exception rather than the rule. One Royal Commission after another recited the different ways in which the power was abused. Many civil servants were advanced without any regard to their qualifications, many owed their promotion to political intrigue, many of the higher offices were filled directly from outside without any attempt to reward those who had been Government employees for a lifetime.[1] Conditions in the Inside Service, however, were much improved after 1908, and the majority of departments promoted for merit. The Act of 1918 extended this principle to the whole service by placing promotions in the hands of the Commission acting in co-operation with the deputy head concerned. But in the following year, when the classification was introduced, all promotions were given to the Commission alone, which could use its discretion in determining the grounds on which advancement should be made.

The process of making promotions under the present system may be briefly stated. When an office is created or becomes vacant, the fact is advertised among those clerks who are the most suitable candidates, and their applications are received. The Civil Service Commission then furnishes the department with paper forms, and the deputy, chief of branch, or some other officer makes thereon a rating for each candidate. This rating includes the applicant's past record and also an estimate of his future ability to fill the vacant office. To this rating the Commission adds another based on seniority. If two or more candidates are fairly close on the totals of these estimates, or if there is any suspicion that the

---

[1] Cf. *supra*, pp. 40, 41, 46, 64, 75.

rating is not given fairly (in one instance a deputy marked one candidate one hundred per cent. in everything), or if the Commission is not satisfied in any other respect, it may order that the candidates take a written examination on what one Commissioner felicitously called 'fitness for future functions'.[1] The written examination, however, is not always demanded, and the ratings given by the deputies or their subordinates are frequently final and conclusive.[2]

This scheme of dealing with promotions is defended on the negative ground that any other plan would be much worse. It is freely admitted by all that, in spite of the theory of ministerial responsibility, a member of the Cabinet should not be allowed to promote employees, partly because he knows nothing about them, but chiefly because he might advance his own party's friends. The advocates of the present plan argue also that the deputy head is likewise unsuited to make promotions because he is subject to party pressure through his Minister. There is probably some truth in this contention. One case was brought to my notice in which a Minister (before 1919) desired his deputy to increase the pay of a certain employee. The deputy refused to comply unless all the men of the same rank received the same treatment, and the result was that six employees got a raise in salary instead of one. One deputy testified in 1923 that during twenty-seven years' service he had never had any pressure put upon him to promote any one, but such complete immunity is rare, and past years have known instances of Ministers using their positions to influence the advancement of subordinates in whom they were personally or politically interested.[3]

It is important to note, however, that the abuses feared arise largely from temporary causes. The service has only recently been cleansed of patronage and some of the mud still clings, with the natural result that there are many politically appointed employees who are able to find friends in the Cabinet and are willing to use them. But this is obviously a

---

[1] *Can. H. of C. Journals*, 1923, Appendix, § 5, pp. 706-7, 822-6, 886-7.
[2] *Ibid.*, p. 888. This is denied by some deputies, pp. 625-6, 794.
[3] *Ibid.*, pp. 614, 822.

condition of the transitionary period and will eventually disappear. So long as appointments were made chiefly by the party, the appointing power had a real interest and motive in helping its protégées in their subsequent careers. But now that these appointments have been largely stopped and men no longer enter the service because of political influence (except in very inferior positions), the use of 'pull' at a later period will not have the same excuse for its continuance. Another temporary condition is the lack of ministerial conscience and the slowness of the public to realize that political influence in the civil service is almost abolished. Both of these factors have strengthened the arguments of those who wish to give promotions to the Commission, but both have begun to lose their force. Such elements in the problem can justify at best only a temporary control by the Commission, and not a permanent relinquishment to them of the promoting power.

The deputy head would appear to be the natural one to determine the advancement of any employee under his control. His is the actual task of running the department, his the responsibility (next to the Minister) if anything goes wrong, his the thankless duty of allowing the Minister to take the credit if things go well, his the direction of the subordinate officers, his, logically, the dispensing of rewards in the form of salary increases and promotions. To quote the words of the Under Secretary of State in 1923:

'It was laid down a very long time ago, as a fundamental principle of conduct, that a man cannot serve two masters. . . . The civil servant at the present time takes his directions from the deputy minister, but he looks for promotion and preferment to the Civil Service Commission. . . . I think, as every business man knows, the person who must distribute favours is the man who gets the work done, and when you get away from that you are putting things on a wrong business principle.' [1]

The argument is difficult, if not impossible, to answer, nor does it stand alone. The qualities which must be weighed in making promotions are for the most part intangible—honesty,

---

[1] *Can. H. of C. Journals*, 1923, Appendix, § 5, pp. 622-3.

reliability, alertness, rapid absorption, quick analysis, resourcefulness, attractive personality, good habits—these are
not easily ascertained by any written examination on 'fitness
for future functions', but they can be readily and accurately
passed on by a superior officer who has had years to observe
the candidates at their work. An occasional lapse into
favouritism is better to endure than the wooden, impersonal
knowledge of the Commission. The latter in the vast majority
of cases knows almost nothing of the nature of the vacant
office or of the offices which the candidates have been holding
save what is written in the *Schedule*, nor are the Commission's
assistants usually qualified to set a promotion examination
without using members of the department.

In short, the transfer of the making of promotions to the
Civil Service Commission has been a great mistake; it is a
complete misreading of the functions for which that body was
created. The *Report of Transmission* considered the judgement of entrance qualifications and of promotions as essentially the same—a supposition impossible to justify. The
most important requirement for selecting candidates on
entrance is impartiality, that for judging candidates for
promotion is an intimate knowledge of the office and the
men. The Commission can, with help, set examinations for
admission: it can do this efficiently and impartially, in a
manner which no other body or person can equal. But to make
promotions demands a different kind of knowledge and an
intimate contact with the work and personnel of a particular
department, which the Commission does not possess, and
which the deputies and their assistants have in an unusual
degree. It is true that the Civil Service Commission is able
to guarantee impartiality, but impartiality so far removed
from other essential qualifications is not worth having. The
Nizam of Hyderabad would doubtless be an ideal examiner
for the Canadian service if the only requirement were independence of undesirable influences, but he would lack a
knowledge of conditions which would make his neutrality of
secondary importance. Control of promotions by the Commission might possibly be tolerated for a few years until the
service is firmly established on a merit basis, but as soon as

this takes place, the power should be given back to the deputy heads where it belongs. If it is still desired to remove all suspicion of partiality, favouritism, or politics from the minds of unsuccessful candidates, the deputy head might act on the advice of a promotion board composed of the head of the branch immediately concerned, the departmental personnel officer, and any chiefs in the department who are well acquainted with the work of the position or the past achievements of the applicants. Any aggrieved candidate or any employee who might feel that he had not been given adequate consideration might be allowed an appeal to the deputy head.

It may be argued, however, that inasmuch as the ratings are now supplied by the deputies, and as these are often accepted without any examination, the power of making most promotions is really not in the hands of the Commission at all. The Commission, however, is the sole judge of the necessity for its own interference: it passes on all ratings, and its opinion is final as to the adequacy and accuracy of the recommendations given. Furthermore, the Act places the deputy heads in a position of definite inferiority in this respect; they resent it deeply, they co-operate half-heartedly with the Commission, and inevitably discipline within the service suffers. Finally, if the deputies really promote—as the Commission alleges—the civil servants are deluding themselves with shadows: they believe that promotions have been taken from the deputies, while in fact no change has been made. The Act apparently discloses a sense of humour no less deep than the promotion schedule.

Promotion examinations were introduced into Canada by the Act of 1882; they remained in force until 1908, when they were made optional; and in the following years they were gradually allowed to die out. The Act of 1919 reintroduced them by giving the Commission the power to require written tests when they were thought necessary, and they now form an important part of the promotion process.

The desirability of any such test at all may be seriously questioned. It has already been suggested that the written test is unable to discover adequately the qualities on which promotions are based, and that other means are available which will do this with relative ease. Also, the age of many candidates would work against their success in a written examination. The younger men would almost invariably do better than those who had spent many years in the service; not because the former would know more about the subject, but simply because they would be intellectually more agile.[1] Another difficulty to be confronted is the subject-matter of promotion examinations. Academic tests are ruled out for they would be unsuited to the aim in view, and would also be quite beyond the ability of any civil servant to pass without a special and arduous preparation. The usual subject assigned is 'fitness for future functions', i.e. the duties of the new office and the candidates' capacity to discharge them, but the written examination is ill adapted to discover merit of this kind with any great accuracy. If the questions are concerned with the duties of the old office, the really able clerk has little advantage over the routineer; if they deal with the duties of the office to which the promotion is to be made, none of the candidates know enough about the subject to make it a fair test, or one man alone in the department may have had unusual opportunities to acquire some superficial knowledge of that office's work.

'Promotion by examination or by any system of mechanical evaluation of record', says Sir Stanley Leathes, 'should, in my opinion, be avoided wherever possible. The human mind, duly fortified by knowledge, experience, and sympathy, is a much more delicate and accurate measure of human beings than any of these devices borrowed from the laboratory. The only effective obstacle to jobbery in promotion is a high standard of integrity in public administration; the only guarantee of wise—which is also fair—promotion is the wisdom and watchfulness of the chief officers; promotion by mere seniority has its own drawbacks hardly less than those of favouritism. We cannot make the judgment of our promoting authorities infallible; methods designed as scientific are, in my opinion, illusory; good will, with a good system of observation and varied trial of individuals, should produce the best results that are humanly possible.'[2]

---

[1] Cf. *supra*, p. 147.
[2] Leathes, Sir Stanley, ' Public Servants at Home and Abroad', *Journal of Public Administration*, 1925, pp. 72-3.

In certain exceptional positions, however, promotion examinations have been used successfully for years. If promotion depends not so much on a general increase in efficiency and the personal qualities already mentioned but more on acquired technical knowledge, the latter may be tested by written or practical examination. The customs and excise have used promotion examinations profitably to measure such things as the officials' knowledge of tariff classification, differentiation, valuation, &c. But even in these special instances it is much wiser to use the test as only a minimum qualification for advancement, and allow the employees' general efficiency, as judged by the deputy head, to be the deciding factor.

The classification of 1919 was intended to check promotions which were made without any conspicuous merit on the part of the civil servant and without any noticeable change in his duties. In this it has been largely successful. Until 1919 it was a very common thing for employees to be advanced in rank for faithfulness and length of service while doing precisely the same work; but to-day there can be no promotion of this kind unless a vacancy occurs in the higher office. This has, however, the opposite fault: while the earlier system was too elastic, this one is too rigid. If the deputy wishes to reward efficiency, and no one above the meritorious official is obliging enough to step out, his only course is to apply to the Commission for the creation of a new 'class'. The Commission thereupon sends to the department an investigator who goes through the motions of studying the situation as an expert, and reports on the advisability of following the deputy's advice. If the Commission decides to create the new class, it reports to the Governor in Council to that effect, and the latter then changes the official's classification. The difficulty of promotions of this kind prevents many unnecessary ones being made, but at the same time it stops many good men receiving the advancement they have earned.

Another bad habit in the service has been the granting of increases in salary as a reward for seniority rather than efficiency. In 1897 this practice had become so common that the Postmaster General asked the Minister of Justice for a

legal opinion whether the civil servants were entitled to
increases as a matter of right, provided they had not been
guilty of misconduct or neglect of duty.[1] Fourteen years
later a civil servant, in an excellent article in the Ottawa
Citizen, described the habit of granting indiscriminate increases of salary as the chief fault of the service:

'It would be supposed that in all matters affecting increases,
promotions or changes, these heads (of branches) would always
be consulted by the deputy. . . . I do not know of a single department in which this is done. . . . It is regarded as the comfortable
plan to give everybody the annual statutory increase, and nobody
a special increase. . . . We are here in contact with the chief
imperfection in the civil service system—the lack of an honest
discrimination in the giving of statutory increases, and the still
more conspicuous lack of a judicial spirit in the dispensation of
discipline.

'The amended Civil Service Act of 1908 made specific provision
for the rewarding of conspicuous merit by the granting of an
annual increment of $100. . . . The service will continue to be un-
attractive as a career so long as it is not the practice to make a
clear and substantial difference between the treatment accorded
to a highly efficient clerk and a mere time server. . . . As a matter
of history not a single $100 increment has been granted to clerks
below the rank of the first division.' [2]

The classification of 1919 provided minimum, intermediate,
and maximum salaries for each class. The *Report of Transmission* (confirmed by the later Act) stated that the increases
should take place only for merit on the recommendation of
the deputy head and with the approval of the Commission,
and that no employee who reached the maximum should
have any increase in salary while he remained in that class.[3]
Thus the Commission has the final word in the granting of
salaries as well as in making promotions, and it may even
demand from the deputy evidence and records to substan-
tiate his recommendations. Necessarily, however, this check
on the deputy is largely nominal, for the Commission cannot
begin to give the time which a careful scrutiny would involve.

[1] *Can. Sess. Pap.,* 1897, § 47. The Minister replied in the negative.
[2] 21 Oct. 1911.
[3] pp. 30–1; *Can. Stat.,* 10 Geo. V, c. 10, section 45B.

The invariable result is that increases in salaries continue to be made automatically every year until the employees reach the maximum for their respective classes. Even this barrier may be passed by promotion to another class with a higher maximum, but such changes are usually made only for really deserving officials. The classification has therefore succeeded in making few improvements save to set a limit to the number of automatic increases an employee may receive.

Salaries in the service, particularly in the higher ranks, are deplorably low; and the results are made even more unfortunate by the statutory provision that an officer must be appointed at the minimum for his class, and by the severe limits imposed in the *Schedule*, which renders any great or sudden increase for conspicuous merit almost impossible.[1] The low salary fails to attract the best men to the service, and fails to retain the best of those who have entered. While the Government cannot be expected to compete with private business concerns in the salaries paid to its officials, it should be able to compete in attractiveness; and the remuneration is one of the most important items. The more secure tenure, greater honour and importance, salary, pension, &c., of public service should make an appeal to the ambitious young man equal to that presented by the larger salary but more uncertain future of private life.

'I am all in favour of paying good salaries,' said Lord Haldane, 'because, in the main, you get what you pay for, and it is still more clear that you do not get what you do not pay for. That is human nature, and it is as strongly implanted in the miner as the State official. The State official, hitherto, has been the patient beast of burden who has been underpaid, and whose salary has risen very slightly compared with the cost of living. Equally good salaries do not mean the salaries which rich men require in order to live as rich men. Your general in the Army, your colonel, your captain, your admiral in the Navy, your commander, live on what the rich man often calls very little indeed, but the reward comes to them in another way. They have social advantages which he has not. They are rewarded by the public, by honours, and by positions which tell. I do not like that being a monopoly of the

---

[1] *Can. Stat.*, 10 Geo. V, c. 10, section 45B; *Can. H. of C. Journals*, 1923, Appendix, § 5, p. 656.

fighting services. I want to see it extended to the other administrative services of the State, and I think it can be. It has been partly extended to the Civil Service, and I want it extended to those larger Civil Services of which we are speaking. . . . There are many kinds of glory. The glory of a popular preacher is very great, but he does not demand a large salary. The glory of a successful politician may be very great, and often he is as poor as a rat, but he does not mind. He has much more. He can dine with millionaires each night if he pleases.' [1]

[1] *Coal Industry Commission, Volume II (Great Britain),* 1919, Cmd. 360, p. 1090.

X. TENURE: REMOVAL: RETIREMENT: WOMEN

'All unaided are you acting,
  Or do they provide assistance?
When you're busy, have you got to
  Get up early in the morning?
If you do what you ought not to,
  Do they give the usual warning?'
                    The Gondoliers.

CIVIL servants in Canada have always held office legally at pleasure, actually during good behaviour. Before the time of responsible government all positions were held under this tenure, and the subsequent introduction of a responsible Cabinet left most offices unchanged in this respect. The new scheme necessarily caused the tenure of the few political heads of departments to become much more precarious; but that of the civil servants proper, as Lord Grey was careful to indicate in 1847, remained undisturbed.[1] This condition has continued to the present time. Although the *Civil Service Act, 1918*, explicitly states that 'all appointments to the civil service shall be during pleasure',[2] nevertheless the customary tenure during good behaviour is retained and applied as before.

This contradiction between custom and law has, of course, its justification. The law retains for the Ministry the ultimate word in the retention of an employee, and should it be necessary to discharge any one for cause, the action can be taken promptly and without friction. A frequent use of the power of removal, however, is considered to be neither desirable nor expedient, and the customary good behaviour tradition operates as a check on indiscriminate dismissals. The permanent tenure, while it undoubtedly tends under some circumstances to lead to laziness and lack of initiative, has certain definite merits. It enables the civil servant to obtain a familiarity with his work which he can acquire only after long experience and practice, and gives him that expertness which the amateur Minister demands of his subordinates. The permanent tenure is therefore absolutely essential in the

[1] Cf. *supra*, pp. 11–12.   [2] Section 10.

scientific, technical, and quasi-judicial branches of the service, and almost as much so for the higher administrative and clerical positions. The spoils system was inefficient, not solely because it appointed poor men to office whose chief qualification was party activity, but also because it meant a complete turnover of personnel with each change of Government, inevitably accompanied by a loss of knowledge and experience. In addition to the above merits, the permanent tenure also attracts men into the service because of the greater security, and the Government is thus enabled to compete more effectively with private business concerns for the acquisition of young talent. Finally, the civil servant is made more independent and free in the execution of his work; he acts more fearlessly, more honestly, more surely, when he knows that his labours will not be made the subject of a political attack, and that he will not be removed from office because his findings or reports do not happen to meet with the enthusiastic endorsement of the Government of the day.

Removals from office are made by the Governor in Council usually on one of two grounds: political activity, or inefficiency. The former has been by far the more common, and dates back to pre-Confederation times, when the ruling was made that active political partisanship constituted 'official misconduct' contrary to the 'good behaviour' tradition and would justify summary dismissal.[1] The habit of appointing only political friends to office, and of expecting them to support the Ministry which gave them their places, led inevitably to ruthless dismissals when the administration changed, in order that the balance of party strength might be restored. In this way the rule which had been originally endorsed by the Colonial Office as an aid to better and purer government resulted somewhat unexpectedly in a 'spoils system' on a moderate scale. This condition persisted as long as appointments were made for party reasons, and when the latter began to diminish, the number of dismissals for political partisanship decreased also. To-day these dismissals are comparatively rare, and are confined almost entirely to those offices which are still filled by party nomination.

[1] Cf. *supra*, pp. 14–17.

The method of testing the truth of the alleged political partisanship of a civil servant is, however, not entirely satisfactory. The old way was to regard with suspicion any of the opposite party's appointments and dismiss them summarily if any partisan activity was charged. To-day the deliberate accusation of a member of Parliament that to his own knowledge the civil servant has been guilty of offensive partisanship will lead to removal, or, if the charge be laid by more irresponsible persons, the Government will appoint commissioners to investigate and report.[1] The best and most impartial method was probably that laid down by an Order in Council in 1918, which gave the power of inquiry and recommendation to the Civil Service Commissioners, who were to be guided in their decision solely by the public interest and the official's record.[2] While any unusual extension of the powers of the Commission should be carefully scrutinized, this procedure had the very great merit of establishing the confidence of the public and of the civil service in the investigating body, and thereby escaping the imputation of partisanship which is apt to be brought against *ad hoc* commissioners appointed by the administration. The Order in Council of 1918 was followed in two or three cases, but the Government apparently found such investigation too impartial for its liking. The Order was temporary and was not renewed, and the practice described above was substituted.

The question of the political activity of the civil servant is now fairly definitely settled. Disfranchisement is not seriously discussed to-day except as a possible part of a scheme to make Ottawa a federal district like Washington or Canberra. The present *Civil Service Act* contains a clause forbidding all public officials to engage in any partisan work and distinguishes between the right to vote and the right actively to support a candidate at an election.

'No deputy head, officer, clerk or employee in the civil service shall be debarred from voting at any Dominion or provincial election if, under the laws governing the said election, he has the right to vote; but no such deputy head, officer, clerk or employee

[1] Cf. *supra*, pp. 102–3.   [2] Cf. *supra*, pp. 91–2.

shall engage in partisan work in connexion with any such election, or contribute, receive or in any way deal with any money for any party funds.

Any person violating any of the provisions of this section shall be dismissed from the civil service.' [1]

A prohibition of such a sweeping nature appears at first glance to be unprofitable to the public and unjust to the civil servants. A democracy should strive to interest all classes of the community in its government, and particularly those who by education and training are best fitted to make intelligent decisions. The civil servants undoubtedly fall in the latter group. They are in constant contact with the country's administration, they understand its faults, they have decided opinions on the possible remedies, they have an especial interest caused by the fact that they may suffer a change of masters; in short, they have the qualities and inducements to form sound judgements and to aid in shaping intelligent public opinion. Yet their share in the election is definitely restricted by law to the casting of a ballot, and any further activity is punishable by expulsion from the service.

The unquestioned fitness of the civil servant to participate in elections is, however, but one phase of the problem. He is not only a citizen and a member of a democracy, but a public official and that democracy's servant; and it is his public position and not his private talents that leads to a curtailment of his political activity. He is no longer regarded, as he was before 1908, or even before 1918, as a member of a partisan body: he is now independently appointed, he owes his position to no political party, and if he has party prejudices he is supposed to be discreetly reticent. This tradition of impartiality, which is necessarily still young in Canada, must be maintained at all costs. The public and the civil servants themselves must learn to regard the service as an unprejudiced neutral body which will give unquestioned allegiance to whatever master the people may wish to choose.

'We think', reported a British Royal Commission in 1914, 'that if restrictions on the political activities of public servants were

---

[1] *Can. Stat.*, 8–9 Geo. V, c. 12, section 32.

withdrawn, two results would probably follow. The public might cease to believe, as we think they do now with reason believe, in the impartiality of the permanent Civil Service ; and Ministers might cease to feel the well-merited confidence which they possess at present in the loyal and faithful support of their official subordinates ; indeed they might be led to scrutinise the utterances or writings of such subordinates, and to select for positions of confidence only those whose sentiments were known to be in political sympathy with their own.

'If this were so, the system of recruitment by open competition would prove but a frail barrier against Ministerial patronage in all but the earlier years of service ; the Civil Service would cease to be in fact an impartial non-political body, capable of loyal service to all Ministers and parties alike ; the change would soon affect the public estimation of the Service, and the result would be destructive of what undoubtedly is at present one of the greatest advantages of our administrative system and one of the most honourable traditions of our public life.' [1]

The British Commission, however, was willing to make a partial exception for subordinate employees in the Post Office and other departments, and suggested that an order forbidding such officials 'using their official positions in any way to influence elections' would be sufficient.[2] Such an exception could not be tolerated in Canada, for it would lead inevitably to a return of the spoils. Indeed, the chief difficulty has always been, not with the highest officers of the service, but rather with the humble country postmasters, lighthouse keepers, lock tenders, &c. These in their little communities represent the Civil Service, and if they be openly partisan, public confidence in the whole organization will be shaken, and one of the greatest benefits of reform will be destroyed. Such a display of partisanship would also give ammunition to the supporters of the opposite party which could be used to besiege their members of Parliament, and the latter would probably, as in times past, surrender ignominiously and demand the removal of the offenders. An unusual case occurred in 1921 when three employees of the Canadian National Railways were dismissed from office be-

---

[1] *Fourth Report of the Commissioners*, 1914, Cd. 7338, p. 97.
[2] *Ibid.*, p. 98.

cause they had been candidates in provincial elections; but they were later reinstated.[1] This would appear to be a legitimate exception to the general rule, for a clear distinction exists between employees in State industrial enterprises and the public service proper.

A second ground for removal is lack of ability; and although many governments have been prompt and even eager to remove for political partisanship, all have shown great reluctance to dismiss for inefficiency alone. In 1881, for example, the Royal Commission, after it had called attention to the shocking condition of the service, due in large measure to faulty appointments, made the following statement:

'We have felt that it would be both arbitrary and unjust to dismiss from the service in a summary manner men who, however unfit, have been in it many years, and who have been brought into a service for which they have little aptitude, by a faulty system for which they are not responsible, and under which there is an implied contract between the government and its employees, that they should not be dismissed except for gross misconduct. To dismiss those men now for causes other than those implied by the practice which prevailed at the time they were appointed would be unjust, and would have the effect of reducing them to penury.' [2]

The same difficulty has existed up to the present time. A Special Committee of the House of Commons, appointed in 1919 to inquire into the Civil Service, reported that 'the method of dismissal provided by section 28 of the Act [3] is too formal and difficult of accomplishment to lead to the results which no doubt were contemplated when the section was adopted, and in consequence the efficiency of the service is impaired.'[4] The Committee further reported that removals were virtually never made, and even when recommendations to that effect were put forward, they were not acted upon. The *Report of Transmission*, which was drafted in the same year, came to a similar conclusion. 'Our contact with the

[1] *The Times (London)*, 3 Feb., 16, 1921.
[2] *Can. Sess. Pap.*, 1880–1, § 113, p. 45.
[3] i.e. by the Governor in Council.
[4] *Can. H. of C. Journals*, July 4, 1919, p. 518.

Canadian Civil Service has given us the impression that employees are seldom removed except by the hand of death. . . .
The impression that we have received is that discharges on account of general unfitness or low standard of efficiency are rarely made.'[1]

The *Report of Transmission*, however, in trying to find a solution of the problem, decided there was no problem at all. 'The process of removal may be considered as the reverse of the process of appointment, and the same principles apply.'[2] Discover the inefficiency, said the Report, keep a record of it, and remove on the basis of this record. 'An employee, no matter how he came into the service, has only a right to a position while that position exists or for the period during which it is necessary to keep it filled.'[3] To this end it was suggested that a policy of 'lay-off' be followed if the position should become unnecessary, that old officials be pensioned, and that the inefficient be speedily dismissed.[4]

Although the subsequent Act [5] was intended to give effect to most of these proposals, dismissals for inefficiency are as rare as before. The law is adequate, but not the practice; nor is it likely to be so. A feeling undoubtedly exists in the public mind that a Government should not discharge employees with the same freedom as private corporations, and that occasional inefficiency is preferable to the harshness of dismissal. What makes the situation more difficult is that this feeling is shared to some extent by the higher public officials, and when they approach the actual point of advising a removal they usually draw back. They are reluctant to be the immediate cause of a man losing his job, and as an alternative will give the employee less important work to perform, and place him where he can do little harm. The story is told of an old man in the British service who had been engaged for years on a certain work, the necessity for which had eventually passed. When he was told that it was no longer needed, he tried unsuccessfully to drown himself in a pond on Clapham Common. He was brought back and told to continue his task, which he did

---

[1] *Report of Transmission*, pp. 53–4.   [2] *Ibid.*, p. 52.
[3] *Ibid.*, p. 58.   [4] *Ibid.*, pp. 52–9.
[5] *Can. Stat.*, 10 Geo. V, c. 10, section 5.

to the increased happiness of all concerned. This type of
case, though fortunately few are as extreme as this, is quite
common; and the Government finds that it is impossible
to discard employees like inefficient machines: there is a
brutality in the act for which few can be found to take the
responsibility.

Prompt dismissal for inefficiency is made more difficult also
by the size and nature of the service itself. Any large business
establishment finds that the discharge of employees is com-
plicated by the diffusion and dispersion that an extensive
organization entails. The real head of the business is unable
to acquaint himself with all the facts of the case, his information comes to him second- or third-hand, he never knows how
large a part may be played by prejudice and personal dislike,
and he is as a consequence most careful in applying so drastic
a remedy as discharge. The Governor in Council is in the
same position, with this additional reason for caution, that
the reverberations following a dismissal, whether it be fair
or unfair, do not subside rapidly, and are apt to have political
results which cannot be ignored.

This statement is no solution of the problem; on the contrary, it is an admission that no satisfactory solution has yet
been found. A scheme of efficiency records and departmental
ratings which would automatically discharge the inefficient
might be worked out as suggested by the *Report of Transmission*, but the attitude of the public and the higher civil
servants would probably render it inoperative. The employee who is clearly unsuited to his work from the time of
entrance can be discharged without hesitation during the
probationary period. The old employee who is guilty of gross
misconduct or dishonesty can also be dismissed without any
grave qualms of conscience. The difficulty arises in its acute
form with those old faithful employees who are duffers, or
who have failed to maintain their usefulness and have developed what Mr. Sidney Webb calls 'potterer's rot'. These
have established a kind of vested right to their office, and
the difficulty of dismissal varies directly with every year of
service. In a great number of instances such an employee's
experience has not fitted him for any position in private life;

he cannot very well get another Government to employ him, and he is unable to set up a post-office or administer a customs tariff of his own. Yet to maintain him in inefficiency is poor economy and tends to weaken the morale of all his associates. Something may be done to jar him into activity and fresh interest by moving him around in the department, by giving him a new kind of work, or by placing him under a more stimulating superior. Another aid which might be invoked is a pension system, which would permit retirement before the normal age to officers who lack sufficient ability to carry on their work. Such a scheme, though nominally expensive, would be in the long run an economy.

Superannuation of old employees is therefore intimately related to the problem of dismissal. Canadian Royal Commissions have paid it constant attention [1] and it has given rise to a number of statutes. In 1870 a *Superannuation Act* was passed granting retiring allowances to those members of the service who had made regular contributions to a fund established for that purpose.[2] This plan was open to the objection that many employees, having contributed for years, might die before retirement, and neither they nor their families could recover any of the payments made. Accordingly in 1898 the Act was repealed for all future civil servants, and a *Retirement Act* substituted.[3] This authorized the deduction of five per cent. of each employee's salary, compounding it twice a year at four per cent. interest, and paying the total to the civil servant or his heirs on retirement, dismissal, resignation, or death. Both these statutes remained in force until 1924, when another *Superannuation Act* was passed which will ultimately supersede the others.[4] Under the provisions of this Act each employee [5] who enters after 1924 must pay five per cent. of his annual salary into a common fund, in return for which he will receive the following privileges:

[1] *Can. Sess. Pap.*, 1882, § 32, pp. 13–84; *ibid.*, 1892, § 16 c, pp. lxxiii–lxxviii; *ibid.*, 1907–8, § 29 A, pp. 21–3; *ibid.*, 1913, § 57 A, pp. 18–19.
[2] *Can. Stat.*, 35 Vic. c. 4; 46 Vic. c. 8.
[3] *Ibid.*, 61 Vic. c. 17.
[4] *Ibid.*, 14–15 Geo. V, c. 69.
[5] He must receive at least $600 a year.

(a) Superannuation at sixty-five years of age.

(b) Superannuation before that age, if he is disabled or incapacitated, or if his office is abolished.

(c) Payment in a lump sum without interest of all money contributed if the employee should leave the service for causes other than misconduct or those above mentioned.

(d) Allowances to widow and children in the event of the death of the civil servant, either before or after his superannuation.

A theoretical justification for some system of superannuation is easily found. The Civil Service cannot attain the highest peak of efficiency unless a constant flow of promotions is maintained, while this in turn cannot be secured unless the old officials are continually and regularly being retired, and new men promoted to their places. An adequate provision for retirement will lead inevitably to the older members being willing to accept a pension and make way for younger and more useful talent. It will also overcome to a large degree the reluctance of the deputy head to advise retirement, for he will know that, even though the official may not wish to resign, no actual hardship need occur if his resignation is forced. Superannuation also pays its own way. The retention of old and inefficient men, which so frequently occurs when superannuation is not available, is expensive; for it is usually accompanied by an increase in the numbers of the staff in order that the normal work of the service may be performed. The men who should retire are naturally the older ones, and they receive the high salary while those below earn it. 'A government', said the Deputy Minister of Finance in 1907, 'simply cannot get rid of those who, worthy in themselves, and who have given years of honest service, have outgrown their usefulness, and must carry them on at high salaries while younger men have to be employed to do the work.' [1]

The more indirect effects of superannuation are equally beneficial. Greater efficiency is secured because the service is made more attractive to those who wish to enter and to

[1] *Can. Sess. Pap.*, 1907–8, § 29 A, p. 214.

those who are already employed. Some candidates, for example, are induced to apply for admission because they desire the security which a pension system gives, while some of the best of the Government officials refuse tempting offers from private enterprise solely because of their reluctance to give up valuable superannuation privileges. The absence of a pension system and the consequent presence of old, inefficient employees weakens the morale of the entire service, and often causes even the most energetic and ambitious officials to become lax and indifferent towards their work. A plan of systematic retirement has the opposite effect: loyalty to the Government, *esprit de corps*, good conduct, freedom from worry—all are probably increased to some degree, and all contribute indirectly to efficiency.

Judged by these criteria the old *Retirement Act* was clearly inadequate. It offered no inducements either at entrance or later; it merely refunded, with four per cent. interest, the money which had been deducted from the salary. It had, however, one good quality: it may have enabled the deputy heads more readily to advise retirements, because they would realize that the employees would not leave the service penniless. But there are obvious disadvantages to the payment of a lump sum which do not attach to the payment of an annual allowance. The result was that the *Retirement Act* was condemned by Royal Commissions, members of Parliament, and the civil servants themselves, and a general wish expressed that the earlier statute should be re-enacted.

The Act of 1924 is really the old *Superannuation Act* with improvements. It is eminently fair, and insures not only the civil servant against want, but his wife and family also. The latter protection was lacking in the early statute, and was its one conspicuous weakness. The chief criticism which might be brought against the present Act is that it makes the civil servant pay in part for the privileges which he enjoys. There would seem to be no reason, save that of economy, why any payments whatsoever should be required of the employee. It does not seem to be too much to ask that any official who has given years of service to the State should be given a liberal pension without any preliminary contributions on his part. It should be a free gift by the Government to its employees for faithful work rendered on its behalf. The salaries are sufficiently low that no one need have any conscientious qualms that the civil servant would receive more than he deserved.

The *Superannuation Act, 1924,* makes retirement compulsory when the allowance is offered to the civil servant, though it is careful to add that 'such offer shall not be considered as implying any censure on the person to whom it is made, nor shall any person be considered as having a right to such allowance, but it shall be granted only in consideration of good and faithful service'.[1] The way is thus made easier for the officials in the department to recommend the superannuation of the inefficient. A further compulsory element in the Act is the section which makes retirement obligatory for any one who has attained the age of seventy years. This rule, like the similar one in the British service, is subject to certain exceptions:

'If the deputy head of any department reports . . . that on account of his peculiar efficiency and fitness for his position the continuance in office of such contributor beyond the said age is in the public interest, and if such report is concurred in by the head of the department and the Treasury Board, the Governor in Council may extend annually the service of such contributor beyond the said age for a period not exceeding five years.' [2]

The general rule, taken in conjunction with the exception, is aimed to produce that combination of rigidity and flexibility which will do the most good and the least harm. Compulsory retirement at seventy might compel a few of the most experienced servants to resign their work at a very critical time or before it was concluded. To allow retirement to be optional would result inevitably in many useless men being retained because the deputies lacked the courage to pension them and did not wish to hurt their feelings. The provisions of the Act steer a middle course. Inefficient employees will be allowed to shift to the superannuation list, exceptionally good men will be retained for a few years more, and yet the process of retention is at the same time made so

[1] *Can. Stat.,* 14–15 Geo. V, c. 69, section 10.   [2] *Ibid.*

difficult that it will be used only when necessary. Occasional instances may arise where the Act will be found too rigorous, but its rigidity in all but unusual cases will be the test of its effectiveness. Compulsion which does not compel is of little use, and the rule must be formulated to meet the ordinary, everyday case. It is therefore far better to retire one very efficient man before his time of intellectual activity is over than to retain ten inefficient men year after year to the detriment of an entire department. One criticism of the Act might be made: the age of retirement is too advanced—sixty or sixty-five would be far preferable to seventy.

'It is believed', wrote the Civil Service Commission in 1925, 'that the *Superannuation Act* [of 1924] will solve many problems that hitherto have yielded to neither classification nor reorganization. As a result, the Government will now be free to retire officers who have outlived their usefulness, a proper flow of promotions will be created, the service will be rendered more mobile, reorganization will be simplified and business administration improved, with greater efficiency and economy in the public service.' [1]

One of the most serious questions which the Civil Service has had to face in recent years has been the general position of women in Government employ. At the time of Confederation no 'woman problem' existed; but each year thereafter it became more and more important. The Royal Commission of 1868 did not mention any positions for women in its theoretical organization of the departments,[2] while a review of the existing staff (as tabulated in the Report) reveals the name of only one woman, and for this an apology was appended in a foot-note stating that 'it is not proposed hereafter to employ female house-keepers.'[3] In 1881 the women in the service were few, they occupied very subordinate positions, and it was generally felt that they were in their proper places. One witness, for example, testified that 'they can work usefully, but it is difficult to make any arrangements for utilizing their work with convenience.'[4] Others also

---

[1] *Can. Sess. Pap.*, 1925, § 24, p. viii.
[2] *Ibid.*, 1869, § 19; *ibid.* 1870, § 64.
[3] *Ibid.*, 1869, § 19, p. 54.   [4] *Ibid.*, 1880–1, § 113, p. 69.

admitted that the women did good work in subordinate positions, but there was a general perplexity felt as to how they could be segregated and at the same time supervised effectively. The Royal Commission gave its opinion somewhat naïvely as follows:

'While we see no reason whatever why female clerks should not be quite as efficient public servants as men, we are forced to confess that there are several obstacles in the way of their employment which we fear it will be very difficult if not impossible to overcome. For example, it would be necessary that they should be placed in rooms by themselves, and that they should be under the immediate supervision of a person of their own sex; but we doubt very much if sufficient work of similar character can be found in any one Department to furnish occupation for any considerable number of female clerks, and it would certainly be inadvisable to place them in small numbers throughout the Departments. Should circumstances hereafter arise warranting the employment of female clerks, we see no objection to their being appointed as clerks of the third class.' [1]

By 1891 the women employed had greatly increased in number; and although they still occupied minor positions, they were accepted as a permanent part of the staff. The testimony before the Royal Commission of that year almost invariably conceded that they were efficient and the equal of male clerks doing similar work.[2] By 1907 the problem had become more serious, though the difficulties encountered had completely changed. The questions of segregation and supervision had become unimportant and had given way to the much more acute ones of promotion and salary. The Royal Commission reported as follows:

'The Commissioners have to draw attention to another set of circumstances which has cropped up during the last few years, and that is the great redundance of women appointed to the junior branches in the inside service. . . . In Ottawa in 1906, out of the 206 candidates who passed the qualifying examination, 121 were women. The lower grades of the Post Office, where there are 366 employees altogether, and the lower grades of the Department of the Interior, where there are some 500 employees, are practically

---

[1] *Ibid.*, p. 29.
[2] *Ibid.*, 1892, § 16 c., pp. 25, 62, 96, 191, 209, 241, 501, 617.

filled up with women. While the Commissioners readily acknowledge that many women are thoroughly entitled to succeed in the public service, yet the influx of such a large number must, if continued, in the course of time utterly swallow up the lower grades of the service, and by limiting the field for promotion to the higher classes prove detrimental to the development of the higher and more responsible branches of the service; for it can hardly be admitted yet that the work devolving on the departments can be carried on with a staff composed entirely of women.' [1]

The evidence taken at this time disclosed three chief difficulties. First: The minimum salary offered was too low to attract good men and yet was higher than most women could obtain elsewhere. Hence the influx of the latter to the inferior positions. Second: Women could not, it was felt, fill the higher posts, and by occupying most of the lower ones they were preventing men from acquiring the valuable experience and training which was necessary for promotion. Third: Admitting that women might be promoted, the great majority of them remained in the service for a few years only, and left when they were married. They did not expect to hold their positions the rest of their lives, and they consequently regarded their work as a temporary alternative which they would abandon whenever the opportunity offered.[2]

In order to meet these difficulties the first annual report of the Civil Service Commissioners in 1910 stated that they 'found it necessary... to limit almost entirely to men appointments in the First and Second Divisions' [3]—a policy which fitted in with the English plan of gradation which was then being tried. Such restrictions, however, were necessarily abandoned during the war, and have never been resumed on the pre-war scale. The *Report of Transmission* made no effort to grapple with the sex question, though the accompanying classification, by its greater definiteness in qualifications, relieved the difficulty to some degree by ear-marking a few offices for women only.

No satisfactory solution to the general problem has yet

---

[1] *Can. Sess. Pap.*, 1907–8, § 29 A, p. 14.
[2] *Ibid.*, pp. 42, 250, 270, 454–5, 1284–5.
[3] *Ibid.*, 1910, § 31, pp. 17–18.

been found, due in a large measure to a lack of facts and to
the prejudice which naturally follows from insufficient knowledge. Everything depends on the answer to the question: Is
a woman as efficient a civil servant in all respects as a man?
To this each sex has its own unhesitating reply, though even
the experience of the war years is by no means conclusive.[1]
It is probably accurate to say, however, that certain offices
can usually be filled more effectively by women, others can,
as a rule, be filled better by men; and a frank recognition of
the superiority of each in its field of service would do much
to clear up the difficulty of their employment. In many
branches of education, poor relief, inspection of factories,
asylums, prisons, and public institutions, librarianship, secre-
tarial and stenographic work, women are undoubtedly to be
preferred to men: they have a greater sympathy, or a more
useful knowledge, or a peculiar talent for such employment.
On the other hand, men are usually better suited and
equipped for administrative, supervisory, technical, and professional duties, and they generally show themselves more
capable of sustained work, more likely to remain long in the
service, and more adaptable and ready to meet emergencies
calling for rapid decision and the assumption of responsibility.[2]

The complete interchangeability of women for men in the
public service will doubtless never be realized. It is undesirable, not only because each sex brings a different mental and
physical equipment to the work, but also because of the temporary nature of most women's employment. Marriage
affects the male and female employees in opposite ways.
When the man gets married, he settles down and clings to his
position more firmly than before, while the woman almost
invariably leaves the service forthwith. The latter has
disastrous results on the efficiency of the staff. The experience and training acquired over a number of years is completely lost, and the reserve of talent available for promotion
is greatly reduced. In short, the departments cannot afford

[1] Cf. *Report of the Machinery of Government Committee (Great Britain)*,
1918, Cd. 9230, pp. 12–14; *Committee on Recruitment of the Civil Service
(Great Britain) Final Report*, 1919, Cmd. 164, pp. 6–12.

[2] *Fourth Report of the Commissioners (Great Britain)*, 1914, Cd. 7338,
pp. 87–92.

the time and effort needed to instruct and train women in the duties of many of the more important offices, for they have no assurance that their staff will be at all permanent. The difficulty seems to be inherent in the woman question, and can be met in only one way: by excluding women, except in exceptional circumstances, from many of the highest posts and those from which the highest posts are to be filled. The equality of salaries, however, should be unhesitatingly endorsed. As long as a woman can do a man's work and do it equally well there can be no sound reason for denying her the man's remuneration.

If the principle of marking off positions for each sex is adopted, the line of division should be drawn with extreme care and with the understanding that the boundary will have to be altered from time to time. The area of female employment is still unduly restricted on account of prejudice and women's present incapacity, although both of these conditions are probably temporary. Prejudice against women occupying the higher positions in the service is still active, especially if these positions involve the supervision of men. This hostility may eventually disappear, but meanwhile it must be considered and an effort made to eliminate it. The best way to begin is by the careful selection and promotion of a few women of exceptional ability to what would normally have been 'male' offices. The promoted few must act as pioneers for their sex, and if they have been wisely chosen they should break down more prejudice than pages of argument. Women's incapacity in certain kinds of work will tend to diminish also. Few women to-day, for example, have the instinct of leadership and the ability to command so well developed as men, but such types are becoming more common as women penetrate farther into business and professional life. The result will be that many more positions will be thrown open to women in the future, and this will continue to increase as their capacities develop and as the prejudice against them breaks down.

XI. THE CIVIL SERVICE COMMISSION: PARLIAMENTARY RESPONSIBILITY

'His eyes should flash with an inborn fire,
  His brow with scorn be wrung;
He never should bow down to a domineering frown,
  Or the tang of a tyrant tongue.
His foot should stamp and his throat should growl,
  His hair should twirl and his face should scowl,
His eyes should flash and his breast protrude,
And this should be his customary attitude.'
                                    H.M.S. Pinafore.

'Now, although we act as one person, we are, in point of fact, two persons.
'Ah, I don't think we can go into that. It is a legal fiction, and legal fictions are solemn things. Situated as we are, we can't recognize two independent responsibilities.'
                                    The Gondoliers.

THE formation of the Civil Service Commission and the introduction of the open competitive examination have been the two most important reforms in the history of the Canadian service. The earliest ancestor of the Commission was the Board of Examiners, which was authorized in the province of Canada ten years before Confederation [1] and two years after the first Civil Service Commission was established in Great Britain. The Board was composed of twelve of the most important civil servants, who, in addition to their regular work, examined candidates and certified to their fitness. The first Dominion body to exercise similar functions was the Civil Service Board, created in 1867 to supervise admissions to the Dominion service. It was made up of the fourteen deputy heads of departments, whose duties in this regard were exactly the same as those of their predecessors. The Board proved decorative rather than useful. After a few years of subdued activity, of examining candidates who had already been appointed, of re-examining the same candidates if they failed to pass, of observing constant infractions of the law by the Government, the Board found itself at last without material to work on. From 1875 to 1880 only one candidate

---

[1] *Can. Stat.*, 20 Vic., c. 24.

was examined, although the deputy heads solemnly met together every month, and the Chairman continued to draw $400 a year for his exertions as convener.[1]

An examining Board which had no one to examine was thus encouraged in its efforts by the Government which had been the chief cause of the travesty. Conceivably the Board had no great desire to enforce the Act, although the Chairman declared in 1877 that it had 'often represented to the Government that the law had not been complied with'.[2] One thing, however, is certain: whatever the desires of the Board may have been, it possessed no powers of initiative, and its usefulness depended entirely on the extent to which the party in power was willing to keep it employed. To this legal inferiority was added a political one; for the members of the Board, being deputy heads of departments, were in no position to argue effectively with their chiefs in the Ministry. In short, the Board lacked the most vital powers, and even the few that it had were dangerously weakened by its close intimacy with the Government. The candidates gradually ceased to appear for examination, and the only authority which could command their attendance was an unsympathetic Ministry which had no desire to hold examinations at all.

The Civil Service Board died in 1882, and was succeeded by the Board of Civil Service Examiners. The latter was composed of three members, appointed by the Governor in Council and holding office at pleasure. The powers of the new body were more extensive than those of its predecessor; but as two out of the three members were engaged elsewhere in the service, its dependence on the Government was much the same as before.

'I must also protest', said George E. Casey, the civil service reformer, 'against the employment of members of the civil service as members of the Board of Examiners. The examiners being dismissible at the pleasure of the Government are sufficiently at their mercy without being selected from men already in the service of the Government, whose whole time is supposed to be bought and paid for by the Government, and who are so much

---

[1] Cf. *supra*, pp. 40–1, 44.   [2] Cf. *supra*, p. 40.

more at the mercy of the Government. A Civil Service Board absolutely at the mercy of the Government of the day is a farce. It cannot, in human nature, be expected to be absolutely fair and unbiased in its transactions.' [1]

The Board of Civil Service Examiners was consequently no great improvement on the older body. Somewhat greater powers combined with a similar dependence on the Ministry were not apt to revolutionize admissions to the civil service. Nor did the members of the Government intend that they should. The chief aim of the Ministers was to clothe a poor system with respectability; and this they did by allowing the Board to set simple examinations calculated to exclude only extreme ignorance, and by appointing to the Board mild, worthy men who would consider it a breach of etiquette to wrangle with the Cabinet. The results were all that a patronage-loving Government might desire—nominal efficiency, strict impartiality, and patronage continuing on its way undisturbed. The Board held its modest examinations and marked the papers with an admirable conscientiousness, while at the same time the Government appointed to office sturdy party men who came at the bottom of the pass list. When the Government wished to avoid the rules, it did so; and the Board respectfully informed it of the infraction. But on most occasions each left the other alone. The Board had little ability and no desire to cause any embarrassment to its masters, for its position was shaky and its members had been chosen for their colourlessness rather than their pugnacity. The different Governments for their part did not tamper with the honest and impartial work of the Board: they had no reason to be dissatisfied, for the activities of the examiners interfered in no appreciable degree with the distribution of patronage.

The introduction of the open competitive examination in 1908 was accompanied by the formation of the present Civil Service Commission. The two (later three) members of the Commission were appointed by the Governor in Council and held office during good behaviour, being removable only by

---

[1] *Can. H. of C. Debates*, 4 Feb. 1890, p. 218; cp. *supra*, pp. 53, 57-8.

the Governor-General on a joint address of both Houses of
Parliament. They were paid a substantial salary, they gave
their entire time to the work, and they supervised the
greater part of appointments, promotions, and general organization of the Inside Service. The later Acts of 1918 and
1919 remedied certain defects in the first statute, increased
the Commission's powers, and extended its jurisdiction to
include virtually the entire service.

The greater usefulness of the present Commission as compared to the earlier Boards is attributable in part to the
genuineness of its functions, and in part also to its independent position. Its powers are no longer imaginary, but real
and vital to the success of the service. It no longer wastes its
time conducting examinations that any one can pass, while
indulging in the futile pretence that the educational standards of the country are being raised as a consequence.
Furthermore, it has the legal power to make its protests
effective if it should encounter opposition in its work. But
these functions, while useful and necessary in themselves,
derive much of their importance and force from the circum-
stance that the Commission is independent of external
control, and is therefore no longer subject to intimidation
by the Government.

The independent position of the Commissioners rests in a
large measure on their tenure during good behaviour. They
are in this respect on an equality with the judges of the
highest courts, and apparently the same broad interpretation
which has been placed on judicial 'good behaviour' is extended to the Commissioners also. Misfeasance in office,
errors in judgement, lack of tact or skill would not constitute 'misbehaviour', but only malfeasance—wrong
deliberately done, partiality or prejudice openly and un-
mistakably shown. An example of the former occurred in
1915 when the Chairman of the Commission made a speech
attacking the Government for its abuse of patronage. The
speech was undoubtedly tactless, and, whatever its truth,
should never have been made by one in the quasi-judicial
position of a Commissioner. A Cabinet Minister described it as
'false and untrue and dishonest in every shape and form. . . .

The statement was made deliberately for the purpose of influencing the electorate of this country politically against the Government.'[1] Other Ministers were no less emphatic in their denunciation.[2] Such a charge, if substantiated, would undoubtedly have constituted 'misbehaviour' and have merited dismissal; but the Commissioner's speech apparently contained more truth than the Government cared to face, and the Ministers made no effort to introduce an address to secure the removal of the offender.

The early Commissioners held office for life, but in 1918 this was changed, so that all future appointments were made for a period of ten years, with compulsory retirement at sixty-five. The change lessened to some degree the independence of the Commissioners. Under the older statute they were quite free to make any legitimate opposition to the Government without fear of the consequences. They remained undisturbed in office until they felt ready to retire. But as the Act stands at present, a Commissioner whose term is almost over may feel it his duty to oppose an influential Minister, while at the same time he may, by his disagreement, ruin his chances of being appointed for another ten-year period. Such a dilemma, while it will occur only at rare intervals, should be made impossible, by a return to the life term. Whenever an official is so placed that he must choose between his duty and his livelihood his independence has completely vanished.

The second entrenchment surrounding the Commissioner's independence is the manner of his removal. He can be dismissed only by the Governor-General after a joint address has been passed by both Houses of Parliament. This in itself makes the process difficult; but if it is applied with the same attendant formalities as used for the removal of a judge (and in the absence of precedent such is a reasonable assumption) the protection becomes far stronger. The custom has now been established that in order to remove a judge there must be a petition for removal, a Select Committee of Inquiry, a

[1] Hon. J. D. Reid, Minister of Customs, *Can. H. of C. Debates*, 4 Mar. 1915, p. 662.
[2] *Ibid.*, pp. 634–87.

report, the passage of the address by both Houses, and the removal by the Governor-General, each of these steps being hedged about with formalities and restrictions.[1] The extension of the same protection to the Commissioners makes them wellnigh irremovable, except for very flagrant cases of misbehaviour. The Civil Service Commissioner 'is not an officer of the Government. The Government cannot remove him; they cannot control him; they cannot give him any orders. The only body which has any authority over him (the Commissioner) is the Parliament of Canada.'[2]

Although this statement is undoubtedly true, the Government can frequently bring about the removal of a Commissioner by indirect methods. Such a policy was followed with the above-mentioned Chairman who had incurred the enmity of the Cabinet. The Ministers hampered and thwarted his work to such a degree, that when he was later offered another position in the service he gladly accepted it and handed in his resignation. Another interesting case occurred in 1926. An investigation of the Customs Department in that year disclosed that two members of the Civil Service Commission had accepted gifts of liquor from the Inspector of Customs at Montreal. The Prime Minister sent for them, and suggested that as their actions had not tended to raise them in the general esteem of the service or of the country they might ask to be relieved of their duties. Their resignations followed.[3] In both these instances the Commissioners might, of course, have retained their positions, if they had wished to await further action. In the first case, it is extremely doubtful whether the Government could have secured a removal, and the actions of the Ministers indicated that they were not disposed to try forcible methods. The later incident was much more serious, and if the matter had been brought to Parliament the joint address would probably have been passed. It is reasonable to assume that this was realized by both the Prime Minister and the Commissioners, and as a result the resignations were handed in without delay.

[1] Cf. Dawson, R. MacG., *The Principle of Official Independence*, pp. 35–9.
[2] Sir Wilfrid Laurier, *Can. H. of C. Debates*, 4 Mar. 1915, p. 635.
[3] *Can. Annual Review*, 1926, p. 80.

'Next to permanency in office', wrote Alexander Hamilton,
'nothing can contribute more to the independence of the
judges than a fixed provision for their support. . . . A power
over a man's subsistence amounts to a power over his will.'[1]
The argument applies to-day equally well to the Civil Service
Commission, and Parliament has indicated its belief by the
policy it has pursued. The Commissioners are paid six thousand dollars a year (seven thousand for the Chairman), and
the salaries are removed from the Annual Vote and paid from
the Consolidated Revenue Fund. Thus in almost every way,
the new ten-year term being the exception, the independence
of the Commissioners is secured like that of the judges, and
no effort is spared to give them a free hand in the administration of the Act. Their position conforms in a striking
degree to the proposed British Commission described in the
letter of Benjamin Jowett to Sir Charles Trevelyan in 1854:

'Considering the nature of the employment, and that everything depends on the fitness of the examiners, their salary should
be liberal. They should be permanent officers, and except for
proved misconduct, irremovable. It is only by the office being
made permanent that all men will in the first instance be induced
to devote themselves to it, or will have the opportunity of
acquiring the experience and facility necessary for doing their work
well. Their irremovability, as in the case of judges, is the best
guarantee for their independence.'[2]

There are, perhaps, certain more intangible factors which
may be used to produce the right kind of independence in the
Commissioners. External surroundings of tenure, removal,
and salary are excellent, and tend to free the members from
the political influence or allegations of political influence
which brought the older examining bodies into disrepute.
But these expedients are only negative: independence must
mean more than a mere removal of interference or a detachment from disagreeable and dangerous influences. It is not
sufficient to check and arrest the disease, the constitution of
the patient must also be built up; positive factors must re-
place those which have been removed. The official must not

[1] *The Federalist*, § 79.
[2] *Can. Sess. Pap.*, 1880–1, § 113, p. 405.

only be protected, but his desire to act impartially must be constantly fostered and encouraged.

Each Commissioner's freedom of will and independent action, for example, are necessarily affected from within by his own personal opinions and prejudices. The manner of appointment and the history of each member before appointment are therefore further points to be considered. The ideal would be for the Government to appoint only the most unbiassed, the most judicial men it could find—men preferably with no definite party leanings and a passion for efficient administration. Their subsequent acts would probably be above any suspicion of undue influence and would command the complete confidence of the service and the public. But Canadian Governments rarely make such appointments, though, on the other hand, they must be given credit for not trying the American device of a bi-partisan board, which seeks to avoid party bias by the strange method of emphasizing it and giving it representation. A number of those who have served on the Commission have been staunch party supporters in early life, and such service has unfortunately not been held against them when their names were mentioned for office. The present Chairman, for example, had previously sat in the Commons for twenty-one years, and had been Secretary of State and Minister of the Interior in the Conservative Government. Preparation of this kind is highly undesirable: a mind trained to party warfare is not easily transformed into one characterized by judicial detachment, and even if the effort to achieve complete neutrality is successful, suspicion will invariably cling to any acts which have the least taint of irregularity. The Canadian Commissioners, however (notably the present Chairman), have been remarkable for their ability to shake off most of the bias and prejudice acquired in their early political careers, but their party history has nevertheless injured the effectiveness of their work and has been the cause of such gibes as the following:

'It is always a most marvellous thing to me that whenever the Civil Service Commission makes any appointment in the part of the country I come from they invariably strike a Tory. . . . If this is an accident, it is a continuous accident in only one direction.'[1]

Commissioners of the proper type having been appointed, they should be surrounded by influences which will stimulate independent and unprejudiced thought and action. They should be made to feel that their position is one of honour and trust, and that they are expected to prove worthy of the responsibility which has been given them. A high tradition in the office is essential if the Commission is to do effective work—a tradition of scrupulous impartiality and justice, of honesty in all its acts, of placing the welfare of the service before any personal or political need. This can arise, of course, only over a long period of years. Further, the Commissioners should maintain a judicial aloofness from all political affairs. They should be forbidden, for example, either by law or custom, to speak on any controversial question or to identify themselves in any way whatsoever with any party matter. In return for this abstention they should be accorded full protection in Parliament against irresponsible criticism, and any attack made on them in either House should be confined to those rare occasions when a member desires to initiate removal proceedings.[2] The proper attitude in making public speeches was clearly illustrated by the present Chairman in 1922. He had given an address in Toronto on the Canadian civil service, and the newspapers of that city, having no reporters present, made up the address and printed it as the original. The invented speech was naturally quite different from the real one, and contained numerous statements which the Chairman hastened to disclaim.

'I was most careful', he said in a letter to the Prime Minister, 'not to reflect upon any party or any Government past or present, dealing merely with general principles and the necessity of educating the people to take a greater interest in matters pertaining to the civil service.'[3]

One of his audience, the Principal of Upper Canada College, wrote the Chairman as follows:

[1] *Can. H. of C. Debates*, 10 Oct. 1919, p. 963.
[2] This protection is given to the judiciary.
[3] *Can. H. of C. Debates*, 16 Feb. 1923, p. 354.

'Your speech . . . was a model of good taste and reticence. No human being could have told from it that you had ever belonged to a political party or whether your relations with the present Government as chairman of the Civil Service Commission were better or worse than they had been with previous Governments. Personally, I had a natural longing for a little more "spice".' [1]

In view of the difficulties that have followed the making of speeches by Commissioners, the simplest solution would be to forbid them entirely. Neither the Commissioners nor the country would be heavy losers by the prohibition.

But why, it may be asked, are all these elaborate negative and positive precautions necessary? The answer is found in the purpose for which the Commission is created. The primary object is to provide a body which will see to it that all appointments are made for merit, tested by open competition, and that any other qualification, particularly party service, is rigorously excluded. To this end the body must set examinations of different types, grade the candidates in order of their qualifications, and exercise a general supervision over admission to the service on a basis of the examinations. The successful performance of this work depends in no small measure upon the judicial detachment and impartiality of the supervising officials. They should have no interest to consider other than the good of the service; they should be untroubled by local prejudice or the imminence of an election; they should have every motive to do wisely, none to do foolishly. Hence the complete failure of the member of Parliament as an appointing agent of any real value and the necessity for finding some other group of men better fitted to do the work. The Civil Service Commission is the body which has been created to meet the need; but if it is to be really effective the conditions surrounding it must be carefully adapted to the end in view. The chief danger the Commissioner will encounter is party influence, and hence he should have as his chief weapon independence from political control of any kind. He will of necessity become unpopular with certain Ministers, he will have to combat many members of Parliament, he will have to endure criticism from the

---

[1] *Can. H. of C. Debates*, 16 Feb. 1923, p. 355.

service and the public. Yet in the midst of the turmoil the Commissioner must preserve a strict neutrality, accompanied by scrupulous fairness and impersonality of decision. The protection and independence accorded him, therefore, can scarcely be made too extreme; for in no other way can he be impartial in decision and at the same time withstand the continuous buffetings of party supporters.

The independence thus given to the Commissioners will have certain advantages other than those for which it was immediately granted. Their freedom from control will inspire a confidence in their work on the part of the service and of the public. The judiciary receives a similar response from its administration of justice, also due in a large measure to the general conviction that its work is undisturbed by any outside influences. Further, the Commission will be in a better position to resent and report any attempt to interfere with its work, whether this take the form of bribery or mere party dictation. The long and secure tenure also results incidentally in the Commissioners acquiring a greater expertness and familiarity with their work. They obtain their knowledge of detail largely through experience, and after this has been secured they are able to devote their entire time and energies to the broader policies of administration. Each Commissioner has also greater powers of initiative and feels more free to experiment than would be the case if he were under the supervision of some political superior, and such freedom is, as a rule, beneficial in bodies of this kind. Finally, the independent position usually develops, or even possibly creates, an acute moral sense; and the Commissioner, who in earlier life had been a strong partisan, often becomes most conscientious and uninfluenced by party when he takes up his new duties. In the words of Burke:

'There have been known to be men, otherwise corrupt and vicious, who, when great trust was put in them, have called forth principles of honour latent in their minds: and men who were nursed, in a manner, in corruption have been not only great reformers by institution but greater reformers by the example of their own conduct.' [1]

---

[1] *Warren Hastings, Speech on the Sixth Charge.*

The creation of an independent Civil Service Commission has inevitably conflicted with the theory of ministerial responsibility in the making of appointments to the public service. Before the reform of 1908 the theory was that a Cabinet Minister took complete political responsibility for all appointments made in his department. He was supposed to have inquired into the relative fitness of different candidates, to have used his own knowledge and that of his assistants and friends, and to have chosen the best applicants. His duty was to run the Department, and it was supposed to be to his interest to pick able officers. If his selections were wise, so the argument ran, he and his colleagues would be rewarded by continuance in office; if the selections were foolish, the Government would be punished for its inefficiency. The Minister was politically responsible to Parliament; it in turn was responsible to the people.

Experience proved, however, that this idea of responsibility was seldom, if ever, realized. The theoretical responsibility remained very theoretical, and did not work out in the exact and faultless manner supposed. While a Minister and his colleagues were undoubtedly held to a strict accounting for their decisions on matters of trade policy, they were never censured in Parliament because they had appointed an inefficient customs officer or an illiterate postmaster. This anomaly was pointed out in 1879 by George E. Casey when pressing for civil service reform:

'The argument in favour of the present system was that we had a responsible government, and that somebody must be responsible for the appointments, and that the gentleman who recommended and the Minister who made the appointments were responsible. He thought there could be nothing more hollow than this sham of responsibility. Had they ever heard of an instance in this House of a Member being called upon to give the reason for an appointment which he had recommended?'[1]

If the system of making appointments could be criticized on these grounds it was no better when tested in other ways. It was very inefficient; for in the majority of instances the Minister knew nothing about the candidate he appointed. He

[1] *Can. H. of C. Debates*, 16 Apr. 1879, p. 1268.

was himself unable to study the merits of all applicants, and he chose the simplest method, of seeking the advice of his party's representative from the district which held the vacant office. This representative might be a member of Parliament, or a defeated candidate at the last election, or the party patronage committee in the constituency. In any event the Minister received a party recommendation for the position, and as he possessed no other information, and probably desired none, he made the appointment as advised. Responsibility in any real sense of the word could not exist. In theory, of course, the source of the Minister's information was of no consequence, the responsibility remained with him and could not be dodged. In practice the responsibility was never enforced, and it consequently became unreal and imaginary—a shadow so faint that it never darkened the political life of the Cabinet, either collectively or individually. The following quotations will show the extent to which the responsible Minister or the member of Parliament participated in the appointments:

'It is a notorious fact that there was a vacancy in the post-mastership at Kingston caused by death, and that the vacancy was fixed on the nomination of the local patronage committee.' [1]

'I represented a constituency about 150 miles long, and if a vacancy occurred at the other end of the constituency I would not know one man in twenty, and I would have to depend upon my political friends. I would probably write to my political committee and ask for a nomination. They might know some poor chap down at heel and say, "Here is a poor chap ; give him the position!" Sometimes he would be a good man, sometimes otherwise. The member of Parliament would act in good faith, but he might have imposed upon him some one who would not measure up to the requirements.' [2]

Old political theories, which are retained even after the circumstances have materially altered, do little harm and frequently much good, provided that the work of government can still be carried on efficiently underneath the pretence. Such, however, was not the case here. The only provision

---

[1] *Can. Sess. Pap.*, 1907–8, § 29A, p. 1329 ; cf. *ibid.*, pp. 274, 441.
[2] *Can. H. of C. Journals*, 1923, Appendix, § 5, p. 837.

against the abuse of party patronage was ministerial responsibility, not as a theory, but as an ever-present and potentially
unpleasant fact; and when the fact disappeared efficiency
went with it. Two remedies were available: the theory could
have been made to work, or it could have been abandoned for
another which would better fit the circumstances. The first
alternative was never seriously tried, the supporters of the
theory being so earnestly engaged in defending it that they
had no time to suggest changes which would give it life. The
evidence taken by the Royal Commission in 1892 contained
an interesting proposal, which might conceivably have saved
the old appointment system from complete condemnation:

'A member of Parliament has too much power in respect to
appointments, and too little responsibility. He can make a recommendation to a Minister on which an appointment is based, and
nobody knows who has made that recommendation. He perhaps
writes a private note, which is destroyed when the appointment
is made. The man appointed may turn out to be a scamp, and
no visible responsibility rests on the member for having recommended him, while the Minister escapes responsibility on the
general ground that he cannot know the character of every man he
appoints. I consider that if a member undertakes to recommend
any one for appointment to the service he should do so, not by
means of a private note, which has no substantial existence, but
he should do so formally, and his recommendation should be a
matter of record. I would even go further, though I know this is
not at all likely to be adopted: I would publish in the *Canada
Gazette* that so-and-so was appointed on so-and-so's recommendation, or I would report it to Parliament. Then a member would
think twice before he would recommend a person for appointment.' [1]

Such a change might have brought about a sufficient
measure of efficiency to preserve for many years the theory
and practice of ministerial responsibility in making appointments. Nothing of the kind, however, was attempted; and
the reform which was ultimately made disregarded the theory
entirely by giving the power to an independent Commission. A theoretically responsible Minister was abandoned for
a theoretically irresponsible Commissioner. Superficially the

[1] *Can. Sess. Pap.*, 1892, § 16 c, p. 615.

substitution might appear to have been unwise; but the new system (combined with open competitive examinations) soon justified itself by showing a great improvement in the quality of entrants to the service.

This disappearance of ministerial responsibility has met with different responses throughout the country, somewhat resembling a child's reception of the truth about Santa Claus. Some people have assented to the disappearance of their idol philosophically, but to others the shattering of the belief has been accompanied by vast disillusionment and general scepticism; it has meant for these people the end of all efficiency, reliability, and order in the official world. They are like Lord John Russell who, when open competition was suggested in England in 1853, thought it would introduce republicanism and destroy the monarchy.[1] One old die-hard deputy Minister gave evidence before the Special Committee of the House in 1923 as follows:

'One reads nowadays the most appalling trash in the newspapers about the "evils of patronage", as though patronage was necessarily an evil to be shunned. I wonder if these sapient journalists ever reflect for a moment who is best fitted to exercise the patronage of the Government—the Ministers, for the most part men trained in public affairs, responsible to the Crown and to Parliament for their every action, or an inexperienced, unrepresentative and irresponsible body such as the Civil Service Commission?'[2]

A third group of people have resolutely rejected the truth, and have stoutly maintained that there still is a Santa Claus. Members of Parliament and even a Prime Minister have been found denying that ministerial responsibility has disappeared, and asserting that the relation of the Cabinet to civil service appointments is the same as before. The following statement, for example, was made by Sir Robert Borden on 16 May 1918:

'*Mr. Burnham:*

'1. Is the Government aware that constituencies hold their representatives responsible for all appointments not made by examination?

---

[1] Moses, R., *The Civil Service of Great Britain*, pp. 84–5.
[2] *Can. H. of C. Journals*, 1923, Appendix, § 5, p. 613.

'2. Is the Government aware that it is impossible to shift this responsibility to others?

'3. Does the Government therefore intend to refer appointments to the representatives concerned for approval?

'*Sir Robert Borden* (*Prime Minister*) :

'The Government, in respect to appointments to the public service, is responsible to Parliament; Parliament is responsible to the people. In making such appointments the Government is, of course, desirous of obtaining the best possible information that may be available as to the qualifications of the persons proposed to be appointed. It will always be very glad to receive suggestions or recommendations from members of this House in regard to such appointments.' [1]

It is extremely difficult, if not impossible, to interpret this statement, for it was made after the passage of the Order in Council of 13 February 1918.[2] Before 1908 the Canadian Ministers were politically responsible for appointments, promotions, &c., inasmuch as they supervised, in theory at least, all such Acts themselves. But by the statute of that year they were relieved of responsibility for most appointments in the Inside Service when their powers were given to the Commission—a delegation which was completed for the remainder of the service by the Order in Council and Act of 1918. In what manner, then, did Sir Robert Borden think that the Government's responsibility worked? The Government was unable to interfere with the work of the Commissioners, for the latter were by both law and convention entitled to complete freedom in making appointments under their regulations. The Government could not set the examinations, nor could it mark the papers, nor grade the candidates, nor offer appointments. The same was true of the other positions that were filled by the Commissioners without written examinations. All appointments were made by them acting under the law and without molestation from the Government, which, had it been attempted, would have been actively resented. If the Ministry had no power to make or influence appointments, it could scarcely be expected to receive praise or blame for

[1] *Can. H. of. C. Debates*, 16 May 1918, p. 2101.
[2] Cf. *supra*, pp. 90–1.

them. But it might be suggested that the Commissioners, if not the Government, were politically responsible for their actions. This raises difficulties of a similar kind. The Commissioners could not be held responsible so long as they kept within their jurisdiction and did no deliberate wrong: Parliament could not intimidate them, nor, without violating the statute, could it remove them. The responsibility was even more remote when they were assisted in their decisions by advisory boards, for as the latter held no official position they could not be held accountable in any possible way. The plain answer to Sir Robert Borden is that the appointments were made, and that no one was politically responsible for them.

The Commissioners, it is true, have a moral responsibility to their consciences, to their sense of duty, to their reputations, to their pride in the office, or to any other influence which may dominate them. They may be free politically, but their actions are influenced and guided by forces which, if more intangible, are nevertheless very strong and very real. Independent of Parliament, they are made dependent on other things. Again, the analogy may be seen between a Commissioner and a judge. The Government takes no more responsibility for an appointment made by the Commission than for a decision rendered by the Supreme Court; and in both instances the same reliance for the integrity of the work is placed on the character of the officials.

'It is a strange doctrine,' said Sir Wilfrid Laurier, 'to preach that the judges are responsible to Parliament. Where is that responsibility? I have always understood that the judges were responsible only to their own conscience, and Parliament has no power over them. . . . They are only responsible to Parliament in extreme cases of malfeasance.' [1]

The Government must take a certain responsibility, as Sir Wilfrid suggested, when the independent official does a wrong thing, maliciously or corruptly, or when he exceeds his grant of legal powers. In such cases it is usually considered to be the duty of the Ministry to initiate proceedings which

[1] *Can. H. of C. Debates*, 15 Sept. 1903, p. 11313.

will lead to the official's removal. But until the malfeasance
or transgression of powers takes place both the Ministry and
Parliament must allow him to carry on his work undisturbed,
and must ratify, when necessary, his recommendations. One
other point should be made clear. Although the Ministry
takes no responsibility for individual acts of the Commission,
it may be considered to take a vague responsibility for the
entire system; for by leaving the *Civil Service Act* on the
statute books it gives to the law a passive approval. The
Ministers are therefore bound to observe the spirit and letter
of the Act by respecting the independence of the Commission,
even though it does many things which to them are distaste-
ful. In a similar manner they take responsibility for the
system of an independent judiciary, though they do not hold
themselves responsible for each decision of individual judges.
The only remedy the Ministers have in either case is to
remodel the entire plan, and hence its responsibility begins
and stops there.

A failure to grasp this idea led to a confused discussion in
the Commons a few years ago. The Minister of Labour was
presenting his Estimates, and the following debate (very much
condensed here) ensued:

'*Sir Henry Drayton:*
'Are any of these salaries too high, and if so, what are they?
'*Mr. Murdock (Minister of Labour):*
'It would be entirely unbecoming under the existing condition
of the law for the Minister of Labour to even hazard a view as to
the consistency of wage rates now in effect with respect to the
various classes of civil service as established and maintained by
the Civil Service Commission, a body appointed under the preceding Government. . . . I have no jurisdiction whatsoever over this
question. . . .

'*Sir Henry Drayton:*
'I would have thought that the Minister responsible for these
payments would be able to give the Committee an idea as to
whether the payments ought to be made or not. . . .

'*Mr. Murdock:*
'It would not be fair . . . to ask me to express my opinion as to
any individual rate paid, because these rates are established by

the Civil Service Commission, an heirloom which has been be-
queathed to us from the previous Government, and whose recommendations we are now following. . . .

'*Mr. Meighen* (*Leader of the Opposition*):
'The Minister of Labour . . . tells this House that, no matter
what may be the will of the Government, or of this Parliament,
these men must get the salaries set opposite their names because
the Civil Service Commission says so.

'*Mr. Murdock:*
'I did not intend to convey any such impression. . . .

'*Mr. Meighen:*
'I do not want the hon. gentleman to get out of the responsibility, although he has been trying hard to. The Civil Service
Commission has a duty . . . to allocate the salary that is in their
view commensurate with the duties and responsibilities of each
office. . . . But no civil servant has a right at all to any salary until
this House passes upon it and decides that it is a proper one. And
when the Minister comes to this House with his Estimates, he says:
"Those are the salaries that I think right, and I ask this House
to vote them." That is his responsibility. . . . When a Minister
comes to Parliament he takes his responsibility for the fairness of
the salaries. He is in a position to say, "The Civil Service Commission recommends these salaries; they believe they are fair and
right, and I have behind me their support." But he cannot say,
"I am bound to put these salaries in the Estimates because that
is the view of the Civil Service Commission"—not at all. . . . Are
we here merely to put our imprimatur upon what the Civil Service
Commission says? Not at all. The Minister's responsibility is that
he recommends these salaries to this Committee, each and every
one of them, and he cannot escape that responsibility. . . .

'*Mr. Murdock:*
'Will the hon. gentleman please not misquote me to this House?
I will assume full responsibility now and ever. . . .

'*Mr. Mackenzie King* (*Prime Minister*):
'The Minister may take one of two courses. He may say: "I am
anxious to keep this whole matter out of Parliament. I am desirous of having the civil service feel a sense of security, knowing that
there will be no interference on the part of the Government or the
Minister. Therefore, I will come to Parliament with the Estimates
exactly as they have been prepared and presented to me by my
deputy minister." That is what my hon. friend is doing at the

present time. On the other hand, he may take the opposite course. He may say: "I am Minister of the department now; I am going to look into the salaries; I am going to cut down so many clerks, promote other clerks, ignore the Civil Service Commission altogether." . . . That is the kind of responsibility that the Minister of Labour has refused to exercise. As my right hon. friend (Mr. Meighen) says, he (Mr. Murdock) as the Minister has the power, but to exercise it is to begin to interfere from a political point of view, and that is what hon. members on this side and members of the Government have refused to do. They have sought to respect the civil service as being outside of politics altogether, and, in the Estimates which they bring before the House, to be governed by the recommendations of the permanent heads of departments who know the service, and by the approval of the Civil Service Commission. . . . There is a great deal of difference between a Minister saying: "I will not take the responsibility of interfering with the recommendations of my deputy head, those recommendations having been approved by the Civil Service Commission," and one saying: "I do not take any responsibility at all." [1]

None of these views expressed the whole truth, though that of the Prime Minister came close to it. The Government, in effect, was giving its silent approval to the *Civil Service Act* and its principles, and took a vague general responsibility for both. There its responsibility ended. The reason that the Minister of Labour did not tamper with the salaries, as passed on by the deputy head of his department and the Commission, was that under the *Civil Service Act* he was not supposed to have anything to say about them. He had, of course, the right as a Minister to recommend, and Parliament had the right to approve, any changes in salary; but to do so would have been tantamount to amending the fundamental statute. The estimates of the Minister simply carried out the law; they did not express his wishes but those of the Act, as administered by the Commission. The general principle of the Act was that appointments and salaries should be made by the Commission; [2] and until the Act was repealed, both Minister and Parliament were bound to observe it and to abide by the Commission's decisions. Parliament could rescind all

---

[1] *Can. H. of C. Debates*, 31 Mar. 1922, pp. 548–53.
[2] The increases in salary being recommended by the deputy head.

civil service regulations, double or halve all salaries, abolish
the office of Civil Service Commissioner, raise every candidate's mark on geography by twenty per cent., and admit all
blue-eyed girls between the ages of eighteen and nineteen
and a half years without any examination whatever. Parliament was legally competent to enact all these changes, and
the Ministry could have recommended them, but the whole
principle of the service would thereby have been altered also.

'No one questions', said a later speaker in the above debate,[1]
'the right of Parliament to repeal any Act, but so long as the
Civil Service Act is in force a Minister cannot, without contravening the spirit of that legislation, reduce any salary fixed by the
Commission, and every one knows that. . . . Hon. members would
have the right to move for the repeal of the *Civil Service Act* if
they wished.'

The whole purpose of creating the independent Commission
and removing the service from any direct parliamentary control is to make certain that the civil servant will be appointed
for merit, and that he and his work will remain completely
separated from party influence and prejudice. Both devices
aim indirectly at creating a non-partisan feeling in the service, an environment quite apart from the disputes and
wrangling of political warfare. The service is bound to have
a will of its own, but this is not supposed to derive any
inspiration from any party will or policy.

Before the merit system was introduced, however, the civil
servants were dominated by quite a different spirit. They
owed their offices to a party, and frequently were willing to
give their first allegiance to their benefactor. The service,
being composed of politically appointed officials, reflected
this partisan feeling and made little pretence of neutrality.
Political bias and sympathy were openly expressed. When
the Government changed the new Ministry was usually confronted by hostile civil servants, whose chief inducement to
politeness and co-operation was the fear of losing their positions. The temptation to bring the administration into
harmony with the Ministry was frequently too strong to be

[1] Hon. George P. Graham. He alone of the speakers in the debate comprehended the actual situation. Cf. *ibid.*, pp. 553–4.

resisted, and the offices thus vacated were filled with members of the opposite party who were no less biassed than their predecessors. Thus if a new Ministry retained the old officials, harmony was almost impossible; if it changed them for members of its own party, it was creating the same embarrassing condition for the next Government. The service was thus described by George E. Casey in 1877:

'Serious complaints are often made of the existence of this evil (of a partisan service), and of the employment of our executive body as electioneering agents, complaints which it is to be feared are not always unfounded. Indeed it could hardly be otherwise. Civil servants are only human beings, and when they have been chosen for zeal and activity in political life they can hardly be expected to be transformed at once into impartial executive machines. Their opportunities for furthering party interests are often considerable, and they are extremely likely to take advantage of them to some extent, often without the slightest idea of impropriety in so doing.' [1]

At the time the above article was written conditions were very bad indeed. The Canadian service was fast building up a little copy of the American spoils by the systematic supporting of supporters. Instead of deprecating the movement, many politicians openly rejoiced at it and advocated its further extension.[2] Sir Richard Cartwright, a Minister in the Mackenzie Cabinet, has described the difficulties encountered in 1873 when the new Government took office.

'We soon found that we lived in a glass hive. Hardly a question could be discussed in Council, and certainly no resolution arrived at, which was not known to our opponents. Nay, it was quite a common case for us to find that measures which had not even been submitted to Council were known to our enemies long before they were considered by the majority of the Cabinet. The fact was that not only almost all the higher offices in the Civil Service, but practically all the subordinate places, were filled with more or less zealous partisans of our opponents. I do not mean to say that all, or even a majority, of these men deliberately betrayed our confidence, but they certainly took no interest in making our Government a success. . . .

[1] 'Civil Service Reform', *Canadian Monthly*, Jan. 1877, p. 85.
[2] Cf. *supra*, pp. 32–4.

'One or two of us . . . made our intention known to the effect that if any secrets leaked out by fault of our officers and the culprit could not be discovered, we would make a clean sweep of every man who could possibly have known anything of the matter, a step which in these particular instances ensured a due measure of reticence. . . .

'Every step they (the Mackenzie Ministry) took, every detail of their administration, was at once reported to their opponents, and in the actual working of their departments very frequently more favour was shown to their political opponents than to their own friends.' [1]

Sir Richard stated also that this extreme partisan feeling continued in the service for many years, and that the census returns of 1891 were deliberately falsified, in order that the Government's failure to curb emigration to the United States might not be disclosed.

'It should be noted', he said, 'that all the census officials, from the highest to the lowest, were strong partisans. They were all aware that the Government had been fiercely attacked on the score of the immense exodus which had taken place, and it was natural that they would try to diminish the number of absentees as much as possible.' [2]

Sir Richard Cartwright was never known to underestimate the villainy of his opponents, and his statements are subject to some discount. But the essential truth remains, that an incoming Government could not trust the honesty or rely on the loyalty of many of the civil servants who had been appointed by its predecessor, and that some of these officials were apt to betray any political knowledge which they might happen to acquire. This partisanship persisted in such a marked degree that the Opposition undoubtedly believed that the census officials had made partial and fraudulent returns. There was, therefore, a possibility and danger that a compliant civil service might have become a mere tool in the hands of the Government, which would inevitably have brought all official reports and statistics under suspicion, and have destroyed the public confidence in all such work. A civil service living in such an environment lacks the morale

[1] Cartwright, Sir Richard, *Reminiscences*, pp. 128–30.
[2] *Ibid.*, p. 327.

and pride in its position which is essential to its success, and
this deficiency was pointed out by a Royal Commission at
this time:

'There is also to be noted, too often, an absence of that *esprit de
corps* which ought to animate and usually does animate the
members of the same body or service. Efforts from time to time,
your Commissioners have been told, have been made by some
members of the service to awaken and stimulate this sentiment,
but it is feared without any marked success. Your Commissioners
believe that one effect of the creation of the Civil Service Commission will be to secure this co-operation, create an *esprit de corps*,
and result in ensuring to the Ministry and the country a zealous
and united service for the conduct of public affairs.' [1]

A civil service, impartially appointed under open competition administered by an independent Commission, occu-
pies a neutral ground between the political parties, an area
which, though surrounded by partisan struggles and clashes
of public opinion, is relatively undisturbed. Like the judiciary the civil service goes on with its work unaffected by the
changing political fortunes. The candidate for admission no
longer looks to a party leader, a member of Parliament,
a Cabinet Minister, a patronage committee, but to himself,
and he takes his position with no debt of gratitude to discharge. He has won his office solely because he has proved
himself better than other applicants, and he will gain promotion for the same reason. An environment of this kind is
certain to raise the morale of the entire official body, and
makes it easy and almost inevitable for the civil servant to be
neutral in politics and give his best to his political superior.
His natural allegiance is not to a party, but to the state. The
following description of a prominent British civil servant,
the late Sir Henry Jenkyns, will indicate the nature of the
qualities most desired:

'A new post, like that of Parliamentary Counsel to the Treasury, is apt to be very much what the holder chooses to make it.
Jenkyns' view of his functions was that he was not merely a
draftsman, but counsel to the Government in its legislative
capacity, and that it was his duty, as such, to bring forward and

[1] *Can. Sess. Pap.*, 1892, § 16 c, p. xxiii.

press any considerations within his knowledge and experience which might assist a Minister in arriving at a sound conclusion, always remembering that it was for him merely to present arguments, and that the responsibility for decision must rest with the Minister himself. To perform this task with efficiency and discretion is not easy. The adviser has often to play the part of Devil's advocate, and to insist on difficulties which the sanguine legislator would prefer to ignore. It is easier to prophesy smooth things, and sometimes more profitable. Micaiah the son of Imlah was not popular in high quarters. The extent and variety of Jenkyns' constitutional knowledge and Parliamentary experience made him a formidable critic of legislative proposals, and the frankness and outspokenness with which he expressed and supported his views, coupled with a certain brusqueness of manner, sometimes gave offence. But those whom his criticism irritated for the moment were usually ready to acknowledge its permanent value later on. And it was not a merely negative and destructive criticism. He was always eminently suggestive and resourceful. He possessed, what is perhaps the most valuable of all qualities for legislative purposes, a constructive imagination. . . . It need hardly be said that his zeal and energy were bestowed irrespectively of political parties. . . . There are occupants of the opposition Front Bench who can testify that his criticisms of weak points in legislative proposals were at least as unsparing during their period of office as in the time of their successors.' [1]

The purified atmosphere that envelops the reformed civil service is thus beneficial to every one concerned. The civil servants themselves gain in independence and usefulness, and their offices acquire a new dignity. The public service becomes a career instead of a temporary sinecure to be relinquished when the opposite party is returned at the polls. The Cabinet Minister, on the other hand, feels that his subordinates are not trying to thwart him, but are conscientiously endeavouring to give loyal service and expert, disinterested advice. Finally, the administration gains enormously in the public estimation. The civil servants are no longer accused of partisanship, they are conceded a professional standing, and they are able by the quality and impartiality of their work to secure the good will and the confidence of the country.

[1] Jenkyns, Sir H., *British Rule and Jurisdiction beyond the Seas*, Preface (Sir Courtenay Ilbert), pp. xiii–xiv.

XII. THE CIVIL SERVICE AS A LARGE SCALE ORGANIZATION

'Oh, philosophers may sing
    Of the troubles of a king;
But the duties are delightful and the privileges great;
    But the privilege and pleasure
    That we treasure beyond measure
Is to run on little errands for the Ministers of State.'
The Gondoliers.

THE civil service, although a large scale organization, differs in many ways from its counterpart in the ordinary business world, and, hence, rules of efficiency which are found to succeed in the latter may prove almost unworkable in a government department. Private business, for example, is almost invariably conducted for profit, and this forms an automatic measure of its efficiency. If it can declare a dividend, it succeeds; if not, it is a failure, and disappears from the commercial world. While the same test might be applied to certain activities of the Government (such as the postal service, for example), to do so would be to emphasize a quite secondary aspect of its function. The administrative departments exist primarily to render a service to the community, and the price that they charge, if they ask any at all, does not necessarily represent the money equivalent of the work which they perform. Even a quasi-business department like the Post Office might not consider that it was justified in raising the letter rate in order to meet a threatened deficit; nor would any one be so rash as to suggest that the fees charged by the courts should be large enough to defray the expenses of the judicial system. In short, there is little or no effort made to estimate the success of a department by its credit balance at the end of the year, nor is it desirable that any such effort should be made.[1]

Closely allied to profit as a stimulus in private industry is competition, both individual and collective. The business firm is constantly struggling for supremacy with its rivals,

[1] Cf. *Fourth Report of the Commissioners on the Civil Service* (*Great Britain*), 1914, Cd. 7338, pp. 82–3.

and the loss of the fight frequently means extinction. Competition pervades also the entire internal organization; each employee endeavours to surpass his fellows, and finds an additional inducement to effort in the thought that if he does well another company is able and willing to make him an attractive offer. Here, again, the Government department finds itself at a disadvantage in its effort to be efficient. It is usually running a monopoly and has no rivals in the field, its life does not depend on its ability to defeat hostile forces, its employees do not feel the sharp stimulus of competition, and many are so highly specialized that few, if any, opportunities arise outside the service. One doubtful advantage is enjoyed by the Government: it gets cheap labour, partly because there is little external competition to force salaries up, and partly also because Parliament and the people are jealous of paying generous amounts to their servants. Despite this motive for leaving the service, the majority of public employees remain there for life, for they find themselves in a blind alley with no exit to the business world. On the other hand, however, the civil servant receives in exchange for his sacrifice more humane and gentle treatment than his brother in private employ; for the lack of competition makes the heads of departments more tolerant of inefficiency and meagre talents. Finally, the department, having little real interest in economy, is apt to become wasteful and extravagant in spending the public money. The general effect, therefore, of the lack of the profit motive and the absence of competition is to accelerate the movement, always present in any large scale organization, towards lower administrative efficiency.

The peculiar conditions under which a government department must work tend in themselves to make its machinery more elaborate, its instruments more complex, than in ordinary business. Every act is subject to public and parliamentary criticism; the officials live in a glass cage, and each movement is apt to be seen and noted. To protect himself the ordinary civil servant hides behind either the exact letter of the law or a precedent, while his superior prepares his defences by issuing orders in quadruplicate and inventing ponderous filing systems. Unfortunately there is a need for all these checks, and for counter checks as well; inspectors must not only inspect, but also be inspected. The civil servant must be ready at all times to meet criticism; he must be prepared to produce documents showing the exact instructions issued to a certain official on a certain day; he must be able to show that the one rule has been consistently followed, and that Tom Jones has been given no more privileges and no different treatment than Joseph Andrews.[1] He is forced into multiplying records, over-emphasizing consistency and precedent, making an idol out of precision and legal-mindedness. The result is officialism and red-tape, all of which is popularly denounced, most of which is regrettably necessary. Those critics who expect to run a public department like an oil company fail to realize that the faults in the service of which they complain are due in a large measure to the requirements of parliamentary government, and are 'part of the price paid for the advantages of public discussion and criticism of public affairs'.[2] If the people's representatives insist on supervising and questioning the work of the civil service (and this must be done in order to avoid bureaucratic government), then they must be prepared to forgo a certain amount of speed and economy in order to maintain their control.

A government department must also submit to many restrictions in selecting and directing its personnel which would be considered intolerable in a private company. The possibility that political influences will be used to affect both the admission of candidates and the subsequent career of those appointed can never be forgotten; and civil service rules must therefore often sacrifice efficiency in order to obtain strict and rigid neutrality. This fear of sinister influence has gone so far in the Canadian service that even promotions and salary increases are no longer controlled by

[1] The necessity for uniformity in government administration is admirably described by Sir Josiah Stamp, ' The Contrast between the Administration of Business and Public Affairs', *Journal of Public Administration*, 1923, pp. 161–8.

[2] *Fourth Report of the Commissioners on the Civil Service (Great Britain)*, 1914, Cd. 7338, p. 83.

the heads of the departments, but are given for the most part
to the independent Commission. This is an extreme example
of the principle that, while the oversight of the service must
be fair and impartial, this in itself is insufficient. The fairness
and impartiality must not only exist: they must be so plain
and evident that they are demonstrable to all. Methods of
this kind undoubtedly prevent political favouritism; but,
by contrast, it is difficult to imagine such enterprises as the
Canadian Pacific Railway and the Bank of Montreal carrying
on their business by creating an administrative authority
with such palpably artificial powers.

A similar want of flexibility appears in other restrictions
placed on the civil service. Employees cannot be discharged
nor laid off for long periods of time without evoking public
protests at the hard-heartedness of the Government. If a
department wishes to retain or secure an exceptionally good
man they find it almost impossible to offer him the necessary
salary, for either the regulations will be so inelastic that no
great change in remuneration can be made, or the salary
which can be offered will be entirely too small to prove
attractive. Private companies can make promotions with a
speed and decisiveness which no civil service dares to emulate. The result is that when a government industry, like
the Canadian National Railways, comes to compete with one
privately owned, it is forced in self-defence to abandon all
civil service regulations, and to follow in almost every way
the freer methods and unrestricted and almost uncensored
practices of the private company.

The civil service and the private commercial enterprise,
while generally resembling each other, thus differ in several
important respects; though as the modern corporation continues to grow in size, it comes steadily nearer to the civil
service in its form and in its problems of personnel administration. Both exhibit the general defects of large scale
organizations: the machinery is usually rigid and cumbersome; conditions and remuneration tend to become stan-
dardized and uniform; the whole body moves, in the language
of the Chancery, 'with all deliberate speed'; the system
shows a general inability to exert a direct and effective

supervision over employees. But the public service, unfortunately, is apt to exaggerate these faults, due to the absence of certain stimuli as noted above. In the earlier pages of the book the problems of the service have been discussed with emphasis on its political and public relationships. In this chapter the chief stress will be laid on those problems which the service shares, for the most part, with other large scale organizations, albeit it shares them with a difference. The most important general question to be answered is the way in which efficiency can be secured. This leads to a discussion of the functional distribution of work, the relations between the head of a department and his subordinates, the stimulation of interest and initiative in the employee, and, in short, anything which will overcome the impersonality, the deadening routine, the mental laxness, which often pervade the service.

The broadest problem that presents itself is the general division of work in the administrative organization. There is almost unanimous agreement on the principle by which the work of government departments shall be allocated, viz., distribution according to the services or functions performed, for example, agricultural, entomological, biological, and allied subjects will be under the Department of Agriculture, the judiciary, penitentiaries, granting of pardons, and similar subjects will be under the Department of Justice.[1] The maintenance of the line of division, however, is not nearly so simple as it might appear, nor is the line, once drawn, necessarily stationary. Civil servants, in common with the rest of humanity, share that strange desire for power for power's sake, and are continually reaching out and trespassing on one another's ground in the effort to make their position more important and indispensable. In some instances, however, the movement may be dictated merely by convenience, a small branch being established in response to a definite need, which gradually enlarges as the demand for it increases. The Department of the Interior, for example, must issue

---

[1] White, L. D., *Introduction to the Study of Public Administration*, pp. 66–9; *Report of the Machinery of Government Committee (Great Britain)*, 1918, Cd. 9230, pp. 7–10; *Can. Sen. Journals*, 1919, pp. 346–9.

maps of the Dominion to indicate the natural resources of the country, and maps are therefore printed and sent out. A few years later, the Department of Marine and Fisheries decides that its work would be helped by a map showing the location of the important fisheries, and it thereupon begins a new branch for the purpose. The Commission of Conservation (now happily dead) issues a conservation map, and the Department of Labour an industrial map. Suddenly some alert official discovers that there are four branches in the service engaged in making maps, which could be more efficiently and economically carried out by one. A realinement follows, and one branch issues maps for the entire service.

There are, of course, many instances when a number of departments must do the same type of work, and when serious inconvenience would result from unification. The decision must naturally depend on whether a change would lead to a gain in efficiency, and if so, whether it would be financially profitable. In the event of the work being left undisturbed, departmental co-operation would probably effect large economies in administration. This suggests one of the most difficult problems in the service: the maintenance of cordial and effective co-ordination between departments. Each unit wants to be self-sufficing, and finds that the simpler and easier way is to go ahead and let the others take care of themselves. This policy, if adhered to, inevitably means duplication and excessive costs, and the only remedy is co-operation.[1] This can be obtained chiefly by requiring the officials to hold interdepartmental conferences which will be devoted to discussions of the problems and the work which they share in common. No rule can be laid down to cover all cases. With some branches, an occasional meeting of the different heads will be sufficient, with others the work will be so closely interwoven that a joint committee of the departments concerned will have to be formed. Above everything else, however, there must be a willingness on the part of the civil servants themselves to deal with other departments in a spirit of genuine co-operation.

A comparatively new device for obtaining greater effi-

[1] *Ibid.*, p. 345.

ciency in administration is by the departments' use of advisory boards or committees. These have been tried in Canada to a very limited degree and with an even more limited amount of success,[1] but they are being extensively adopted in England and the United States.[2] The object is to enable a department both to utilize the information and experience of outside interests and to obtain a more accurate idea of what the public wants and needs. The committees thus give technical and expert advice, and also act as a link between the public and the Government. They are valuable as guarantors of the acceptability of the departments' administrative measures, and in many cases are able to anticipate and smooth out many objections before the final decisions are made.[3] 'So long as advisory bodies are not permitted to impair the full responsibility of Ministers to Parliament,' said the Machinery of Government Committee in 1918, 'we think that the more they are regarded as an integral part of the normal organization of a department, the more will Ministers be enabled to command the confidence of Parliament and the public in their administration of the services which seem likely, in an increasing degree, to affect the lives of large sections of the community.'[4] One of the most successful of such advisory committees was that used by the British Ministry of Food during the war. Its purpose was thus described by two civil servants a few years later:

'The Ministry of Food during the war realized how great the danger was that a machine which had to be created post-haste might inevitably become too elaborate and too bureaucratic; and that it might leave out of account the most vital factor of all, viz., the psychology of the ordinary man. To correct this a body was set up which was called the "Consumers' Council". I will admit that sometimes this council gave us a great deal of work and anxiety and sometimes wasted a great deal of valuable time. But there you had a small body of men and women of various classes

---

[1] e. g. the Lighthouse Board and the Commission of Conservation, cf. Dawson, R. MacG., *The Principle of Official Independence*, pp. 127–34, 146–50.

[2] *Report of the Machinery of Government Committee (Great Britain)*, 1918, Cd. 9230, pp. 11–12; Selby-Bigge, Sir L. A., *The Board of Education*, pp. 203–6.

[3] Cf. *The Development of the Civil Service*, pp. 107–9, 219–22.

[4] *Report of the Machinery of Government Committee (Great Britain)*, 1918, Cd. 9230, p. 12.

of the general public, sitting once a week, and sometimes more, in the Office, with access to all papers, with power to summon any official at any moment to explain what he was doing and why he was doing it, which was able to express forcibly and with knowledge what the public wanted. It educated the Office as to the mind of the public, what it would stand, what was troubling it, and, on the other hand, it educated the public as to what the Department was doing, why it adopted particular methods, and what the obstacles were that prevented other methods from being adopted. I am not sure which particular aspect was the more useful. Certainly the Department was saved from much ignorant and from much uninstructive criticism. On the other hand, it was able to adjust its schemes to meet reasonable and instructive criticism without the disabilities attendant on changes of policy. At the same time, however, it should be remembered that full responsibility for executive action continued to rest on the Department.' [1]

'The Consumers' Council', writes Sir William Beveridge, 'was an interesting and useful addition to the constitution of the Ministry. It met as a rule weekly; matters directly affecting consumers—in particular, proposals to raise prices and rationing schemes—were regularly brought before it; it might of its own motion bring forward questions, complaints, or suggestions. It was purely advisory and thus did not interfere with the ultimate responsibility of the Food Controller; his right to override the advice given was unquestioned. It was also a confidential body; its proceedings were private and the Food Controller never tried to avoid his own responsibility by quoting its authority for some unpopular measure; this assured him of a frank and fair expression of opinion. . . .

'In more than one way the Consumers' Council recalled another well-known revising body. Like the House of Lords, it gave an opportunity to officials of correcting mistakes of drafting; like the House of Lords it could delay a proposal it did not like, once or even twice, and so might make it worth while for any section of the Ministry in a hurry to compromise for the sake of a quick passage; like the House of Lords it gracefully yielded to fixed determination on the part of the really responsible body—the Food Controller or any official whom he was prepared to support.'[2]

[1] Wise, E. F., 'The Civil Service in its Relation to Industry and Commerce', *The Civil Servant and His Profession*, pp. 86–7.
[2] Beveridge, Sir William H., *British Food Control*, pp. 71–2.

The functions and composition of advisory committees have been carefully described by Professor H. J. Laski.[1] He believes that the members of each committee should represent special knowledge in a particular field, so that 'the opinion of those members cannot be weighed lightly even by the most sturdy bureaucrat', in other words, if they are to advise, they must advise intelligently and with an authority derived from a real knowledge of the subject. The committee should be composed of two kinds of members: 'a majority chosen by representative associations in the different interests, such as industries, affected by administration, and a minority chosen by the Minister to represent the public and special bodies sufficiently, though indirectly, concerned to need the protection of representation.'[2] The committee is not, of course, to direct administration or to control or define policy—that would interfere with the political responsibility of the Minister—but its advice is to be sought on proposed bills and on general administrative problems, while it is expected to make suggestions of all kinds for ministerial consideration. Professor Laski even endorses the participation of the committee in the issuing of administrative orders under statutory authorization, and, in the event of disagreement with the Minister, thinks it might be given a suspensory veto over the Minister's power to issue such regulations. An extensive use of advisory committees would probably do much to commend the administration to the people, it would undoubtedly add to the efficiency of the Government departments, and it would at the same time stimulate and improve the whole civil service by subjecting it to constant surveillance and criticism.

Another idea which has met with growing favour in Great Britain is that the House of Commons should choose from its members a Standing Committee for each department of the Government. Each committee would keep in close contact with the work of its assigned department: it could demand full information on any subject, and the civil servants and even the Minister would appear before it to defend and

[1] *A Grammar of Politics*, pp. 376–87.
[2] *Ibid.*, p. 378.

explain their acts. The committee would also review the departmental estimates, and when these came before Parliament they could be subjected to much more intelligent criticism than is possible under the present system. The members of the committee might be chosen so as to reflect the strength of the parties in the House, or because they possessed special knowledge in that particular field, or for both of these reasons combined. The activity of the committee would in every case be definitely limited by the necessity of preserving intact the Minister's political responsibility, so that under no circumstances would the committee directly assume any policy-forming functions. Its chief duties would be to acquire information for Parliament, to make suggestions to the Minister, to offer criticisms of the administration, and to make Parliament's oversight of the executive and the bureaucracy a reality instead of a form.[1]

The particular scheme of organization and control which is used within each department may be left to it to decide in the way best adapted to its needs. All employees should be assigned work which will demand their maximum ability, and which will be given them under such conditions that their skill can be used in the most effective manner; and this rule should govern the relations between a Minister and his officers, as well as the relations between these officers and their subordinates. The undeviating political custom has been that the Minister takes the responsibility for all acts within his department, whether these acts have been done with or without his knowledge or direction. He is supposed to defend the civil servants when they are criticized in Parliament, the only exception being on those rare occasions when the offence is so serious that it has necessitated the dismissal of the official. The rule of responsibility does not mean, of course, that the ideal Minister will be cognizant of all that goes on under his authority; on the contrary, the most successful administrators will usually be those who are skilled in choosing trustworthy and expert assistants and who know the proper time to leave them alone. The same

[1] Cf. *Report of the Machinery of Government Committee (Great Britain)*, 1918, Cd. 9230, pp. 14–15 ; Muir, R., *Peers and Bureaucrats*, pp. 81–5.

principle that is applied to the Minister may be extended to the chief officials and the heads of branches. Each of them is compelled to delegate powers, and is forced to rely to a large degree upon the discretion, judgement, and knowledge of his inferiors.

'Each permanent official performs a double service for his immediate superior. He collects all the material that bears upon a question, presenting it in such a form that a decision can be readily and quickly made ; and he acts to a certain extent as a reader, examining a mass of papers that the superior would be quite unable to go through, and making up his own mind how far they contain anything that requires his chief's attention. This system runs throughout the department, from the junior first-class clerks to the parliamentary head, each official deciding what he will submit to his superior in the same way that the Minister himself determines what matters he will settle on his own authority, and what he had better lay before the Cabinet. No doubt a subordinate, in undertaking to decide a question, occasionally makes a mistake for which the Minister must assume the responsibility ; but that is not a serious danger. The besetting sin of bureaucracy is the tendency to refer too much to a higher authority, which cannot become familiar with the facts of each case, and finds its only refuge in clinging to hard and fast rules.' [1]

The extent of the decentralization will vary from one department to another, from one branch to another within the same department, and from one official to another within the same branch. Some Ministers are reluctant to abandon any matters for other people's decision, others are willing and sometimes even anxious to allow their subordinates to go ahead and refer only the most important things to them. The different deputy heads and those under them vary in the same way. Decentralization to some degree is, of course, imperative in almost every office ; and even a simple delegation of authority on quite unimportant matters usually gives to the inferior the power of deciding what things are and what are not 'important'. In all cases the character, reputation, and experience of the civil servant are of very great consequence in measuring out his independent powers. If in the

[1] Lowell, A. L., *The Government of England* (1912 ed.), i, pp. 184–5.

past he has shown that he possessed a shrewd judgement and sound common sense, or if his reputation for infallibility is strong, or if he has tact, a pleasing personality, and an ability to get things done and done well, he will be allowed to proceed and do his work with little interference. Thus the same office, occupied by different men, may be granted widely differing degrees of freedom. The danger is not that the decentralization will be too great, but that it will be too small; for the superior official is always tempted to endeavour to control everything that is done within his jurisdiction. The following acute maxims on the subject have been stated by Sir Charles Harris of the British service:

'Don't regard centralization as anything but a necessary evil at best—not even if you are at the centre; and if you are not, don't think decentralization should stop at yourself.

Don't think the central point of view must be right in every case because it is central. Like other generalizations and abstractions, it may have lost touch with the concrete particular. Don't forget that the executive man on the circumference sees things that the centre doesn't, but give him his head whenever you can.

Don't wait for the man below to extract from you a little freedom, grudgingly given, but develop your integrating machinery and then give him all he can carry.

Don't cut down the discretion of the man below, or his class, by requiring submission to higher authority in future, because he has made a mistake. Teach him and try him again; but if he is unteachable, shunt him. Delegation cannot be successful unless there is power to select and to weed. All branches and grades of the public service suffer from carrying passengers in the boat, because it requires less determination to go on than to stop and put them ashore. And for this reason, don't let Whitley Councils or anything else deprive a Head of the control of his staff.' [1]

The amount of freedom given to each official will depend also on the kind of knowledge possessed by the supervisor and the supervised: if both are expert and technically trained, then the control of the superior may be close and detailed; if the head is a layman and the inferior an expert, the super-

[1] Harris, Sir Charles, 'Decentralization', *Journal of Public Administration*, 1925, p. 133.

vision will probably be slight. Further, if the work to be done is varied or extremely complex, or if the field in which he is an authority is very limited, the freedom accorded him will be uncommonly large. A frequent solution is for the superior to indicate the thing desired, and allow the expert to choose his own methods to achieve that result. The conditions in each office vary so widely that any very exact definition of the relationship is impossible.

The civil servant has thus a double independence. He enjoys, in common with his fellows, a collective independence from external and political control, obtained through the impartial appointment, the permanence of tenure, the difficulty of removal, and any other means which may be used to render him secure from outside interference. To many civil servants this collective independence is sufficient, for their work is such that there is little scope for unsupervised and original effort. A typist, a filing clerk, a grain scooper, are all performing tasks where initiative is almost unknown, and where any great indulgence in independent ideas is apt to cause trouble and inconvenience to others. But as the offices become more technical, or more important, or higher in rank, a larger freedom and independence in research, or method, or general administration, is desirable. Whatever the speciality of the officer may be, he should be so placed and so untrammelled that his usefulness will not be impaired by excessive control by a conscientious though ignorant superior.

The allotment of work among the departments and the general organization of each one are but the first steps in creating an efficient large scale organization. The variety and multitude of offices, however, make it extremely difficult to submit further suggestions for improvement, though a number of proposals may be put forward which, if not applicable to all positions, nevertheless may fit the needs of a large number. The most important question to be faced is the manner in which bureaucratic lethargy can be dispelled. How is the service to maintain its efficiency, how stimulate its officials, how keep a proper perspective, how cut superfluous red-tape while retaining that which is useful and necessary? These can be accomplished to a limited degree by the expedients noted above—the lay influence of the Minister, the organization of the departments, the granting of a certain amount of independence to the officials—but help must be sought also in the service itself.

It has been said that the entrance to the civil service should bear the inscription, *All hope abandon ye who enter here*, a thought which has been frequently repeated in Canadian civil service history. The sentiment expressed in the following quotations, for example, is scarcely encouraging:

'I have had some knowledge of the Civil Service for a few years, and, from my experience, my advice to my friends and acquaintances has been to keep clear of the Civil Service above everything else. If you have any ambition ; if you ever expect to make any headway in the world ; if you place any value on your initiative, your freedom, then, for Heaven's sake, steer clear of the Civil Service. If you want to become part of a machine by which you move along, without exercising your initiative, then the Civil Service is the proper place for you.' [1]

'*Commission:* You thought there was a prospect before you?
'*Witness:* Yes.
'*Commission:* You had evidently not studied the Civil Service.' [2]

'*Commission:* Is there any inducement for any brilliant boy to stay in the department?
'*Witness:* No. There is every inducement for him to go out. I think a young man is unwise to go into the Government service.' [3]

The colours are not cheerful ; and, unfortunately, they have been to a large degree true to life. A young man has entered the service, bright, eager for advancement, ready to work, confident in his future, and has emerged twenty or thirty years later an old, discouraged automaton, fussing wearily over routine papers, his horizon limited to the four walls of his office. Year after year the service brings about the same metamorphosis, until one is almost forced to conclude that

[1] *Can. H. of C. Debates*, 10 May 1918, p. 1740.
[2] Royal Commission on the Civil Service, *Can. Sess. Pap.*, 1907–8, § 29a, Evidence, p. 114.   [3] *Ibid.*, Evidence, p. 293.

the change cannot be prevented. There would seem to be something in Government work that insidiously unfits a person for Government work, that creates a man of routine in precisely the sphere where men of routine ought not to be. The difficulty confronting the service is that it must attempt the complex task of administering a country largely through the impersonal means of correspondence and book-keeping; and the whole tendency is to allow the forms to displace the reality, to lose contact with the actual events and persons, and to view men as memoranda walking. The excessive leaning towards formalism invariably results in a worship of routine and a lack of initiative, which are probably fostered to some extent by the conditions under which the civil servant holds office. The feeling that he has a secure position for life, his lack of worry as to the future, the leisurely character of the work, the general placidity of his existence, all may encourage faults which in any case would be present to a limited degree. In short, while making the civil service independent of politics and ridding the administration of one pest, another has inadvertently been cultivated.

Happily this is not true of all the expedients which may be used to promote the external independence of the civil servant; on the contrary, several of these devices, if properly applied, may also be made to stimulate his intellectual activity and his initiative. The entrance examinations, for example, will eliminate party appointments; but if the examinations are given on the proper subjects and carefully planned with a view to selecting unusual general ability, they will have the further effect of providing the service with men who are least likely to be cramped by routine in later life. If promotions and salary increases are made for genuine merit and future promise instead of party affiliation, seniority, or mere faithfulness, not only will undesirable influences be excluded but the service will have in its chief offices men who are the least likely to fall into mental ruts. Even security of tenure may work against as well as for routine, inasmuch as it attracts and keeps in the service many good men who might otherwise go elsewhere, and also because in some men it calls forth their very best work:

'Security of tenure . . . enables a man to feel from the first that he is undertaking a serious and worthy lifework ; it lets him grow into his work, and settle down to it calmly, without the feverish unrest which belongs to the kind of work that a man does not for its own sake but for what it will bring ; and this is of great value in an organization which is dealing, as most State officers must deal, not with mere affairs of money-making, but with subtle and complex questions of human action and interaction, questions which have to be dealt with primarily with a view to justice, never with a view to gain. To apply, under such circumstances, the simple and crude test of efficiency—"get on or get out"—which is generally adequate in money-making concerns, would be merely disastrous.' [1]

The scheme of gradation is no less important in its influence on the mental life of the civil servant. The English two-fold division,[2] coupled with the difficult academic examination, is best calculated to develop the highest type. The upper grade of the service will perform most of the intellectual work, and the lower grade the routine and mechanical work, promotion from one grade to the other taking place only in exceptional instances. The result of this division is that the able young men who enter immediately from the universities will not have their initiative and freshness of outlook dulled by years of uninspiring drudgery, but will be trained from the outset to use their talents to the best advantage. The objection may be raised that this classification does not abolish routine work, but merely segregates it and locks it up in the lower division. Until the time arrives, however, when monotonous tasks can be taken over by labour-saving devices, the reasonable plan is to confine the evil effects of routine to one class rather than allow the entire system to be poisoned.

Admirable though the above methods may be, routine and lack of initiative cannot be successfully overcome without other assistance. The struggle against the original sin of bureaucracy must be more unremitting than that against patronage, for, while the latter can be largely curbed by law,

[1] Muir, R., *Peers and Bureaucrats,* p. 55.
[2] Cf. *supra*, pp. 156–8.

the former depends for the most part upon the constant
activity of the officials themselves. They must be ever on the
alert to invent new methods of co-operation with each other,
new expedients for counteracting indifference, new ways of
encouraging initiative in their subordinates. No one scheme
will be sufficient to this end, and even a number and variety
of schemes must be carefully watched and fostered, if they
are to provide the creative minds which the service needs in
order to maintain its efficiency.

'In the case of the Government offices, most of those who have
had dealings with them would say that they need to be "human-
ized". The official should be a man, should be known as a man,
and should be expected to behave as a man. From the beginning
he should do part of his work by oral methods. If, however, half a
dozen clerks are merely placed round an office table and then told
that they are to think with the same kind of effort that would be
made by a newly elected Town Councillor, or a Cabinet Minister
faced with the opportunity of his lifetime, disappointment will
inevitably follow. Civil servants require, not only opportunities,
but motives for thought.' [1]

Professor Graham Wallas has indicated not only a great
cause of bureaucratic lassitude and impermeability to new
ideas, but also the means which may be used for its removal.
If the official is treated as a machine and expected to function
like one, he will probably do so and produce machine-like
thoughts and actions. The remedy, however, is not the mere
creation of opportunities for initiative: this, though important, is inadequate by itself and will not produce the desired
response; one must go deeper and provide a stimulus for
thought as well. The problem then becomes: What ' motives
for thought ' can the public service provide? The private
business corporation answers the question by offering an
opportunity for rapid promotion, the hope of acquiring great
wealth and all that it implies. This is a field in which the
civil service cannot compete effectively. The private business
offers other incentives, though these are not so frequently
stressed, in its emphasis on the importance of the individual,
in its encouragement of his initiative and its reward for his

---

[1] Wallas, Graham, *The Great Society*, pp. 273-4.

response, in the love of power, in the feeling of the importance of high position, in the sense of achievement, and in the love of the work for the work's sake, the business equivalent of the craftsman's delight in his skill. All these latter inducements the civil service should be able to hold out in as tempting a fashion as private industry, though unhappily in the past it has not chosen to do so.

The personal relationships in a public department form naturally the basis for 'humanizing' it and for creating the 'motives for thought'. The official's individuality is of enormous importance to himself, and he must be led to feel and believe that it is important to others as well. To this end care must be taken that he will not become completely lost and merged in his work or his office; he must not be a mere mechanical unit but rather a part of a living organism. One obvious way of keeping his individuality distinct and of increasing his self-respect is by limiting the number of employees in each of the groups into which the department is divided. The smaller the group, the more will each member feel his responsibility and importance in it. The exact number should be determined in part by the requirements of effective supervision and administration, and in part also by the facility of obtaining those personal contacts which will inspire loyalty, affection, co-operation, and individual interest.[1] These qualities will tend to appear more readily when the group is composed of members sharing approximately the same traditions, social background, and educational training. Many superficially unimportant things will likewise work towards better personal relationships. The ability of a chief to call his subordinates by name, to know something of their outside activities, to show a genuine concern for their personal welfare, acquires a new significance when considered as an aid to *esprit de corps*.

The higher official, for his part, may have his interest aroused and maintained by similar treatment. The Minister

[1] 'The number of his fellows with whom a man can maintain easy personal intercourse varies with individual variations, with the conditions of work, and with the time which any body of workmen spend together. Perhaps it does not often exceed eighty, and is normally about twenty or thirty.' *Ibid.*, p. 333; cf. also pp. 332-7.

may ask him to lunch at the Rideau Club, and introduce him to fellow Ministers or other reputed celebrities as 'a coming man in the department'. The deputy head may invite him and his wife to a game of bridge, or play golf with him at the Country Club, or in some other way give him a social recognition which helps to break down the rigid barriers of departmental discipline and makes the subordinate feel on terms of potential equality with his official superior. The Minister or the deputy may also summon him to attend a conference committee in the department 'to help us out of a difficulty'; or his opinion may be requested on an important matter of policy; or his advice may be accepted on some subject which he has made his particular study. In short, small unexpected attentions, trifling though they may seem, are likely to have a salutary effect out of all proportion to their apparent insignificance. The official cannot but derive a subtle pleasure at being singled out for attention. The implication of equality and the deference to his opinion convey a new idea of his place in the department and the importance of the office he holds. He will probably experience a desire and an ambition to compel more notice in the future, and will look forward to the time when such events will occur every day in the week. He sees in these incidents a recognition of his personality and his merits, and he comes to regard himself more and more as a partner in a great state enterprise.

The deputy head and his chiefs, if they could be persuaded to take the trouble, could do a great deal to promote original thought and work by the young ambitious men in the department. The difficulty that is usually encountered is that the official in charge is more concerned with getting things done than with instructing his inferiors and thinking out ways in which their initiative might be stimulated. To this reluctance is occasionally added the fear that if he takes his assistants into complete confidence they will soon know as much about the work as he does himself, with the probable result that his prestige and authority in the department would be lessened. The more generous policy will, however, ultimately pay; for if the superior desires skilled help and eager co-operation, one of the surest ways of obtaining them is to place responsibility on his juniors while they are young enough to give an adequate response. Special attention is given in Great Britain to this part of a department's work:

'The incoming letter,' writes Sir Thomas Heath, former Joint Permanent Secretary to the Treasury, 'after the routine processes of registration, search for previous papers, &c., have been completed, passes to the Division concerned, where it will frequently fall to be dealt with by the junior officer of the Division, an Assistant Principal, who may be a man quite recently appointed. This junior officer starts with a clean slate, as it were ; and he can, according to his lights, make his contribution towards the preparation of the case for a decision by his superior officers, or himself suggest what the decision should be. There is no period at the beginning of his service during which he is confined to mere routine or mechanical work ; he can plunge at once *in medias res*. Any paper which is beyond his competence he sends forward to the Principal under whom he works. The Principal will, as a rule, be a man of some years' service, with considerable experience. He will naturally overhaul what the junior has written, and will see how far he has got on the right lines or failed through inexperience to do so ; he will give him hints as to how to deal with a future case of the kind, what particular points to look for, and so on ; for it is a special duty of the Principal to help the junior to learn his work. The Principal will then either dispose of the paper himself or submit it with any further observations to the Assistant Secretary in charge of the Division.' [1]

A Canadian deputy minister has told me that he made a custom of discussing important problems with those under him, and that he found that both he and they profited enormously. He discovered that his own thoughts on the subject became more precise and distinct, while he frequently received valuable ideas or was able to look at the question from a new angle. The subordinate, for his part, derived pleasure from feeling that his comments were really desired, and that he was exerting a direct influence on the policies of the department. But encouragement of this kind is rare. Too often the young official spends all his time at routine work, and the only response that his suggestions evoke is a stiffening of the barriers of inertia and indifference. Even if he is able

[1] Heath, Sir Thomas L., *The Treasury*, pp. 16–17.

to arouse interest in a reform, he frequently must convince his superiors not only that the change would be beneficial, but also that they had thought of it themselves. Finally, if the idea should prove successful, he sees the one in authority receive the greater part of the credit while his part in the affair is almost entirely ignored.

Deputy heads and their immediate subordinates should be the first to realize that if the young civil servants are to exercise large powers and to show initiative in the future, they must be given early responsibilities and opportunities for creative thought. If this encouragement is not offered, all their training will foster those traits of mind and character which will hamper them in later years. Excessive centralization and control will inevitably breed a lack of imagination and a weak initiative in subordinates. The necessity of referring all important matters to a superior, the reluctance to take a personal responsibility for any act, the habit of emphasizing the sectional rather than the broader views— these characteristics, once acquired, are hard to shake off. Thus the civil servant, while apparently training for a high position, may unconsciously be unfitting himself for it; he will have spent so much time learning to dodge responsibility that when he finally reaches a position of command, his instinctive policy will be to keep himself clear of trouble and to follow rule and precedent as the safest means of self-protection.[1]

The freshening of the official's mind and the encouragement of his initiative may be done collectively as well as individually. One of the most common methods is by the frequent use of group meetings within the department. These may be lunch-hour gatherings which have as their main purpose the creation of better feeling and closer acquaintance, or the more formal business meetings, which consider the common problems of the branch or some particular scheme which is being proposed at the time. The change from written to oral work is psychologically a great aid to efficiency, and the mental stimulus given by discussion and argument is of

[1] Cf. Harris, Sir Charles, ' Decentralization ', *Journal of Public Administration*, 1925, pp. 117–33.

enormous benefit. But if the meetings are to reap the maximum of profit, many small points of detail must be watched. Continual vigilance must be used to keep the discussion full of life and relevant to the main subject; each member at the conference must be prodded by occasional questions in order to sustain his interest; each must be encouraged to express his own opinions without fear of ridicule; and an acute psychologist will even take care to arrange the order of seating around the room.[1] Such meetings have a further merit in that they help to disclose unexpected ability in some of the subordinates and enable the chief to mark them out for future advancement, while he himself is apt to come from the conference with the realization that he knows much more about the subject than he did before the discussion began.

The general morale of the service is of enormous importance in determining the interest of the official in his work. By morale is meant 'a spirit which expresses itself in enthusiasm, loyalty, co-operation, devotion to duty, pride in the service'.[2] Just and able administration, deserving promotion, impartiality and fairness of treatment, security of tenure, a sense of loyalty to a superior and a desire to emulate him, a spirit of competition within the service, social intercourse, pride of accomplishment, enthusiasm, jealousy of the department's reputation—all these both cause and constitute morale. It may be nourished by such little things as a bowling league or a service billiard room, or by such great things as a lifetime of devotion to duty. It may be enfeebled by an unjust criticism, or by an undeserved promotion, or by an insidious growth of a tradition of indifference and mental laxness. The success or failure of any administrative department, and particularly the degree to which it is able to call out the best efforts of its employees, will depend in a very large measure upon the extent to which these widely different factors have been fostered or discouraged.[3]

It is important to note that while private business is as

[1] Wallas, Graham, *The Great Society*, pp. 260–74; *Human Nature in Politics*, pp. 263–4.

[2] White, L. D., *Introduction to the Study of Public Administration*, p. 237. For an excellent account of morale in the public service cf. pp. 234–50.

[3] Cf. *Report of Transmission*, pp. 37–8.

a rule at an advantage in competing with the public service, in some very significant ways the latter can make the strongest appeal. The peculiar nature of the civil service and its unusual position in the country are frequently able to furnish greater incentives for thought and industry than any temptation that can be offered by a private company. The prestige of the nation's business and the honour attached to public offices of importance make the high positions in the service prizes which usually are coveted and eagerly pursued. Moreover, the Government service is bound to bring the officials into close contact and association with the leading men of the country in a manner and to a degree which no private business can rival. The civil servant also enjoys the feeling that he is doing the really big things, and is making decisions which profoundly affect the destinies of the whole nation—a sense of combined power and patriotism which is somewhat enhanced by the short and uncertain tenure of the ministers. All these are stimuli of no mean order; and they call forth not only the best talents of the public officials but their self-sacrifice and devotion also. Lord Haldane, who spoke with no common authority on such matters, was emphatic in his declaration of the important part played by these incentives:

'Profit-making is not the only nor the most powerful motive. I doubt much whether it is the most real source of inspiration. If you look, for example, at that wonderful living structure, the British Navy, you find a set of motives more dominant, in so far as self-sacrifice for the sake of public duty is accepted as more important than life itself. Right through the Navy, as our great wars have shown, there has been continuity of this spirit from generation to generation. The cause comes first, the individual second. . . . I have seen the same spirit in the Army, and I have seen it in the Civil Service itself. But on the whole the Navy seems the best field in which to study it. For it is there as the outcome of a long tradition, and of a natural aptitude which was as marked in the days of the Armada as it is to-day. The spirit is one which is at least as efficient as that of profit-making, and it is the result of tradition and education. It is the outlook and attitude of the best naval and military officers which make their leadership welcomed by the men, men who are trained to look for and to expect it.

'This attitude is the result of tradition based on the preference of duty to the State, extending to the sacrifice of the life itself of the individual concerned. It is a motive which has shown itself to be potent and dominant. It is the outcome of training and habit of mind based on it. I do not believe that the practicability which experience has demonstrated of encouraging it, is any monopoly of the fighting services. I have seen something analogous, but hardly less marked, in the refusal of civil servants to exchange modest salaries for lucrative employment in commercial and industrial profit-making concerns. Such a refusal when it is made generally comes from a deep sense of duty to the State as the higher choice. It is the result of a habit of mind which I believe we might see yet more of in other departments if we took the proper steps to stimulate it. It is most common among those who have cultivated the high ideals based on that larger outlook which is the result of knowledge of the meaning of life.' [1]

'Does anybody imagine that any private firm or company could run the British Navy? They could not. You would not get the public spirit that is required in the British Navy from any private concern. Not only does your great Admiral laugh at the notion that because he is paid on a by no means high scale, he should therefore look about for civil employment which would be offered him on much more remunerative terms. No; he is there for the glory of the thing. Now you can have that in the same way, if you appeal for it, in every department of the State Service. A man there may be as proud of his work, and feel the same devotion to the State, as he can in the other services. It is only a question of tradition and training.' [2]

The inelasticity of mind, the narrowness of vision, and the love of formalism, which so often hamper the civil servant, are frequently due in large measure to the fact that he is kept year after year in the same office doing the same general type of work in the same way. This can be counteracted to some extent by an interchange of positions. Managers of private companies are constantly on the alert to find new promising material, and having found it, they move it wher-

[1] Haldane, Lord, 'An Organized Civil Service', *Journal of Public Administration*, 1923, p. 14.

[2] Haldane, Lord, 'The Machinery of Government', *The Civil Servant and His Profession*, pp. 39–40.

ever it can be used to the best advantage. But the Government organization is more inelastic, and transfers from one department to another are almost impossible, even though an employee may be a misfit in his position and show promise of succeeding somewhere else. Transfers within the limits of one department are more common, though they usually are made with another purpose in view. They aim at exchanging the old position for one which is different in type though closely allied in subject-matter, in order that the official's knowledge and experience of the department's work may be varied and enlarged. Lord Milner stated a few years ago that one great difficulty he had observed in the Colonial Office was that most of the Downing Street clerks who dealt with places like Jamaica or the Straits Settlements had never been there, and they thus lacked a practical acquaintance with a very important part of their work. The few in the department who had had the actual contact with some of the colonies enjoyed a very noticeable advantage over the others.[1] A similar need for transfers between the Inside and Outside Canadian Services has frequently been experienced and commented on; as, for example, in the following evidence given before the Royal Commission in 1891:

'I think that when a chief officer discovers a man employed in the outside service, who to his knowledge exhibits extra cleverness and ability, and a man of that kind is required for special and very important duties in his office, he should be allowed to secure that man's services by having him transferred to the inside service for trial and permanent appointment, if he was found satisfactory. There have been many good men in the outside service who would have been found after trial invaluable in the inside service. In the city post offices and custom houses you can find men equal to, if not superior to, some in the inside service of their departments, and who, from having been located in business centres, mixing with the public and knowing its wants, and having a knowledge of commerce and business transactions, could render valuable assistance in many directions, if placed in the inside service.'[2]

[1] Milner, Lord, 'The Aims of the Institute of Public Administration', *Journal of Public Administration*, 1923, p. 90.
[2] *Can. Sess. Pap.*, 1892, § 16c, p. 142; cf. *ibid.*, 1880–1, § 113, pp. 30, 44–5.

A regular system of transfers and promotions from practical work to clerical and administrative work should be
included as an essential part of the policy of many departments. If a certain number of clerks in the Customs Department, for example, were exchanged with an equal number
of inspectors, the change would be beneficial to all. The
official who issues orders on immigration and the care of
immigrants should spend some time at Halifax or Quebec;
he should see them arrive, and try his skill at applying the
rules he has helped to formulate. The clerk who writes letters
from Ottawa about Indian affairs would write much more
intelligently if he had seen an Indian and had some first-hand
experience of a reservation. Things which had been merely
names to him would take on a new significance and a changed
importance. The bored bureaucrat, who dictates regulations
somewhat glibly in the West Block, would discover after a
brief contact with the realities of practical work that regulations were much easier to dictate than to execute; and he
would gain an understanding of what rules were difficult to
enforce, and the causes of the difficulty, and the necessity for
giving a little more or a little less discretion to the official in
charge. On the other hand, the civil servant in British
Columbia, who has been impatient of red tape and has been
unable to comprehend the reason for the delays at the capital, would begin to grasp some of the difficulties of administration after he had spent a few weeks in the Inside Service.
In short, the training of every one would be greatly improved
and broadened, and when each returned to his original work
he would be a much more valuable employee than he had
been before.

Unfortunately these transfers have been made very sparingly in Canada, due partly to short-sightedness, partly to the
bother of putting them through and of making the necessary
readjustments afterwards, and most of all to the incredible
stupidity of the present *Civil Service Act*, which treats transfers as an invention of the devil which must be outwitted at
all possible cost. The only way in which a transfer can be
made from one department to another is by the agreement
of the two deputy heads; and even when the agreement is

reached, they must secure the approval of the omnipotent Civil Service Commission, which body will not consent unless the transfer is within the same class. Should a deputy desire to make a transfer within his own department, his powers without the Commission go no farther than moving a man from one position to another of the same class—a generous concession, inasmuch as the multitude of classes makes a transfer under these restrictions quite meaningless. He cannot, for example, move a Clerk-stenographer to the position known as Book-keeper-stenographer, though he has the privilege of moving the Clerk-stenographer in one branch to the position of Clerk-stenographer in another.[1] And yet the Chairman of the Commission remarked that the system had 'a good deal of elasticity'.[2]

A further stimulus of the same kind might be given by sending some men from Ottawa to hold inquiries throughout the Dominion, and by granting to others leave of absence with pay in order that they might have an opportunity to learn at first-hand the nature of the work in the field. Occasional groups of civil servants might be sent to the United States or to Great Britain to make a comparative study of administrative methods and other problems common to both.[3] A more ambitious scheme would be to work out a civil service copy of the academic sabbatical year, whereby leaves of from six to twelve months (with full salary) would be regularly granted to the highest officials after each seven or ten years of service. The assistant deputy minister from the Department of Trade and Commerce might profitably spend his leave in the West Indies or South America with an idea of seeking out new opportunities of trade development. A chief of division in the Finance Department might study the methods of Treasury control in England or the banking system of the United States. The head immigration officer might visit Europe, and see exactly how the immigrants are secured and to what extent the most desirable classes are

---

[1] *Can. H. of C. Journals,* 1923, Appendix, § 5, pp. 74–7, 446, 641, 686, 843.
[2] *Ibid.,* p. 843.
[3] This has been done unofficially in England by the Society of Civil Servants sending delegations of this kind to France.

attracted to Canada, while a colleague might spend several months examining American methods at Ellis Island. All these journeys would bring a broader intellectual outlook and a new perspective, while forming at the same time additional rewards to the highest officials. It might also be possible to recruit a limited number of Dominion civil servants from the provincial services, if and when the latter become reformed and make merit the only basis of admission. Certain offices at Ottawa could be set apart for limited competition from the local services, and they could be filled from the provinces as they became vacant. The mingling of civil servants, somewhat differently trained and performing somewhat different work, would lead to an interchange of ideas and a comparison of experiences which could not fail to be helpful.

A great deal might also be accomplished through the formation of a general civil servants' organization along the lines of the Institute of Public Administration in Great Britain. The Institute is endeavouring to promote the study of public administration and to develop central and local civil services as recognized professions. These aims are being pursued more explicitly by: (1) The development of high ideals and traditions of the public service. (2) The study of public administration, of the machinery necessary for its practice, of the principles of history, economics, and political science with special reference to public administration and constitutional law and practice. (3) The exchange of information and thought on administrative questions with a view to increasing the efficiency of the public services and to create a well-informed public opinion regarding these services, to develop the technique of administration, and to disseminate useful information regarding the public services of Great Britain and other countries. (4) The expression of the view of the services on questions of public duty and professional etiquette. (5) The promotion of good relations between different branches of the public service and the encouragement of interest in their profession, and to this end the establishing of central headquarters with committee rooms, library, and other amenities for study and social intercourse. (6) The publication of a periodical journal.[1]

The more material interests of the civil servants might very profitably be entrusted in part to a Canadian edition of the Whitley Council. The idea was suggested by the *Report of Transmission* in 1919, which also pointed out that a Council's primary purpose was to give expression to the views of the different groups in the service and not to serve merely as a grievance committee.[2] This caution the civil servants of 1923 apparently forgot; for while urging the necessity for an organization of the Whitley type, they envisaged Councils which would deal with and determine individual questions of discipline, hours of work, leave, organization of work, classification of positions, efficiency ratings, and even dismissals, salaries, promotions, and appointments.[3] The Councils can be of real benefit to the service as representative bodies having as their main objects the securing of more information, the promotion of a better understanding, the free exchange of ideas, and the creation of a spirit of co-operation and helpfulness. They will succeed not in proportion to the grievances they adjust, but according to the number of grievances which never arise. Their great contribution to the service will be the increased morale which naturally comes from the consciousness that an impartial mediating and representative body exists.[4]

The desirability of the civil servant supplementing his knowledge by an intensive study of suitable university subjects is being increasingly recognized. This is in no way an acknowledgement of the failure of the academic examination to form a satisfactory gauge of entrance qualifications. Such examination is beyond reasonable doubt the most prophetic test of a candidate's ability; it secures competition over a more extended field than any examination on special sub-

[1] Corner, H. G., 'The Aims of the Institute of Public Administration', *Journal of Public Administration*, 1923, p. 50.

[2] *Report of Transmission*, pp. 60–2.

[3] *Can. H. of C. Journals*, 1923, Appendix, § 5, pp. 207–8, 222–32, 293–4, 368–94.

[4] Cf. Bunning, G. H. S., 'Whitley Councils in the Civil Service', *Journal of Public Administration*, 1924, pp. 172–83.

jects; it obtains men with a cultural background and a type
of mind which is not likely to become narrow and bureaucratic in later years. These facts, however, do not prevent
the official's training after admission being carried along
special lines. Hitherto he has picked up his information
largely as he has happened to encounter it in the department—a haphazard arrangement which has been both inefficient and slow. 'The general remedy', says Sir William
Beveridge, 'is to develop the idea that there is really an art
of public administration. The civil service is now a profession, and I should like it to become and realize itself as a
learned profession.'[1]   To this end every encouragement
should be given to officials to attend university courses on
selected subjects; and those who have been ambitious and
intelligent enough to take and profit by such opportunities
should be singled out for promotion. The completion of any
particularly good piece of research or the writing of an
exceptionally able report might be rewarded in a similar
manner, partly because the employee has earned it, and also
because the service will be the gainer by placing him where
his abilities may be used to better advantage.[2]   The Canadian Civil Service Commission has gone so far as to suggest
that a board of university professors in science should be
named, whose duty would be to recommend for recognition
those civil servants who had done original research work of
conspicuous merit. The recognition might take the form of a
promotion, a money grant, or a generous superannuation.
The Commission gave as an illustration the case of Dr. Saun-
ders, who recently was compelled to retire on a small pension,
despite the fact that he had added millions to the country's
wealth through his discovery of Marquis wheat. [3]

The idea that civil servants may be trained for administration as others are trained for law or medicine has been
most forcibly expressed by Lord Haldane, who based his

[1] 'The Civil Servant of the Future', *The Development of the Civil Service*,
p. 242. Cf. Gibbon, I. G., 'University Education in Public Administration',
Journal of Public Administration, 1926, pp. 434–7; Robertson, C. Grant,
'University Education in Public Administration', *ibid.*, 1926, pp. 438–42.

[2] Cf. Laski, H. J., *A Grammar of Politics*, pp. 403–7.

[3] *Can. H. of C. Journals*, 1923, Appendix, § 5, pp. 921–2, 1044–9.

arguments on his own experience as a Cabinet Minister from 1905 to 1912. As Secretary of State for War he brought about a definite separation between the General Staff, or those in the fighting service, and the administrative officials, such as those in the Army Medical Service, the Quartermaster's Department, &c. This separation being made, he then set himself to the task of developing administrative officers, whose outstanding characteristics would be self-reliance, initiative, and an ability to think and act for themselves. Academically trained men were taken and put through a number of specialized courses at the London School of Economics, such as contract law, local government, administrative law, general economics, public administration, comparative government, and railway management. The results proved to be enormously successful, and would have been even better had the war not brought the scheme to a premature close. Every effort was made both in the academic work and in practice to encourage the men to take responsibility and to use their own talents, to depend less on their superiors and more on themselves. The college courses were designed to give them the information and the proper starting point, as well as to suggest possible solutions and possible lines of thought. In practice the emphasis was the same: a man would be assigned a definite piece of work, and he would be held responsible for its performance in the speediest, most economical, and most efficient manner.[1]

Initiative, power to take responsibility, freedom to act, knowledge, decision, and the instinct for coming out right— these qualities Lord Haldane named as necessary to the highest type of civil servant. Nor can the requirements be seriously denied or questioned. What the service must have if it is to be genuinely alive and adequate to the tasks which the future will impose upon it, is an officer class composed of men equal in power and imagination to those in the business world, and greater than they in devotion to duty and singleness of purpose. They do not need to be masters of petty detail or experts in every branch of their department. They

[1] *Coal Industry Commission, volume* ii (*Great Britain*), 1919, Cmd. 360, pp. 1082–5.

do need to have a large amount of natural talent, a knack of working with men and of drawing out the best efforts of their subordinates, a flair for getting to the heart of a matter, an ability to confront difficulties and a genius to surmount them. These are admittedly exceptional qualities, and exceptional means must be used to obtain and encourage them. The official must begin with an excellent education, he must augment it with a specialized training in administration and similar problems along the lines suggested, he must be given constant encouragement to use his own judgement and inventiveness, his mind must be continually freshened by an interchange of ideas, and he must be surrounded by an atmosphere where initiative is not only expected but rewarded.

'Initiative', said Lord Haldane, 'is a matter of the spirit and a matter of temperament. Like courage and temperament, initiative can be developed. I should like to see a school of the State teach the necessity of that and the necessity of a man relying upon himself and making his own decisions. I should like to see encouraged what the best officer already knows by instinct, the absolute necessity of treating his men as equals, getting on with them, understanding them, and making their concerns his, and working with them in such a fashion that, although he was their guide, philosopher and friend and their commander, yet when it came to a moment of decision, while they felt it was their own spirit which was embodied in him, in taking the initiative in what he was doing, he was not taking an arbitrary initiative, but an initiative based on knowledge. As you see, I put education in a very wide and broad sense as the foundation of the question whether you can train administrators for the service of the State.'[1]

[1] *Ibid.*, p. 1085.

XIII. CONCLUSION

'It's an instrument rare,
To be handled with care,
And ought to be treated as such.'
The Yeomen of the Guard.

A REVIEW of the history and present organization of the Canadian service shows that its life has been dominated throughout by one, it might almost be said by only one, thing, viz., political patronage. Patronage came in with the earliest Government, it merely changed hands with the introduction of a responsible Cabinet, and the history of the service since Confederation has been largely concerned with its abolition. A reasonable measure of reform has finally been adopted, and the ward heeler and his associates are now kept out of all but the meanest positions. But patronage is still the dominant influence in the service, or, to put the situation more accurately, patronage has been largely eliminated, but the fear of it still governs the service throughout its entire structure.

The present organization of the Canadian service is built upon fear—fear that party supporters will be appointed, fear that they will be promoted even though they obtain office legitimately, fear that they will be transferred from a poor position to a good one, fear that the deputy minister may be open to unworthy suggestions from the minister, fear that the chief of a branch may be influenced by party in recommending the reclassification of a position, fear that the salaries of Liberals may be increased while those of Conservatives remain unchanged. The result of this attitude has been a search for objective tests and the placing of an undue reliance upon the Civil Service Commission whose thankless task it is to administer such tests. An attempt is made to measure objectively things which by their very nature cannot be satisfactorily gauged by mechanical methods, and the Commission is given functions to perform for which it has neither the aptitude, nor the facilities, nor the necessary information.

Examples of this have been given in earlier chapters. Promotions are made by the Commission, although they have no first-hand knowledge of the candidates' qualifications, and they lack familiarity with the nature of the work which would give them the ability to use second-hand knowledge effectively. The reclassification of positions is done by one of the 'experts' of the Commission, who knows nothing of the work of a particular department, but who goes down to the office and asks earnest questions. Fortified by the information thus obtained, the 'expert' makes his recommendation to the Commissioners, who nod their heads wisely and acquiesce in the report. The Commissioners also exercise a nominal oversight over salaries, although it is somewhat difficult to understand how they are expected to know whether a particular employee, out of the tens of thousands in the service, should be granted or refused an extra sixty dollars a year. A similar omniscience is expected in making transfers within a department or from one department to another. In arriving at all these decisions the Commission is using second- or third-hand information, and is relying largely upon objective and mathematical methods to measure such intangible things as the civil servant's tact with the public and other employees, ten years of faithful service, his ability to seize upon essentials in a letter, an interview or a departmental problem, his entire trustworthiness and willingness to assume responsibility, his calm and power of decision in an emergency, the need that may have arisen for giving him a mental stimulus, &c. The Commissioners peer owlishly at reports made by subordinates, who are in most instances as conscientious and as ignorant as the Commissioners themselves; they labour through files of correspondence, reports, efficiency cards in varying colours and sizes, recommendations from inferiors with additional comments attached; and at last they give a ponderous judgement affecting some harmless little fellow who has asked to be moved from Medicine Hat to Ottawa. All this circumambulation, delay, waste of energy, ineffectiveness, occur because of the patronage bogey. Can one wonder that the deputy heads of departments, whose task is to get things done, throw up their hands in despair and growl imprecations against the crimes that are committed in the name of reform?

But, it will be argued, the history of the Canadian service conclusively proves that however bad the present condition may be, political control is much worse; and even admitting that Commission rule is undesirable, it is better than rule by a patronage committee through a Minister. The truth of this contention must be granted; but the choice need not lie necessarily between the two extremes. A misleading comparison is usually made between the Canadian service of to-day and that before 1917, in other words, between a reformed service and one largely unreformed, a comparison which inevitably favours the former. A reformed service without complete control by the Commission existed only from 1917 to 1919; and there is every reason to believe that had this been given an extended trial, it would have been more successful than the present system of Commission rule. It is, in other words, possible to retain open competitive examinations and similar devices as the means of entrance, and yet hand back to the deputy ministers control in all those matters which naturally and properly come under their authority.

It must be remembered that the device of using a Civil Service Commission was originally invented not to manage the civil service, but to obtain an impartial supervisory body which could set examination papers and grade them. This function they were well suited to perform, for they were applying an objective test on subjects within their knowledge; and while the underlying motive was the discernment and weighing of unusual natural ability, no other test was as suited to the purpose, and the Commissioners were at least as well equipped as any one to decide the matter justly. Any addition to the functions of the Commission demands therefore the most careful scrutiny, and the onus of proof must be placed on those advocating the change. This has never been done. The narrowness of the Commission's proper task has been lost sight of in the frantic desire to curb the spoilsman, and its functions have as a consequence become warped and twisted out of their original shape.

Another point frequently forgotten is that the great opportunity for patronage occurs before and not after entrance, and party influence concentrates largely on appointments. If the entrance to the service is carefully guarded by really difficult examinations and impartial control over them, then few political adherents will be able to get in, and the danger of subsequent wire-pulling becomes slight. The young man who wins his office by merit will usually have no political influence to invoke, nor is he, as a rule, the type which wishes and tries to invoke it, nor has he the same right as the political appointee to make demands on the party for further support. In short, the use of impartial appointment for genuine merit removes the greater part of the political menace.

The attitude of fear towards undue party influence in the service is up to a certain point praiseworthy, but it must not be allowed to become a phobia. No one can be blamed for being afraid of robbers, but it is foolish to carry that fear so far as to insist on an armoured car whenever one wishes to go for an airing. It is impossible for the service to do its best work when its chiefs are hampered and restrained and suspected at every step. Surroundings of this kind inevitably ruin the work of the chiefs and undermine the discipline and morale of the entire service. The deputies and their assistants must be given back their natural powers, and they must be trusted to resent and oppose any attempts at undue influence, should such attempts be made. If necessary, the position of the civil servant might be defined more exactly by a public pronouncement of the Cabinet to the effect that it was pledged to support and encourage an independent, non-political service, and that it desired no advice on questions of personnel. A pledge of this kind and a conscientious attempt to live up to it is not, I think, too utopian in view of the present state of Cabinet and public opinion.

'As matters now stand', said the Northcote-Trevelyan Report in 1853, 'the Government of the country could not be carried on without the aid of an efficient body of permanent officers, occupying a position duly subordinate to that of the Ministers who are directly responsible to the Crown and to Parliament, yet possessing sufficient independence, character, ability, and experience to be able to advise, assist, and, to some extent, influence those who are from time to time set over them.' [1]

Word for word this is even more true to-day than when it was written, and it still involves the solution of the same fundamental problems: the good men must first be obtained, and they must then be encouraged and given the opportunity to use their best efforts in the service of the state. The first problem has in Canada been so linked up with patronage that it has absorbed all attention to the virtual exclusion of everything else. As the merit system becomes more firmly established, greater care and attention can be paid to the solution of the second problem, viz., the creation of a more efficient administrative body.

Before either problem can be properly approached, however, democracy must begin to make up its mind as to exactly what qualities in a civil servant are desired and what place the civil service is expected to fill in the modern government. The difficulty, as noted in an earlier chapter, is due in a large measure to the almost simultaneous appearance of popular rule and a complex society in whose affairs, according to modern theory, the governing authority must take an increasingly important part. Had either democracy or the complexity of governmental functions appeared without the other, the solution would have been comparatively simple. It is their concurrence which has caused the difficulty. If, for example, the popular control were applied under more simple social and economic conditions, the Jacksonian idea that one man was as good as his neighbour and equally well fitted to occupy public office, might be adequate. Officials might conceivably be chosen by lot or by election or by party appointment, and inasmuch as their work would consist of little more than the simpler kinds of regulation and the preservation of public order, they would be able to perform it with moderate success. But the growth of a complex civilization and a new conception of the state's place in that civilization has changed the whole problem, for the demands on the civil service have increased enormously

[1] *Can. Sess. Pap.*, 1880–1, § 113, p. 393.

in number and variety and difficulty. Men of little ability and of ordinary intelligence are unequal to the task; and as a consequence a method of selection which does not eliminate men of this type is useless. Popular election and party appointment do not stress the necessary qualifications, nor is a scheme which has the single merit of impartiality, such as drawing lots or competing in a simple examination, very much better. The method of selection must go farther: it must be not only impartial and unaffected by irrelevant considerations, but it must also pick out, so far as is humanly possible, real ability in an unusual degree.

The mere selection of a civil service, however, as this book has tried to show, is but the first step if the administration is to do its work properly in the modern government. The elimination of patronage simply ropes off the area and keeps the interested spectators from taking an active part in the game that is to be played. But if the game is to be worth the playing, the participants need more than an assurance that the spectators will not jump on the field, they must have a real interest in the struggle and feel that it warrants their utmost exertions. The object of the new democracy must be to discover the best environment, the most suitable conditions of tenure in its broadest sense, the most adequate stimuli, which will produce the intense mental and volitional effort in the different officers of Government, while preserving in the last resort popular control over the whole.

If this end be steadily kept in view, it will lead to a varied use of widely different political expedients for different offices. The members of Parliament, for example, must be given those conditions which will be most apt to aid them in their work of reflecting, yet at the same time leading, public opinion. They must be elected by a wide electorate; their term of office must be for so many years; their right to freedom of speech must be given unusual protection; they should have the spur of political ambition; their numbers should not be immoderately large or small; and if a high standard of personnel is to be maintained, they must be given generous powers. These and many other conditions are designed to produce the proper response in the members of Parliament, to make the House of Commons attractive to the highest type of candidate, to give the members the best atmosphere for genuine political effort, to keep them in touch with public opinion, to obtain from them, in short, the kind of effort which the country desires.

But a different kind of ability and a different kind of effort are required in other parts of the Government service, and different means must be used to obtain them. The office of the judge cannot be treated the same as that of a Senator or of a member of the Montreal Harbour Commission. Nor can the civil servant be adequately chosen by election, nor will he do the best work if his term of office is limited to five years, nor should he try to reflect public opinion. He belongs to an organization primarily concerned with thought rather than will;[1] the conditions of his office, the environment in which he performs his tasks are peculiarly his own, and should be carefully adapted to his needs. Hence some civil servants will be appointed by the Government, some will be chosen by competitive academic examination, some by competitive special examination, some by competitive tests of varying kinds and degrees of difficulty. Furthermore, it is likely that the majority will do better work if the tenure of office is long and moderately secure, if promotion is based on merit, if salaries are generous, and if allowances are made for retirement in old age. Even these will not yield the maximum of intellectual effort, and many other devices must be tried in varying degrees to encourage initiative, independent thought, and general freshness of mind.

Careful selection and the presence of the proper stimuli, however, will do little good unless provision is made at the same time for the adequate utilization of the civil servant's special knowledge and inventiveness. How much freedom and independence should be accorded him in the performance of his work? The problem is by no means a new one, but it is becoming more urgent each year as the complexity and difficulty of administration increases. The Minister is still theoretically accountable to Parliament for the work of his department, but it is common knowledge that he has little or

[1] Cf. Wallas, Graham, *The Great Society*, pp. 235–319.

no control over enormous areas which nominally are subject to him. In the past the theory and fact of ministerial responsibility corresponded very closely, for the governing power and the administration were virtually one; but to-day the two lie far apart. The separation has been brought about largely by the multiplication of governmental offices and by the imperative demand for *expertise,* both of which have destroyed the Minister's immediate contact with his work. He is forced to rely more and more upon assistants, who, as their work grows in technical and administrative difficulty, become less and less subject to direct or indirect popular scrutiny.[1]

All this, however, disturbs the simpler kind of democratic theory, which looks upon election and appointment by the people's representatives as the only orthodox ways of filling public offices, and expects the popular control over these offices to be continually and rigidly maintained through the Ministry. The idea of a sovereign people issuing impressive commands to its servants has never been very close to the facts; it is even more misleading and inaccurate to-day. Democracy in the Great Society cannot be reduced to such simple terms; and if the machinery of government is to be adequately understood, the old theory must be accepted with generous reservations and a somewhat different and more complex idea substituted. The control of the people and their representatives must be retained as a final check on all officers of Government, but both people and Parliament must learn when to interfere and when to abstain. In the future even more than to-day the most efficient Parliament and Cabinet will prove to be those which will concern themselves with essentials and matters of broad policy, which will be content to judge the administration largely by results not incidents, and which will abstain from poking and prodding unduly into departmental minutiae. There must be a genuine division of talents; Minister and civil servant must supplement the qualities of each other, while Parliament maintains a general oversight and final control. Democracy and its political representatives will do well to be suspicious

[1] Cf. *supra,* pp. 119–24, 229–32.

of any bureaucratic vices, but they should at the same time give to the civil servant their willing co-operation, avail themselves of his special knowledge, trust him as far as they are able without dropping completely all power of restraint. Trust, not suspicion, confidence, not fear, must be the guiding spirit of the new régime—yet behind it all must be in the last resort the supervision of Parliament. It is this contradiction which makes the whole relationship not only difficult to work but also difficult to describe: Parliament and the Ministry must trust the civil service; but they must trust it with a whip in their hands, or at least with the consciousness that the whip is where they can grasp it at a moment's notice.

All this assumes that ministerial responsibility, as it is generally understood, must be greatly slackened in practice even though it may be still retained in theory. Many of the most skilled civil servants must be left free to cope with the problems which they alone can solve, while the function of the lay political superior will be reduced to that of supervision of a very vague kind. More and more power must pass, as it has been passing for years back, into the hands of the permanent officials; greater and greater allowance must be made for the growing authority of knowledge which they alone can command and which they alone can apply intelligently. This development may even go so far that within certain well-defined areas ministerial responsibility may be virtually abolished. Work of a non-controversial character, or work of a very special nature which would demand a judicial detachment from outside influence, or work demanding unusual administrative or technical skill, may be cut off almost entirely from ministerial and parliamentary control. This has already been done, for example, with the Civil Service Commission, with many other boards and commissions, and with the office of auditor-general. These officials have usually been isolated from the civil service proper by different conditions of appointment and tenure, but similar islands of authority will probably emerge within the ordinary departmental organization. There will be, in all likelihood, little or no uniformity; some will be given a great deal of freedom, others much less, the degree of independence in each case being determined solely by the nature of the work to be performed.

But how, it may be asked, is the country to be saved from the clutches of an irresponsible bureaucracy? In many ways. In the first place, an almost complete independence would be the privilege of very few, and consequently only a small proportion of the civil servants would be given a position of such impregnability that they could do much harm. Further, no matter how great the freedom given, Parliament would retain the power of intervention in the last resort if it needed to be exercised. This would not only halt the wayward civil servant, but the mere possibility of interference would make him less likely to stray very far off the path of official rectitude. But by far the most important security must be sought in the character of the men who occupy these important positions, in precisely the same way as we find our best guarantee for unselfish and conscientious service in the character of the judiciary. In both cases we rely on something higher than threats—personal attributes, the tradition of the profession, the pride in the work done, and many other intangible but in the mass enormously important constraining forces.[1]

Such a conception in Canadian government is by no means revolutionary; much of it, indeed, is merely a recognition of a freedom which is tacitly given and exercised in the service to-day, though not quite openly admitted. The experience in another branch of government has been extensive. The judiciary have enjoyed their independence for a century, and no very alarming abuses have occurred. Democratic control exists; but is at most times wisely held in abeyance, and is invoked only in rare instances when the confidence and trust has been betrayed. A country which has not only tolerated but prided itself on the excellence of its independent judiciary should have little difficulty in becoming reconciled to having part of its civil service founded upon essentially the same general principles.

[1] Dawson, R. MacG., *The Principle of Official Independence*, pp. 12–27; cf. Lord Haldane, *supra*, pp. 242–3.

It is clear that the problem of the political control of the administration, while not new, has been greatly altered by the emergence of new conditions. The difficulties which have thus arisen are still largely unsolved and can be worked out through experience alone. The Government must grant a large amount of influence and power to its technical and administrative experts, though retaining ultimate control; it must be willing to mark out important areas of administrative activity and free them from external meddling, while reserving to itself the right to meddle in rare emergencies; it must obviously depend to an enormous degree on the advice of its employees, yet for a while, at least, it must accept a nominal responsibility in Parliament for all acts of the administration. The Minister will be compelled to consult his assistants at every step, he will try to develop their initiative and encourage them to come to him with plans of their own for bettering the condition of the country and the department, he will continually bow to their judgement on technical and administrative matters, he will have to be content to relinquish some policies while retaining only the most essential for his own decision. Both Minister and civil servant must frankly recognize the delicacy of the relationship, they must cautiously feel their way, they must show a willingness to experiment and to try out the possibilities of each situation as it arises, they must show a mutual respect and confidence, each considering the rights and province of the other. The result will be, perhaps, a new science of public administration, a new method whereby a democracy can carry on its work without losing its ultimate control or diminishing the skill and effectiveness of its servants.

INDEX

Abbott, Sir J. J. C., 61–2.
— Government, 61–2, 67.
American Telephone and Telegraph Co., 131 n.
Appointment of civil servant, *see* Selection.
— of Civil Service Commission, 79, 199.
Assembly, Legislative, 4, 7, 8, 9, 13, 17.
Auditor-General, 61, 67, 68.

Bagehot, Walter, 112, 114, 117.
Bagot, Sir C., 14.
Baldwin, Robert, 13–14.
— La Fontaine Government, 6–8.
Bennett, Arnold, 115–16.
Beveridge, Sir W., 227, 249.
Blake, Edward, 53 n., 60 n.
Board, Advisory to the Civil Service Commission, 104, 148–51.
—, Advisory to the Ministry, 226–8.
— of Civil Service Examiners (1857–67), 195.
— — (1882–1907), 51, 53, 56–9, 62, 67–71, 86, 196–7.
— of Hearing and Recommendation, 96.
Borden, Sir Robert L., 209–10.
— Government, 82–3, 90.
British North America Act, 1867, 3, 19, 24.
Bryce, Viscount, 25, 28.
Bureaucracy, evils of, 112–14, 221–2.
—, checks on, 114–17, 232–51, 261.
Burke, Edmund, 205.

Cabinet, *see* Ministry.
Calder Act, *see* Public Service Retirement Act.
Cartwright, Sir Richard, 216–17.
Casey, George E., 38, 42–3, 47, 48, 57, 196–7, 206, 216.
Chandler, E. B., 16.
Christie, R., 8.
Civil Service, compared to private corporations, 220–4.
—, faults of, 112–14.
—, function of, 117–24.
—, importance of, 124–6.
—, place in future government, 256–62.

Civil Service Act (1868), 19, 21, 23, 24, 28, 30, 38.
— — *(1882 and 1885),* 24, 50–1, 59, 64–6, 71–2, 74–6.
— — *(1908),* 79–81, 88–9, 142, 197, 210.
— — *(1918),* 92, 96–7, 142, 149, 162, 168, 178, 180–1, 198, 210.
— — *(1919),* 96–7, 102, 162, 172, 175, 184, 198, 212–15, 245.
Civil Service Board (*see also* Board of Civil Service Examiners), 20, 40, 44, 66–7, 195–6.
— Commission, *see* Commission, Civil Service.
— Federation, 96.
Classification, 92, 95–6, 104, 143, 149, 159, 162–8, 174, 253.
Classification of the Civil Service of Canada, 95–6, 159–62, 165–7, 171, 176.
Commission, Civil Service (Canada), 46–7, 79–81, 84–9, 91–2, 94–5, 97–9, 101–4, 144, 148–53, 161–4, 167–72, 174–5, 180, 190, 192, 195–206, 208–15, 223, 246, 249, 252–4, 260.
— — (Great Britain), 24, 36–7.
—, Coal Industry (Great Britain), 176–7, 250 n., 251.
Commission, Royal, on the Civil Service (Canada).
— (1868), 21–4, 190.
— (1880), 24, 43, 44–51, 52, 136, 183, 190–1.
— (1891), 62–7, 152, 191, 208, 218, 242.
— (1907), 74–7, 78, 152, 191–2.
— (1911), 83.
— (1912), 83–5, 157.
Commission, Royal, on the Civil Service (Great Britain) (1914), 132, 181–2, 193 n., 220 n., 222 n.
Committee, Advisory to Ministry, 226–8.
— on Class I Examination (Great Britain), 134 n., 135, 138 n.
— of Deputy Ministers (1922), 105, 150.
—, Select, of House of Commons (1877), 38–41, 47.
—, Special, of House of Commons (1919), 105, 183.

Committee, Special, of House of Commons (1921), 98, 105.
— — — (1923), 105, 163–4, 209.
— —, of Senate (1919), 104.
— — — (1924), 105.
—, Standing, on Public Accounts (1891), 61.
— —, Permanent, 228–9.
Council, Consumers', 226–7.
—, Executive, 5, 7, 9–13, 16, 17.
—, Legislative, 7, 13.
—, Whitley, 231, 248.
Customs and Excise, Department of, 22–3, 40, 200.

Daly, D., 6.
Davidson, J., 6.
De Celles, A. D., 56.
Decentralization, 229–32.
Department of (Canada), Customs and Excise, 22–3, 40, 200.
— —, Finance, 85.
— —, Inland Revenue, 40, 46–7, 94, 152.
— —, Interior, 163, 191–2.
— —, Labour, 69.
— —, Marine and Fisheries, 39–40.
— —, Post Office, 40, 69, 191, 220.
— —, Public Works, 45.
— —, Soldiers' Civil Re-establishment, 94.
— (Great Britain) Agriculture and Fisheries, 144–5.
— (Great Britain), Food, 226–7.
Departmental co-ordination, 224–5.
Deputy Ministers, 20, 51, 53, 95, 98, 150, 151, 162–3, 169–72, 174–5, 187, 238–40, 245–6.
—, Committee of, 105, 150.
Disfranchisement, 60–1.
Dismissal, see Removal.
Draper Government, 6.
Drayton, Sir Henry, 212.
Dufferin, Lord, 42.
Durham, Lord, 4, 5, 7.

East India Company, 36.
Electoral Franchise Act, 1885, 60–1.
Examination for entrance, academic, 20, 36–7, 51–5, 84, 130–41, 146, 234.
— —, competitive, 36–7, 46, 49, 71, 74, 77, 79, 91, 129–30, 195, 197.
— —, pass, 20, 22–3, 37, 40–1, 51–5, 59–60, 63–4, 67, 70–1, 87.
— —, professional or technical, 79, 81, 86, 91–2, 104, 146–51.

Examination for entrance, special, 77–9, 103–4, 141–6, 147.
— for promotion, 46–7, 49–51, 64, 68, 70, 74, 85, 172–4.
Executive Council, see Council, Executive.
Experts, 110–11, 178–9.
—, relation to non-experts, 111–12, 114–16, 117–24, 231–2, 258–62.

Family Compact, 4, 7, 11, 17, 126.
Federalist party in United States, 25.
Finance, Department of, 85.
Fish, C. R., 26 n., 27, 28 n.
Floud, Sir F. L. C., 119–20, 144–5.
Foster, Sir G. E., 82–3.

Glenelg, Lord, 4, 9–10, 13.
Government, parliamentary, 109–10.
Governor, colonial, 4, 7.
Governor-General in Council, 19, 20, 51, 56, 66, 68, 79, 91–2, 97, 105, 149, 151, 174, 179, 185, 189, 196–7.
Gradation in Canada, 20–1, 46, 49–50, 65, 72, 79–80, 84–5, 92, 154–68.
— in Great Britain, 37, 49, 156–8, 235.
— in United States, 158.
Graham, G. P., 215.
Great Britain, civil service in, 34–7, 189, 195, 209.
—, influence of, 9, 11–12, 18, 34, 38, 44, 47–50.
Grey, Lord, 9, 11–12, 13, 15, 16, 112, 178.

Haldane, Lord, 122–3, 132–3, 176–7, 242–3, 249–51.
Hamilton, Alexander, 201.
—, P., 16.
Harris, Sir C., 231, 240 n.
Harvey, Sir J., 11.
Head, Sir F. B., 9–10.
Heath, Sir T., 239.
Huntington, L. S., 31.

Independence of civil servant, 42, 48, 215–19, 229–32, 258–62.
— of Civil Service Commission, 36, 47–8, 57–8, 80, 198–206.
Inertia in civil service, 113–14.
Initiative, encouragement of, 232–51.
Inland Revenue, Department of, 40, 46–7, 94, 152.
Inspector-General, 61–2.

Institute of Public Administration, 247–8.
Insurance Act, 72.
Intercolonial Railway, 28–9.
Interior, Department of, 163, 191–2.

Jackson, Andrew, 25, 26.
Jacksonian democracy, 25, 33, 256.
Jenkyns, Sir H., 218–19.
Jowett, Benjamin, 138–9, 201.

King, W. L. Mackenzie, 102–3, 200, 213–14.
— Government, 102.

Labour, Department of, 69.
La Fontaine, *see* Baldwin-La Fontaine.
Langevin, Sir H., 52, 55 n.
Laski, H. J., 228, 249 n.
Laurier, Sir Wilfrid, 73, 200, 211.
— Government, 74–5, 81–2.
Leathes, Sir S., 173.
Legislative Assembly, *see* Assembly, Legislative.
— Council, *see* Council, Legislative.
Le Sueur, P., 56.
Lewis, Sir G. C., 124.
Lippman, W., 112–13.
Lowell, A. L., 230.

Macaulay, T. B., 130–1.
Macdonald, Sir John A., 29–31, 39, 60 n., 73.
— Government, 31, 42–3.
— Sandfield, 32.
Machinery of Government Committee (Canada), 104.
— — (Great Britain), 193 n., 224 n., 226, 229 n.
Mackenzie, Alexander, 32, 33.
— Government, 31, 216–17.
MacLean, A. K., 96.
Marcy, Senator, 27.
Marine and Fisheries, Department of, 39–40.
Meighen, Arthur, 213.
Metcalfe, Sir C. (Lord), 6, 7–8.
Milner, Lord, 121–2, 244.
Minister, Cabinet, faults of, 117–19.
— —, function of, 114–16.
Ministerial responsibility, *see* Responsibility, parliamentary.
Ministry, early, in Canada, 5, 6.
—, relation to civil service, 5, 6, 84, 114–16, 206, 258–62.
—, Abbott, 61–2, 67.
—, Baldwin-La Fontaine, 6, 7, 8.

Ministry, Borden, 82–3, 90.
—, Draper, 6.
—, Laurier, 74–5, 81–2.
—, Macdonald, 31, 42–3.
—, Mackenzie, 31, 216–17.
—, Tupper, 72.
Minute, Treasury (1879), 63.
Moses, R., 37 n., 209 n.
Muir, R., 35 n., 112 n., 123, 137, 229 n., 235 n.
Mulgrave, Lord, 16.
Mulock, Sir W., 73–4.
Murdock, J., 212–13.
Murney, E., 13–14.
Murray, Sir George, 83–5, 157.

Newcastle, Duke of, 16–17.
Northcote, Sir Stafford, 36.
Northcote-Trevelyan Report, 24, 36–7, 39, 49, 156 n., 255–6.

Ogden, C. R., 6.
Order in Council (Canada) (1904), 69.
— — (1907), 74.
— — (1914), 88.
— — (1918), 90–2, 102, 104, 180, 210.
— — (1919), 97, 99, 104, 151.
— — (1921), 99, 151.
— — (1922), 99, 151.
— (Great Britain) (1870), 37.
Organization of government work, 224–5.
Overseas service and entrance, 91–2.

Parliament, control over civil service, 116–17.
Parliamentary government, 109–10.
— responsibility, *see* Responsibility, Parliamentary.
Party activity of civil servants, 31–2, 63, 80.
Party influence in civil service, in Canada, history of, 3, 6–9, 23–4, 25, 29–34, 38–41, 54–5, 58, 60, 73–7, 86–9, 92–3, 99–102, 168.
—, inefficiency of, 34, 45–6, 63, 120–1, 128–9.
—, present results of, 252–6.
— in Great Britain, 34–6.
— in United States, 25–8.
Patronage, *see* Party influence.
— Committee, 99–101.
Pensions, *see* Retirement.
Post Office, Department of, 40, 69, 191, 220.
Printing Bureau, 93–4, 104.
Probation, 79, 152–3.

Professional Institute of Civil Service, 151.
— positions, 51, 79, 81, 86, 91–2, 98–9, 104, 146–51.
Promotion, 20, 40–1, 46, 49–51, 63–5, 68–70, 74–5, 80, 165–74, 234, 253.
— examination, see Examination, promotion.
Public opinion, 53–5, 66, 78–9.
Public Service Retirement Act, 105.
Public Works, Department of, 45.

Railways, Canadian National, 182–3, 223.
Reade, A., 8.
Reform of civil service (Canada), 19–21, 38–9, 41–2, 46–53, 61–2, 66–7, 77–80, 84–5, 90–3.
— — (Great Britain), 36–7.
Removal of civil servants, early difficulties, 9, 13–17.
— for inefficiency, 183–6.
— for party activity, 31–4, 72–3, 82–3, 90–2, 102–3, 179–83.
— of Civil Service Commissioners, 79, 199–200.
Reorganization of departments, 104.
Report of Transmission, 141, 143, 165, 171, 175, 183–5, 192, 248.
Republican party in United States, 25.
Responsibility, parliamentary, 47–8, 121, 206–15, 229.
Responsible government, effect on civil service, 3, 6–17.
—, paradoxical features, 109–11.
Retirement, 47, 71, 76–7, 105, 186–90.
Retirement Act (1898), 71, 186, 188.
Retirement Act, Public Service (1920), 105.
Roosevelt, Theodore, 142.
Rotation in office, 25–6, 33.
Royal Commission, see Commission, Royal.
Russell, Lord John, 10, 14, 209.

Salary of civil servants, 21, 64, 76, 174–77, 213, 253.
— of Civil Service Commission, 201.
Secretaries, private, 20, 152.
Select Committee, see Committee, Select.
Selection, 6–9, 29–31, 46–9, 51–2,

58, 73–5, 79, 81, 82–3, 86, 91, 97–104, 128–52, 206–11.
Smith, Goldwin, 30–1, 60.
Soldiers' Civil Re-establishment, Department of, 94.
Spinney Bill, 97–8, 105.
Spoils system, in Canada, 28–34, 42.
—, in United States, 25–8.
Stanley, Lord, 9.
Superannuation, see Retirement.
Superannuation Act (1870), 47, 71, 186.
— *(1924)*, 186–90.
Sydenham, Lord, 6, 14.

Technical positions, see Professional positions.
'Temporary' employees, 22, 65–6, 76, 84, 86–9.
Tenure of office, civil servant, 3, 9–13, 32–3, 178–9, 234–5.
—, Civil Service Commission, 79, 199, 205.
Thorburn, John, 56.
Transfers, 51, 63, 245–7, 253.
Treasury Board, 68, 189.
— — Minute (1879), 63.
Trevelyan, Sir Charles, 36, 139 n., 201.
Tupper, Sir Charles, 31.

Union Government, 90.
United States, influence on civil service, 4, 18, 25–8, 34, 38, 44, 158–9.

Veterans, see War Veterans.

Wallas, Graham, 236, 237 n., 241 n., 258 n.
War, effect of, on civil service, 88–9.
War Measures Act (1914), 88.
War Veterans, 91–2.
— — Association, Great, 100.
Webb, Sidney, 185.
White, L. D., 224 n., 241.
Whitley Council, see Council, Whitley.
Willison, Sir J., 73.
Wise, E. F., 226–7.
Women in civil service, 76, 190–4.

Young, Arthur, and Company, 95, 104.

PRINTED IN GREAT BRITAIN AT THE UNIVERSITY PRESS, OXFORD
BY JOHN JOHNSON, PRINTER TO THE UNIVERSITY